THE CRISIS OF MEDIEVAL RUSSIA
1200 – 1304

LONGMAN HISTORY OF RUSSIA
General Editor: Harold Shukman

*Already published

LONGMAN HISTORY OF RUSSIA

The Crisis of Medieval Russia
1200 – 1304

JOHN FENNELL

LONGMAN
London and New York

Longman Group Limited
Longman House, Burnt Mill, Harlow
Essex CM20 2JE, England
Associated companies throughout the world

*Published in the United States of America
by Longman Inc., New York*

First published 1983

British Library Cataloguing in Publication Data

Fennell, John
The crisis of medieval Russia 1200 – 1304.
– (Longman history of Russia)
1. Soviet Union – History
I. Title
947   DK40

ISBN 0-582-48150-3

Library of Congress Cataloging in Publication Data

Fennell, John Lister Illingworth.
The crisis of medieval Russia, 1200 – 1304.

(Longman History of Russia)
Bibliography: p.
Includes index.
1. Soviet Union – History – 1237-1480.   2. Mongols – Soviet Union.
I. Title.   II. Series.
DK90.F44   1983   947'.03   82-14962
ISBN 0-582-48150-3 (pbk.)

Set in 11/12pt Linotron 202 Garamond No. 3
Printed in Singapore by
Huntsmen Offset Printing Pte Ltd

Contents

List of genealogical tables

List of maps

Glossary

baskak (pl. baskaki)   Tatar overseer, official
chern'   common people
Chernye klobuki   Black Caps (Turkic tribe. **Karakalpak**)
chislenniki   Tatar census officials
Chud'   Estonians
Desyatinnaya tserkov'   Church of the Tithe (Kiev)
detinets   Novgorod kremlin
druzhina   bodyguard, detachment of troops, private army.
dvoryanin (pl. dvoryane)   servitor, service-man
Em'   Finns
grivna   coin
izvod   chronicle redaction
konets (pl. kontsy)   city district of Novgorod
kramola   sedition
kuriltai   Mongol national assembly
myatezh   rebellion, upheaval
namestnik (pl. namestniki)   governor, lieutenant-governor
otchina (pl. otchiny)   patrimony
posadnichestvo   office of posadnik
posadnik (pl. posadniki)   mayor, chief executive (Novgorod, Pskov)
posol (pl. posly)   Tatar agent, plenipotentiary
povest'   tale, narrative
rat'   army, war
samoderzhets   autocrat
sluga (pl. slugi)   service-man
snem   council
Sovet gospod   Council of Lords (Novgorod)
Sum'   Finns
Svei   Swedes
Svod   Chronicle compilation, codex
tamga   customs tax
tiun, tivun (pl. tiuny, tivuny)   administrator

tuska   ? tax
tysyatskiy   local commander and police chief
veche (pl. **vecha**)   town assembly
voevoda (pl. **voevody**)   general, commander
volost' (pl. **volosti**)   district, Novgorod administrative unit
yarlyk   patent for throne, Tatar document of privilege
zhit'i lyudi   well-to-do people

Abbreviations

A.N.SSSR Akademiya nauk SSSR
DDG	*Dukhovnye i dogovornye gramoty*
E	*Ermolinskaya letopis'*
GVNiP	*Gramoty Velikogo Novgoroda i Pskova*
Ipat	*Ipat'evskaya letopis'*
L	*Lavrent'evskaya letopis'*
LPS	*Letopisets Pereyaslavlya-Suzdal'skogo*
L' v	*L'vovskaya letopis'*
M	*Moskovskiy letopisnyy svod kontsa XV veka*
MAK	*Suzdal'skaya letopis' po Akademicheskomu spisku*
MGH	*Monumenta Germaniae Historica.*
N1	*Novgorod First Chronicle*
N4	*Novgorodskaya chetvertaya letopis'*
Nik	*Patriarshaya ili Nikonovskaya letopis'*
NPL	*Novgorodskaya pervaya letopis'*
P1L	*Pskovskaya pervaya letopis'*
P2L	*Pskovskaya vtoraya letopis'*
PSRL	*Polnoe sobranie russkikh letopisey*
RFA	*Russkie feodal'nye arkhivy* (L. V. Cherepnin)
RM	*Russia Mediaevalis*
S1	*Sofiyskaya pervaya letopis'*
Sim	*Simeonovskaya letopis'*
T	*The Trinity Chronicle*
TL	*Troitskaya letopis'*
TODRL	*Trudy Otdela drevnerusskoy literatury*
Tv. sb.	*Tverskoy sbornik* (=*Tverskaya letopis'*)
UL	*Ustyuzhskiy letopisnyy svod*
VFR	*Vneshnepoliticheskie faktory razvitiya feodal'noy Rusi* (V. V. Kargalov)

Preface

This book covers a period in which two momentous events, the one dependent on the other, altered the whole course of Russian history: the Tatar invasion and the eclipse of Kiev and most of what had once been the great Kievan empire of the south. The first of these events was to dominate Russian history for nearly two and a half centuries; the second had a lasting effect on Russia's destiny: while a drastically weakened South Russia became an easy prey for the vast expanding state of Lithuania and Poland, the virtual disappearance of Kiev from the Russian political scene freed the Mesopotamian area of Suzdalia from the constant need to preoccupy itself with territories outside its natural area of development. Rid of the necessity to watch over and to guard itself against the South, the district of Suzdal'–Vladimir–Rostov was able eventually to develop its own resources, to acquire inner strength and, in the fifteenth century, to free itself at last from its Tatar overlords.

The available Russian sources provide remarkably little information on the social and economic conditions of the age: in them we find practically no details of agrarian conditions, of trade, of landownership, of legal administration, of the tax and tribute system in Russia. But from the chronicles, our main source of information for the period, we do learn a considerable amount about the relationships of the numerous rulers of the separate principalities with one another: their conflicts, their alliances, their family connections, their military ventures. Consequently much of this book is taken up with the political activities of the descendants of Vladimir I and with the complex interaction of the various autonomous or near-autonomous districts that went to make up the Russia of the thirteenth century.

The main aim of the book is to chronicle, and seek an explanation for, the gradual decline of princely power from the heyday of Vsevolod III's rule at the beginning of the century to the nadir of the authority of the grand prince of Vladimir at the end of it. To do this it is necessary to investigate the minutiae of inter-princely relations and to attempt to disentangle the complicated web of available information. All the conclusions reached are based exclusively on a study of the primary sources – for the most part, the chronicles – and on an investigation of the interrelationship of these sources.

The chronicles themselves present considerable difficulties. Not one was contemporary to the events described, that is to say not one received its *final* redaction in the thirteenth century. It is therefore at times necessary to reduce the earliest accounts to their original versions by stripping them of later accretions. It is also essential to establish the bias not only of the contemporary chronicler but, often more important still, of later editors of the text as well. The trouble is that so often the skilled compilers of the great codices of the fifteenth and sixteenth centuries, while collating a number of conflicting – and often inadequate – versions and trying to make sense out of what was often contradictory nonsense, tended to rewrite history in the spirit of *their* age. In Appendix A I have described the relevant chronicles and have shown their origins, their history and their relation with one another.

In books in English on early Russian history problems are often posed by place names, proper names and titles. Throughout I have used the terms 'Russia' and 'Russian' rather than 'Rus″' (which in the sources relating to the twelfth and thirteenth centuries tends to denote the *south* of the country rather than the north-east and north-west) and the ill-sounding 'Rus′ian' favoured by some historians. I have adopted the chroniclers' habit of using 'collective patronymics' to denote members of this or that clan: thus, the 'Ol′govichi' are the descendants of Oleg Svyatoslavich of Chernigov, the 'Rostislavichi' – those of Rostislav Mstislavich of Smolensk. As for Lithuanian names, I have given the Russian version first, then the Lithuanian in brackets, e.g. Voyshelk (Vaišvilkas), Zhemaytiya (Žemaitija). Estonian and Livonian place names present more of a difficulty: in most cases I have given the Russian name followed by the local (Estonian or Lettish) and German names in brackets, e.g. Rakovor (Rakvere, Wesenburg). However, Kukenois (German: Kokenhusen) and Gersicke, both on the Western Dvina, have been left in the local form, there being no accepted Russian forms; Kolyvan′ (Tallinn, Reval) I have called by the commonly accepted Russian version 'Revel″'; Lake Chudskoe (Peipsi Järv, Lake Peipus) is 'Lake Peypus' passim. In the spelling of Tatar names I have omitted diaeresis throughout: thus Hulagu *vice* Hülägü, Ogedey *vice* Ögedey; I have also used the commonly accepted Russian version of 'Baty' rather than 'Batu' throughout.

For the transliteration of Russian words I have used the 'British' system of latinization advocated in the *Slavonic and East European Review* (*see* W. K. Matthews, The Latinisation of Cyrillic Characters', vol. xxx, no. 75 (June 1952), pp. 531–49). I have made one or two minor exceptions to this system: (i) e and ë are always transliterated e (thus *Ermolinskaya*, not *Yermolinskaya*); (ii) the endings -ый and -ий are rendered by -y in modern surnames (*Gorsky, Ilovaysky*) and first names (*Vasily, Dmitry, Yury*). In adjectival endings, however, -yy and -iy are used (*Novyy, Nevskiy, Nizhniy, Dolgorukiy*); (iii) in the spelling of feminine names ending in -iya, the spelling -ia has been used throughout (*Maria*).

The second section of Chapter 4 has appeared in a slightly modified form in *Oxford Slavonic Papers* (New Series), vol. xiv, 1981.

Finally I would like to express my gratitude to the Rockefeller Foundation for enabling me to spend four idyllic and prolific weeks at the Bellagio Study and Conference Center in 1979. I would also like to thank those of my colleagues in this country, the United States and the Soviet Union who have helped and advised me, especially Dr G. L. Lewis, Eric Christiansen, Michal Giedroyć and Professor Ya. S. Lur'e.

Oxford
December 1981

CHAPTER ONE

Russia in 1200

At the beginning of the thirteenth century few of the territories that had once made up the state of Kiev showed signs of such healthy political stability as did the north-eastern district of Suzdalia – that is, the territory of Suzdal', Rostov and Vladimir, bounded roughly by the upper Volga in the north and the Oka in the south. The authority of its ruler, Vsevolod III, one of the shrewdest and most farsighted of all the descendants of Vladimir I, was widely acknowledged among his fellow-rulers. 'All lands trembled at his name and his fame spread throughout the whole country', wrote his chronicler, who, though using the conventional fulsome clichés of the adulatory obituary, probably represented the views of most of his contemporaries. All Suzdalia owed him allegiance of some kind or other; the great city-state of Novgorod with its vast subject lands to the west, north and north-east had, for the first eight years of the thirteenth century, only his sons as its rulers; Kiev's eastern neighbour, Southern Pereyaslavl', was firmly under his control; and the princes of Murom and Ryazan' to the south were little more than his vassals.

If at the turn of the century the northern half of the country of Russia enjoyed a certain degree of stability, the southern half did not. By the year 1200 a three-cornered struggle for power had begun between the princely family of Smolensk (the descendants of Rostislav Mstislavich: the Rostislavichi), the descendants of Oleg Svyatoslavich of Chernigov (the Ol'govichi) and the formidable Roman Mstislavich of Volynia. It was a fight for supremacy over the whole of the south of Russia, from Volynia and Galicia in the west to Chernigov and Pereyaslavl' in the east, and for control over the 'mother of the Russian cities', Kiev, and it was to continue off and on until Kiev fell to the Tatars in 1240.

This did not mean, of course, that at the turn of the century Kiev was in a state of complete political and economic decline or that the hegemony of the new centre of Vladimir-on-the-Klyaz'ma was finally established and recognized by all: indeed, the bitter feuding was soon to give way to relative stability in the south (from 1212 to 1235), while in the north Vsevolod III's death in 1212 was followed by a period of violent internecine war, and it is doubtful if at that time the prince of Kiev considered himself in any way the inferior of his cousin in Vladimir. But by 1200 Suzdalia was showing distinct signs of political strength, and the southern princes tended to look up to the grand prince of Vladimir as *primus inter pares*, if not as the senior of all the descendants of Ryurik.

Why was this so? In order to find an answer we must consider briefly the political organization of the various territories which made up the whole of Russia at the turn of the century and glance at their previous history.

* * * *

The agriculturally rich 'land beyond the forests' (*Zalesskaya zemlya*) or Suzdalia, as it is convenient to call the federation of principalities in north-east Russia ruled by Vsevolod III and his numerous sons, was situated in the basins of four major rivers, two running west–east, two running north–south. Through the centre of the district flowed the Volga from Zubtsov in the west – the extreme upper reaches of the river from Rzheva to Lake Seliger ran through Smolensk territory – to its confluence with the Oka in the east. In the south of Suzdalia was the river Klyaz'ma, running from its source north–west of Moscow to where it flows into the Oka and on the central reaches of which stands the capital Vladimir. In the north-west and the north-east of the district were the two northernmost tributaries of the Volga, the Sheksna, which links the Volga with the White Lake, and the Unzha, which formed the easternmost boundary of Suzdalia. Apart from Beloozero near the influx of the Sheksna into the White Lake and Ustyug at the confluence of the Sukhona and Yug rivers in the far north-east, most of the major cities were situated either on the Volga (Tver', Uglich, Yaroslavl', Kostroma) and the Klyaz'ma (Vladimir, Starodub), or between the two (Suzdal', Pereyaslavl' Zalesskiy or Northern Pereyaslavl', Rostov, Dmitrov, Yur'evPol'skiy).

A glance at the map will show just how favourably Suzdalia was situated with regard to these river routes. Most of the main rivers flowed form west to east, and three of them, the Klyaz'ma, Moskva and Oka, were linked with the Volga near the beginning of its great sweep southwards to the Caspian Sea, thus providing trade routes with the markets of the East. At the same time the Moskva and Ugra rivers, both tributaries of the Oka, provided waterways to Smolensk in the south-west and thence to the Baltic and the Black Sea, while the great western commercial centre of Novgorod was linked to Tver' by the Msta and Tvertsa rivers. Furthermore, a number of tributaries bisecting at regular intervals the area between the Upper Volga and the Klyaz'ma provided routes between most of the major towns in the mesopotamian area and also gave them outlets along the main rivers.

The first mention of the 'Trans-forest Land' as a political entity occurs in the Novgorod First Chronicle where Suzdalia is described as an appendage to the *otchina*, or patrimony, of Southern Pereyaslavl' left by Yaroslav I to his third eldest surviving son Vsevolod in 1054: 'Vsevolod [received Southern] Pereyaslavl', Rostov, Suzdal', Beloozero and Povolzh'e [the Volga district]'.[1] Virtually uncontested, it remained the possession of Vsevolod and his son Vladimir Monomakh and the latter's descendants. Curiously enough, in the eleventh century little attention seems to have been paid to this vast and rich area, which was later to become the centre of the great Muscovite state from the fourteenth to the seventeenth centuries – indeed, before 1093 or 1094 neither Vsevolod nor his son Vladimir even appointed princes to rule there. But from the beginning of the twelfth century Vladimir Monomakh began to show a keener interest in this the jewel of his family possessions. Perhaps it was because of the need to defend the southern borders of Suzdalia against the princes of Chernigov or perhaps it was because he had to counteract the growing menace of the Volga Bulgars on his eastern borders, who in the early twelfth century were penetrating further and further west along the Volga?[2] Whatever the cause, we find Vladimir Monomakh founding the city of Vladimir-on-the-Klyaz'ma (1108), the future capital, and appointing his son Yury Dolgorukiy prince of Suzdal'. By the time of his death in 1125 Suzdalia was virtually independent of Kiev under its sovereign ruler Yury.

For the rest of the century the district grew and strengthened under its three tough and remarkable rulers, Yury Dolgorukiy (1120–57) and his two sons Andrey Bogolyubskiy (1157–74) (so called from the palace built at the village of Bogolyubovo near Vladimir) and Vsevolod III (1176–1212). Yury, that veritable 'Christopher Columbus of the Povolzh'e', as one historian has called him,[3] can truly be called the founder of the Rostov-Suzdalian state. During his 37-year rule Suzdalia took shape. Its frontiers with Chernigov in the south and Novgorod in the west became fixed; towns sprang up: Ksnyatin at the mouth of the Western Nerl', Yur'ev-Pol'skiy, Pereyaslavl' Zalesskiy (Northern Pereyaslavl'), Dmitrov, Moscow; throughout the country churches and monasteries were built and decorated; colonization was vigorously fostered; links between Suzdalia and the south were strengthened; and Yury's sons were established in the major cities, often while at the same time holding districts in the south. When he died in 1157 he was succeeded by an even more single-minded and autocratic ruler, his son Andrey Bogolyubskiy, whom the local boyars of Rostov, Suzdal' and Vladimir proclaimed as their prince.

Suzdalia was immensely strengthened by Andrey. Not only did he have far less *southern* aspirations than his father, who had twice been prince in Kiev, or his sons and brothers – it was a son of his (Mstislav) who seized Kiev in 1169, not Andrey, and it was the same son who put Andrey's brother Gleb on the throne of Kiev in the same year – but also he was aware of the danger of having too many relations to share power with and too many of his father's boyars to advise him on how to use that power. In his desire to be 'autocrat (*samoderzhets*) of all the land of Suzdal'', he chased out four of his brothers, two of his nephews and the 'senior boyars of his father' (1161).[4] He even attempted to assert ecclesiastical independence from the see of Kiev by proposing (in vain) to set up a metropolitanate of the north. Again, the frontiers of Suzdalia were widened. Andrey's reach extended eastwards, mainly along the Klyaz'ma, in an effort still further to stem Bulgar aggression: he founded the easternmost outpost of Gorokhovets on the Klyaz'ma as a jumping-off place for the great campaign against the Volga Bulgars in 1164.[5] In the north his influence was beginning to be felt in the vast territories under the nominal control of Novgorod – in the district of Zavoloch'e, the lands 'beyond the portage' between the White Lake and Lake Kubenskoe, watered by the Northern Dvina river.[6]

He was murdered in 1174, and for two years there was confusion and unrest in Suzdalia while two of his nephews and his brother Mikhalko briefly ruled Rostov and Vladimir. But on Mikhalko's death in 1176 the youngest son of Yury Dolgorukiy, the great Vsevolod III, took over, the first prince ever officially to adopt the title of grand prince.[7] His long reign (1176–1212) was marked not only by a great increase of his authority as ruler of Vladimir, both internationally and amongst his southern relatives, but also by a significant increase of territory. In the west Vsevolod reached an agreement with Novgorod whereby the Novgorodian territories of Torzhok and Volok Lamskiy were held in joint control by both Novgorod and Suzdalia,[8] while at the same time he moved further westward along the Volga, building the town of Zubtsov on the southernmost bend of the upper Volga and thus creating a wedge of Suzdalian land between Novgorod territory proper and the shared district of Volok Lamskiy. In the east his defences against the Volga Bulgars were strengthened: Kostroma, Nerekhta and Sol' Velikaya, all on or near the middle Volga, were founded to provide further bulwarks against attacks from the east or to serve as collecting points for campaigns against the Bulgars, as was Unzha, built on the middle reaches of the Unzha river. In the far north further incursions into Novgorod territory were made in the Pechora and Northern Dvina river districts, and the town of Ustyug, at the juncture of the Sukhona and Yug rivers, was founded in 1178.[9]

By the end of the century Vsevolod III's power was firmly established. Furthermore it was recognized by the third and fourth generations of descendants of Monomakh, who saw in him the senior 'amongst all cousins in the tribe of Vladimir [Monomakh]' (see p. 22). Whoever wrote the *Tale of Igor's Campaign* – whether at the beginning of the thirteenth century or later – singled him out amongst all the princes of Russia: 'Grand Prince Vsevolod! Should you not fly here [i.e. to Kiev] in thought to watch over your father's golden throne? For you can splash dry the Volga with your oars and empty the Don with your helmets! Had you been here, a slave-girl would be worth a farthing and a male captive a mite' – an exaggeration, perhaps, of Vsevolod's military capacities, but at any rate an indication of his formidable reputation and of the power of Suzdalia at the turn of the century.

* * * *

The principality of Kiev in the south presented an altogether different picture. At the end of the twelfth century it consisted merely of the lands watered by the middle reaches of the Dnepr, by the western tributaries of the Dnepr from the Uzh in the north to the Ros' in the south and by the southern tributary of the Pripyat', the Sluch'. In total area it was smaller than Suzdalia, Chernigov, Smolensk, Polotsk or Volynia. In the south there were virtually no boundaries at all and it is hard to tell where Kiev ended and the territory of the steppe nomads, the Polovtsians, began, but an approximate, though fluid, line between the two could be drawn south of the Ros' river and the upper reaches of the Southern Bug. The eastern frontier between Kiev on the one hand and Chernigov and Pereyaslavl' on the other ran along the Dnepr, although a 15-kilometre-wide slice of land east of the Dnepr from the Desna to the Trubezh belonged to Kiev. In the north the frontier with the principality of Turov-Pinsk ran south of the Pripyat' river, while in the west that with Volynia ran in a line east of the upper reaches of the Goryn' river.

The town of Kiev itself was ideally situated. Militarily it enjoyed excellent defences thanks to its hilly position; economically the Dnepr provided not only a direct route to the Black Sea, but also links with the Baltic via the Berezina and the Western Dvina, with the Oka and Don via the Desna and Seym and with the basins of the Dnestr and Neman via the Pripyat' and Western Bug. Close by were the strongly fortified cities of Vruchiy (or Ovruch, as it was sometimes called), Vyshgorod and Belgorod commanding the approaches to the capital from the north-west, the north and the south-west respectively. From the south Kiev was shielded by a system of forts along the Dnepr and a series of strongly defended towns on the Ros' river.[10]

At the beginning of the twelfth century the frontier situation was much more fluid. Indeed it is hard to say whether under the great rulers of the early twelfth century, Vladimir Monomakh (1113–25) and his son Mstislav the Great (1125–32) boundaries even existed between what later became known as the 'principality of Kiev' and Volynia, Turov-Pinsk, Smolensk and Southern Pereyaslavl', all of which were held by close relatives (and subjects) of the prince of Kiev. Kiev *was* 'Rus'', and 'Rus'' consisted of all the southern lands excepting Galicia and Chernigov-Ryazan'. Even parts of Polotsk in the north-west were subject to Monomakh and Mstislav. But the unity of the Kievan land, resuscitated by Vladimir Monomakh after the civil wars of the eleventh century, was shortlived. Already the reign of Yaropolk (1132–39), who succeeded his brother Mstislav, was clouded by fragmentation and soured by the struggle within the clan of the Monomashichi themselves: the younger sons of Vladimir Monomakh, who could expect to follow Yaropolk on the throne of Kiev according to the rules of lateral seniority (brother succeeding brother), were incensed by the fact that Yaropolk placed his *nephews* (Mstislav's sons) in Pereyaslavl', by now the accepted seat of the prince next in line for Kiev (see p. 10). The intestine strife was intensified by the intervention of Vsevolod, the son of Monomakh's old rival, Oleg of Chernigov. It became a three-cornered struggle for power between the princes of Chernigov, the powerful sons of Mstislav the Great and the latters' uncles, Yaropolk and his brothers. Civil war was now the order of the day in southern Russia, just as it had been in the last three decades of the eleventh century. Power swung from family to family: from one clan of the Monomashichi to another, from one branch of the princes of Chernigov to another, until eventually a sort of compromise was reached in the curious duumvirate of Svyatoslav Vsevolodovich of Chernigov and Ryurik Rostislavich of Smolensk, who virtually ruled the principality of Kiev jointly until the former's death in 1194. Families themselves became more and more fragmented the greater their expansion. Separate branches began to concentrate on areas which each gradually came to recognize as its inalienable heritage: thus

5

the grandchildren of Izyaslav Mstislavich (prince of Kiev 1146–54) built up their patrimonies in the west – Vladimir in Volynia, Lutsk, Dorogobuzh, Shumsk, Peresopnitsa; the descendants of Rostislav Mstislavich (prince of Kiev 1159–67) kept to Smolensk, which the family had held since 1125[11]; Yury Dolgorukiy's family, as has been mentioned above, concentrated its energies in Suzdalia; the Ol'govichi of Chernigov split into the senior clan (the descendants of Vsevolod Ol'govich, prince of Kiev 1139–46) with its claims to Chernigov itself and the cadet branch (the descendants of Svyatoslav Ol'govich) which settled for the lesser portion of Novgorod Severskiy.

All this meant, of course, considerable variations in the actual power wielded by whoever was prince of Kiev. Yaropolk, for example, indecisive and only too willing to accept a compromise and a disadvantageous peace, undermined the authority won by his elder brother Mstislav and his father Monomakh; Mstislav Izyaslavich (1167–69), for all his energetic and successful defence of the southern frontiers against the steppe nomads, the Polovtsians, was opposed by the majority of the princes and saw his capital taken by the troops of Andrey Bogolyubskiy's son (1169); under Rostislav Mstislavich (1159–67) and Svyatoslav Vsevolodovich (1177–94), on the other hand, a certain stability was achieved, there were few feudal clashes and successful anti-Polovtsian campaigns were undertaken. But in spite of the constant waxing and waning of the authority of the numerous princes who occupied the throne of Kiev from the death of Mstislav the Great in 1132 to the death of Svyatoslav Vsevolodovich in 1194, Kiev never lost its importance as the centre of the south and as the magnetic attraction for the Monomashichi and the princes of Chernigov, nor was it to lose it for the first four decades of the thirteenth century. Much has been written concerning the political and economic 'decline' of Kiev in the twelfth century, and much attention has been paid to Andrey Bogolyubskiy's unwillingness to rule in Kiev after his son's armies had taken the city in 1169. But there is little to show that the authority of Kiev, both as a centre and as a principality, diminished noticeably in the twelfth century, and the fact that neither Andrey Bogolyubskiy nor his brother Vsevolod III chose to rule there is evidence of their determination to concentrate their attention on Suzdalia rather than of their 'contempt' for Kiev. The 'mother of the Russian cities' remained the great prize of the princes until shortly before its capture by the Tatars.

*　*　*　*

Of all the southern districts independent of Kiev the strongest and the least fragmented by the beginning of the thirteenth century was undoubtedly Smolensk. The principality enjoyed an enviable geographical position, situated as it was on the upper reaches of most of the major rivers of Russia. From north to south flowed the head waters of the Dnepr, on which the town of Smolensk was located, as well as the Dnepr's two large tributaries, the Sozh and the Desna. Westward flowed the Western Dvina and its various tributaries, and to the east the upper Vazuza, a major tributary of the Volga, and the upper Ugra, which joined the Oka in Chernigov territory. Thus Smolensk was linked by its waterways with Kiev in the south (along the Dnepr, Sozh and Desna), with the Baltic (via the Western Dvina), with the Gulf of Finland (via various portages between the Dnepr and the Lovat') and with the main routes east (Volga and Oka). Shaped like a tilted triangle, Smolensk shared a boundary with Chernigov in the south, with Polotsk in the west, with Novgorod in the north and with Suzdalia in the east.[12]

In the last forty years of the eleventh century and the first quarter of the twelfth Smolensk appears to have been a dependency of Kiev: in other words, the ruler of Smolensk was the appointee of whoever was prince of Kiev.[13] It passed from prince to prince among the descendants of Yaroslav I, but for most of the last quarter of the eleventh century and the first quarter of the twelfth it was the possession of, or in the gift of, Vladimir Monomakh. Only after Monomakh's death in 1125, when his grandson Rostislav Mstislavich was given Smolensk, did the principality become an independent political unit with its own prince, who could, and did, confine Smolensk to his own descendants. From then on, until the early fifteenth century, Smolensk was ruled exclusively by the family of Rostislav – the Rostislavichi.

Throughout the remainder of the twelfth century the Rostislavichi controlled Smolensk with tact and discipline. From time to time their power was such that they were able to place their nominees – usually close relatives – on the throne of Novgorod and sometimes on that of Pskov as well. Smolensk became a bishopric in 1136. In 1165 the town and district of Vitebsk was temporarily acquired at the expense of Polotsk. Rostislav and two of his most powerful sons, Roman and Ryurik, frequently occupied the throne of Kiev. Most important of all, the Rostislavichi managed to build up strong family connections in the fortress towns near Kiev itself – in Vruchiy, Belgorod and Vyshgorod – thus facilitating the eventual takeover of the city and district in the thirteenth century.

The reasons for the strength of Smolensk at the end of the twelfth century are not hard to find. The principality enjoyed a flourishing economy thanks largely to its links with Eastern Europe along the Dvina river: there is evidence of strong commercial connections with Riga and with the main trading centres of Germany – Lübeck, Dortmund and Bremen. There were no squabbles among the members of the ruling dynasty, nor are there any signs of separate *otchiny* being formed: a member of the clan might temporarily hold a provincial centre, but there was no question of the establishment of *separate* branches of the family outside the capital of Smolensk itself. The princes, it seems, were always at the disposal of whoever was senior member of the family. Above all, Smolensk was virtually free from attacks by external enemies: Polotsk and the south-west corner of Novgorod territory shielded it from Lithuanian and German inroads, while the Polovtsians had to penetrate Kiev, Pereyaslavl' and Chernigov before reaching the frontiers of Smolensk.[14]

*　　*　　*　　*

Smolensk's southern neighbour Chernigov, surrounded by Kiev and Turov in the west, Smolensk and Suzdalia in the north, Murom and Ryazan' in the north-east and Pereyaslavl' in the south, enjoyed a less favourable geographical position in that its southern and eastern frontiers were more vulnerable to attack: the southern half of the eastern border, for instance, was open to the Don steppes. The principality, however, was provided with a system of waterways which linked it with Smolensk (via the Dnepr and Sozh), the south (via the Dnepr) and the east (via the upper Oka). Throughout the southern and central regions flowed the Desna, on which the major cities – Chernigov, Novgorod Severskiy, Trubetsk, Bryansk and Vshchizh – were situated. In the south of the district ran the Desna's tributary the Seym, which constituted a natural barrier against inroads of steppe invaders, while in the west, from Lyubech to Rogachev, Chernigov held the middle reaches of the Dnepr, thus controlling the main water route from Smolensk to Kiev.

Unlike Smolensk, Chernigov, ever since the mid-eleventh century, was recognized as the family possession of one branch of the descendants of Yaroslav I, and one branch only. In 1054 Yaroslav bequeathed it to his second eldest surviving son, together with Ryazan' and Murom: 'Svyatoslav received Chernigov and all the eastern land even as far as Murom.'[15] For the first twenty-two years it was the undisputed possession of Svyatoslav, but during the age of bitter civil war from 1077 to 1097 it changed hands no less than seven times, alternating for the most part between Svyatoslav's sons and Vladimir Monomakh. In 1097, at the great congress of Lyubech, at which the territorial problems of the Kievan state were temporarily solved, Chernigov was confirmed as the *otchina* of the Svyatoslavichi: 'Let each one hold his own patrimony (*otchina*). . . . Let David, Oleg and Yaroslav [the three surviving sons of Svyatoslav] hold Svyatoslav's [patrimony]',[16] and in the hands of the Svyatoslavichi it stayed as long as Chernigov remained an independent principality.

Throughout the twelfth century the family grew and splintered. David, as the eldest son of Svyatoslav, held Chernigov; Oleg made Novgorod Severskiy his capital, while the third son, Yaroslav, eventually (1127) settled in the district that was probably allocated to him at Lyubech and in which his descendants were to remain – the separate joint principality of Ryazan' and Murom. Chernigov and Novgorod Severskiy passed from one branch of the family to the other, from David and his children to Oleg and his. But the branch of the Davidovichi died out in the second generation, and only the Ol'govichi remained. By the seventh decade of the twelfth century the Ol'govichi themselves divided into two lines: the descendants of Vsevolod Ol'govich, the senior branch, and the descendants of Svyatoslav Ol'govich, the cadet. It meant that the territory of Chernigov itself was virtually split into two: only members of the senior branch acceded to the throne of Chernigov, while Novgorod Severskiy was the centre of the lands held by the cadet branch. How exactly the whole territory was divided into the districts of Chernigov and Novgorod Severskiy is hard to say: most of the western and northern lands were seemingly under the control of Chernigov, while the *otchina* of the princes of Novgorod Severskiy consisted of the southern half of the country. Unfortunately there is not enough clear evidence to show how the various minor members of the two families were assigned to the smaller towns. Nor do the sources reveal whether any branches managed to establish firm patrimonial possessions in the less important districts. All we know is that 'lateral seniority', according to which brother succeeded brother, appears to have been the principle observed for succession to the two major thrones of Chernigov and Novgorod Severskiy. But whether Putivl', say, or Kursk, or Kozel'sk were handed down vertically from father to son we cannot say.

All in all, in spite of the numerous family clashes in the mid-twelfth century, the Svyatoslavichi emerged as a reasonably united family by the end of the century. Nor were they unsuccessful in the political upheavals of the age. From 1138 to 1194 various Svyatoslavichi ruled as princes of Kiev for no less than a total of twenty-six years, eight years more than the Ryurikovichi of Smolensk managed over the period 1158–1202. The territory of Chernigov was considerably enlarged: the area on both sides of the Seym, including the important towns of Kursk and Ryl'sk, a district which for a hundred years after Yaroslav I's death had belonged now to Southern Pereyaslavl', now to Chernigov, finally became incorporated in Chernigov territory at the end of the 1150s,[17] while the district of Kletsk (Klechesk) and Slutsk (Sluchesk) (the so-called 'Dregovichi land'), which formed a large wedge in the principality of Turov-Pinsk west of the Dnepr and north of the Pripyat', seems to have been ruled by the princes of Chernigov during much of the twelfth century.[18] Most indicative, however, of the latent power of Chernigov at the turn of the century is the fact that the chronicles record no major feudal wars within the territory during the last quarter of the twelfth century or the first quarter of the thirteenth.

But the power of Chernigov was indeed latent. As will be seen later, at the beginning of the thirteenth century the Ol'govichi were not yet strong enough to play a decisive role in the war for supremacy in southern Russia. This was due in the main to the relative weakness of the two successors of the last of the Ol'govichi to rule in Kiev in the twelfth century, Svyatoslav Vsevolodovich; and it was only when Svyatoslav's powerful son, Vsevolod Chermnyy, became prince of Chernigov in 1204 that the Ol'govichi were able to make their mark in the power struggle which ensued.

*   *   *   *

Southern Pereyaslavl' had little in common geographically or politically with Chernigov. Its western boundary with Kiev ran in a line roughly halfway between the Dnepr and the lower Desna in the west and the Trubezh in the east. At Osterskiy Gorodok, at the mouth of the Oster, the line ran due east, forming a common frontier with Chernigov. In the south-west the Dnepr separated it from the nomadic steppe-land. The Sula river, with its system of fortified strongholds, including Rimov, Lukol'm, Lubno and Romen, formed the obvious barrier in the east against steppe invaders from the Don area, although probably by the end of the twelfth century the land controlled by the princes of Pereyaslavl' extended as far east as the upper reaches of the Severskiy Donets and included much of the basins of the Psel and Vorskla rivers as well. All the main rivers which traversed Pereyaslavl' territory – the Trubezh, Supoy, Sula, Psel and Vorskla – gave access to the Dnepr, the main route south to the

9

Crimea and the Black Sea, while the Donets linked Pereyaslavl' with the Sea of Azov.[19]

Politically, economically and militarily Pereyaslavl' faced south and west. Its main links were with Kiev and its main function – from the point of view of whoever ruled Kiev – was to defend Kiev from steppe invaders from the east. For much of the eleventh and twelfth centuries wars were fought on Pereyaslavl' soil against Pechenegs, Torki and Polovtsians, wars to contain the nomads in their relentless drive westwards. There was little business conducted with Chernigov in the north except for the periodical transfer of the Kursk area on either side of the Seym river from principality to principality in the hundred years following Yaroslav I's death (see p. 9). It is true that the princes of Chernigov again and again attempted to seize control over Pereyaslavl' in the first half of the twelfth century, but they were never successful, and Pereyaslavl' remained firmly in the hands of the descendants of Vladimir Monomakh, even when the Svyatoslavichi held Kiev.

Unlike Smolensk and Chernigov, Pereyaslavl' seems never to have enjoyed any degree of real independence from Kiev until the middle of the twelfth century. The district was assigned to Vsevolod by Yaroslav I in 1054 along with Rostov and Suzdal' (see p. 2) and for the next hundred years was ruled either by Vsevolod himself or by his sons Vladimir Monomakh and Rostislav. From Monomakh's accession to Kiev in 1113 to the end of the twelfth century Pereyaslavl' was ruled only by members of the vast family of Monomashichi – by four of Monomakh's sons (Yaropolk, Vyacheslav, Andrey and Yury Dolgorukiy) and by various descendants of Mstislav the Great and Yury Dolgorukiy. The Monomashichi, of course, looked on it as a springboard for Kiev: the prince of Kiev tended to place his nominee for succession to the throne of Kiev in Pereyaslavl', and indeed of the various princes who sat in Pereyaslavl' from 1054 to 1187 seven eventually acceded to the senior throne. That this was an accepted principle is shown by the events of 1132: when Yaropolk moved from Pereyaslavl' to Kiev on the death of his brother Mstislav the Great, he appointed not one of his brothers in his place, but his nephew Vsevolod Mstislavich. This was immediately taken by his brothers as a breach of the system of seniority; it implied that Yaropolk had designated a nephew rather than a brother as his eventual successor to Kiev. Yury Dolgorukiy, Yaropolk's youngest brother, straightway ousted Vsevolod, but was in turn ousted by Yaropolk, who then added insult to injury by replacing him with yet another nephew, Izyaslav Mstislavich. It was only when Yaropolk's brother Andrey was finally installed in Pereyaslavl' in 1134 that honour was restored and the uncles were satisfied.

For twenty years after Andrey's occupation of the throne, Pereyaslavl' passed from hand to hand amongst the Monomashichi, from Monomakh's sons Vyacheslav and Yury Dolgorukiy, to Mstislav the Great's son (Izyaslav) and grandson (Mstislav), to Yury Dolgorukiy's son Gleb. After Gleb had been placed for the second time on the throne of Pereyaslavl' in 1154, the chroniclers' concern for Kiev's eastern annexe suddenly and inexplicably lapsed. For thirty-three years little that happened there was recorded. The princes of Kiev seem to have lost interest in its ruler as a possible successor to the senior throne. Both Gleb (1154–69)[20] and his son Vladimir (1169–87) ruled undisturbed and managed successfully to defend the principality from Polovtsian attacks.

By the end of the century Pereyaslavl' was out of the clutches of the prince of Kiev. Although the chronicles of both Kiev and Vladimir throw remarkably little light on happenings in the south-east from Vladimir's death in 1187 to 1200, it is quite clear that control over the principality had passed into the receptive hands of Vsevolod III of Suzdalia. The last twelfth-century prince of Pereyaslavl', Yaroslav Mstislavich,[21] was, like his predecessor, a nephew of the grand prince of Vladimir. So confident of the absence of disaffection in the principality was Vsevolod III that he was able to appoint his ten-year-old son Yaroslav to the throne in 1200. His aim was clear. It was to ensure that no prince should gain control over the entire south of Russia from Galicia to Pereyaslavl'.

*   *   *   *

Vsevolod III, like his brother Andrey Bogolyubskiy, entertained similar designs with regard to the most easterly of the south-Russian districts, Murom and Ryazan'. His aim, however, was not only to prevent the spread of power of any one prince over all southern Russia, but also to isolate the rulers of Murom-Ryazan' from their closest cousins, the princes of Chernigov.

Situated on the middle reaches of the Oka and the upper reaches of the Don and Voronezh, Murom-Ryazan' bordered Chernigov in the west and Suzdalia in the north; the eastern and southern frontiers are hard to define more than vaguely, melting as they did into Mordvinian and Polovtsian territory. Like Pereyaslavl', the district was subject to constant Polovtsian aggression from the south; but it faced a further danger from the east – marauding parties of Volga Bulgars. There were few defences in the east: the vulnerability of the area is illustrated only too well by the ease with which Baty's armies swept into Ryazan' in 1237 and into Murom in 1239.[22]

Murom-Ryazan' was considered part of the principality of Chernigov when in 1054 Yaroslav I left 'Chernigov and all the western land even as far as Murom' to his son Svyatoslav (see above, p. 8). A separate principality was formed only in 1127 when Svyatoslav's youngest son Yaroslav was ousted from Chernigov and formally became sole ruler of Murom-Ryazan'. After his death in 1129 Murom-Ryazan' remained in the family of his descendants: it never reverted to the princes of Chernigov or Novgorod Severskiy. Curiously enough, the senior throne was the more remote Murom, the junior was Ryazan'. Although there is little information on the district during the first half of the twelfth century, it looks as though the first two generations of Yaroslavichi occupied the two thrones in strict rotation, according to the rules of lateral seniority, that is. By the end of the twelfth century, however, the family had split into two, and so too probably had the territory of Murom-Ryazan': the descendants of Yury Vladimirovich held on to Murom in the north-eastern corner of the district and, to judge from the scant and often oblique references in the sources, were little more than passive and subordinate allies of the rulers

11

of Suzdalia; while those of Gleb Rostislavich, the cadet branch, clung, with striking tenacity and resilience, to Ryazan' and its various minor districts until what remained of the principality of Ryazan' was formally taken over by Vasily III of Moscow in 1521.

During much of the twelfth century Ryazan' struggled to achieve a measure of independence from its stronger neighbours to the west (Chernigov) and to the north (Suzdalia). But somehow nothing went right. Although after Yaroslav Svyatoslavich's death in 1129 the whole province had shaken off the tutelage of Chernigov, yet on more than one occasion it was obliged to look to its western neighbour for assistance, as though the blood ties had never been broken. But it was north-east Russia – the lands of Suzdal' and Vladimir – that caused the princes of Ryazan' most headaches in the second half of the twelfth century, and subservience to the grand prince of Vladimir replaced their previous subservience to the princes of Chernigov. Andrey Bogolyubskiy and Vsevolod III seized every opportunity to keep their economically weaker neighbours in submission. By obliging them to participate in their campaigns against Kiev, Novgorod, Chernigov and the Volga Bulgars, they reduced them at times to a state of near-vassalage; and by interfering in Ryazan''s internal affairs – if not indeed by deliberately provoking internecine strife – they made sure that Ryazan' was kept firmly under their control.

Only one prince of Ryazan' in the twelfth century had strength enough to resist, and that was Gleb Rostislavich; but he was only able to make his presence felt in the north during the confused period following the death of Andrey Bogolyubskiy (1174). His vain attempt to put his own creatures on the throne of Vladimir led to war in 1177, and Vsevolod's decisive victory over the Ryazanites on the river Koloksha near Vladimir in February 1178 put paid to Gleb's quest for autarchy. For the next thirty years Ryazan' was looked on more or less as a vassal by Vsevolod III: he forced the Ryazanites to fight on his side (against Chernigov in 1180 and 1197; against their old allies the Polovtsians in 1199); he meddled in their internal affairs (1180, 1186); he isolated them politically and perhaps even ecclesiastically from Chernigov – so much so, indeed, that in 1198 they requested and got a separate eparchy (formerly the principality had been under the jurisdiction of the bishop of Chernigov).[23] Vsevolod, it seemed, had only to lift his little finger to be obeyed.[24] At the turn of the century Ryazan' was as much under his sway as was Pereyaslavl'. There was, however, one major difference. Whereas Pereyaslavl' was ruled by Vsevolod's close relations on whom he could rely, Ryazan' had its own homebred princes, many of whom were to prove intractable in its future relations with Suzdalia.

* * * *

The western extremities of the old Kievan state, the agriculturally rich and economically powerful district of Volynia and Galicia, presented a formidable and united power-block at the beginning of the thirteenth century. Before the vigorous Roman of Volynia annexed Galicia in 1199, however, the two principalities had each gone their way, seemingly independent one from the other.

Both had one feature in common which distinguished them from the other south-Russian districts: together they had the longest frontiers adjoining non-Russian territory. On the south-west was the vast kingdom of Hungary, separated from Galicia by the Carpathian mountains; in the west the federation of Poland, split into the provinces of Great Poland, Little Poland, Silesia, Mazovia and Kuyavia; to the north and the north-east lay the lands of the Teutonic Knights. The whole of the vague and indefinable southern frontier separated the two districts from the Polovtsian steppes. Small wonder, then, that their early history differed radically from that of the other Kievan principalities.

Throughout the eleventh and twelfth centuries both districts suffered from the covetous attention of their non-Russian neighbours, especially the Poles and the Hungarians. Galicia, facing both Poland and Hungary, was the most exposed: Peremyshl' and Cherven', in the extreme west, exchanged ownership between Poles and Russians no less than five times in the hundred years before the 1080s, while the Hungarians almost continuously throughout the twelfth century supported Volynia against Galicia and attempted to infiltrate into the country. In the confused period following the death of Yaroslav Osmomysl (1187) King Béla III of Hungary even managed to place his son Andrew for a brief period on the throne of Galich. Nor was Volynia free from Polish interference. From the early eleventh century Volynian-Polish relations alternated between marriages and alliances on the one hand and open hostility on the other.

The westernmost of the two districts, Galicia, was situated on the north-eastern slopes of the Carpathians and in the basin of the river Dnestr. Its main towns were connected via its rivers with the Black Sea and with the Baltic: Galich on the Dnestr, Terebovl' on the Dnestr's northern tributary the Seret, and Kolomyya on the Prut, all had direct access to the Black Sea and thus to Constantinople and the Crimea. Peremyshl' on the San, which flows into the Vistula at Zawichost, had close links with eastern Poland and the Baltic. Volynia was likewise linked with the Baltic via the Vistula's other great tributary the Western Bug, but it also had access both to the Black Sea via the upper waters of the Southern Bug and to Turov and Kiev along the Styr' and the Goryn', tributaries of the Pripyat'. The economic importance of the two countries can be gauged from their geographical location. Not only did trade flow down the rivers to the Black Sea and the Baltic, but overland routes linked Galicia with Hungary across the Carpathians, while the two main dry-land routes from Kiev to Cracow and Prague ran through Vladimir in Volynia in the north and through Terebovl' in Galicia in the south.[25]

The early political history of Galicia – that is to say of its main towns Terebovl' and Zvenigorod; Galich is not mentioned in the sources before the twelfth century – is shrouded in obscurity. Yaroslav I's so-called 'will' of 1054 makes no mention of the district. However, some historians claim that he left it to his grandson Rostislav, the son of his firstborn Vladimir, who predeceased him in 1052. Whatever happened to Galicia in the first thirty years after Yaroslav I's death, it is clear that Rostislav's three sons, Ryurik, Volodar' and

Vasil'ko, managed in the 1080s to carve out for themselves areas of Galicia centered probably on Peremyshl', Terebovl' and Zvenigorod. At any rate at the Congress of Lyubech in 1097 it was decreed that Peremyshl' was the *otchina* of Volodar' and Terebovl' that of Vasil'ko (Ryurik had died in 1092).They were already powerful, with far-reaching reputations: in 1091 Vasil'ko had helped save the Byzantine empire from the Pechenegs[26]; he had led successful campaigns against the Poles and the Hungarians and, in 1097, was preparing expeditions against Poland and the Danubian Bulgars[27]; furthermore, he planned, or so it was alleged, to occupy northern Volynia and the district of Turov and Pinsk.[28] In 1098 Volodar' and his brother, by nullifying Svyatopolk of Kiev's attempt to bring Galicia to heel, effectively freed themselves from the interference of Kiev and put Galicia outside the control of its prince.

Volodar' and Vasil'ko both died in 1124, and during the rest of the twelfth century the former's descendants ruled Galicia. Towards the end of the century, however, the authority of this the first house of Galicia was clearly on the wane. Vladimir Yaroslavich, the last member of the dynasty to rule in Galicia (1187–99), a man 'addicted to heavy drinking and bigamously married to a priest's wife',[29] was humiliated both by his boyars, who ousted him, refusing to 'bow down to a priest's wife',[30] and by the king of Hungary, who, when asked for asylum, promptly imprisoned him.[31] Yet he managed to escape from Hungary in 1190 and to return to Galicia with the help of Frederick Barbarossa and the Poles. Somehow he clung to the throne for another nine years. But his hold on Galicia must have appeared precarious at first. Roman of Volynia was biding his time in expectation of an opportunity to join Galicia to his own principality, while the Poles and Hungarians were waiting in the wings for a chance to pounce. Vladimir had little choice but to seek a suzerain and protector in the most powerful of Russian rulers. As soon as he returned to Galich he sent an envoy to Suzdal': 'Father and lord,' are the words he is alleged to have addressed to Vsevolod, 'keep Galicia in my possession and I shall be God's servant and your servant together with all Galicia. And I shall always be obedient to your will.'[32] It was a wise move. Vsevolod obliged 'all the princes and the king of the Poles' not to attempt to take Galicia from him. He was evidently successful. Vladimir, according to the Kievan chronicle, 'firmly established himself in Galicia, and from that time on there was no one to oppose him.'[33] It was only after his death in 1199 that Roman was able to occupy Galicia and to unite it with Volynia.

The political history of Volynia differed sharply from that of Galicia in that the district only appears to have achieved a measure of independence from Kiev in the second quarter of the twelfth century. Furthermore, the northernmost areas of Berest'e (modern Brest Litovsk) and Dorogochinin seem to have been little more than an annex of Kiev before their incorporation into Volynia in the second half of the twelfth century – in 1142, for instance, we find the Chernigovan prince of Kiev, Vsevolod Ol'govich, allocating them to his relatives.[34]

In the eleventh century Volynia was the possession of no one branch of the family for long. In 1054 it was left by Yaroslav I to his sixth eldest son Igor', but neither he nor his son David held it for any length of time, and David's descendants were eventually pushed out to the tiny peripheral principality of Gorodno (Gródno) at the extreme northern tip of Volynia. After passing from family to family, Volynia finally came to rest in the hands of Vladimir Monomakh and his descendants. For a while it was held by Monomakh's son Andrey (1125–34), but then it passed to Monomakh's tough and energetic grandson Izyaslav Mstislavich. Once in his possession, Volynia ceased to be the *otchina* of whoever was prince of Kiev. It was now the family possession of Izyaslav and his descendants. Under his two eldest sons Mstislav and Yaroslav the district was split into two, Vladimir and the western half falling to Mstislav, while Lutsk on the Styr' and the eastern half became the patrimony of Yaroslav and his sons. At the end of the century Mstislav's great son Roman joined the whole of Volynia to Galicia, thus forming the powerful south-west Russian state which was to play so big a role in the history of southern Russian in the thirteenth century.

* * * *

The district of Turov and Pinsk, watered by the middle Pripyat' and its numerous tributaries, densely wooded, marshy and agriculturally unproductive for the most part, was curiously neglected and at times ignored by all the early chronicle-writers, so much so that it is almost impossible to trace its history in the eleventh and twelfth centuries. And yet, for all its agricultural backwardness, it must have been a region of considerable importance. The Pripyat', on which the town of Turov was situated, was, after all, the main route from Kiev to Poland and the Baltic. Furthermore, Turov was an episcopal see, the most celebrated incumbent of which, Kirill, who flourished in the twelfth century, was distinguished as the author of sermons couched in the most florid and elaborate of Byzantine rhetoric. Culturally and commercially, the region can hardly have been the backwater suggested by what looks like the contemptuous refusal of the sources to mention it.

The boundaries of the district are hard to determine, more so than any other south-Russian principality. All its four neighbours, Kiev, Volynia, Polotsk and Chernigov, controlled parts of it at various times. It is difficult to say, for instance, whether at any time Pinsk formed the northern slice of Volynia together with Berest'e, or for how long Chernigov controlled the central wedge of Kletsk and Slutsk in the twelfth century (the so-called 'Dregovichi land', see above, p. 9), or to what extent Turov was looked upon simply as an annexe of the principality of Kiev or even as an eastern extension of Volynia. All we can say is that Yaroslav I's second eldest son Izyaslav and his descendants seem to have had some sort of claim on much of the region and to have looked upon Turov as their own family possession. Izyaslav certainly ruled there,[35] as did his two sons Yaropolk and Svyatopolk. After Svyatopolk's death in 1113 Turov, like so many other south Russian districts, fell into the grasp of Vladimir Monomakh and his son Mstislav. Until the mid 1150s it passed from hand to hand amongst Vladimir's sons and grandsons. Then, by some quirk of fate, it reverted to Izyaslav's branch. Yury Yaroslavich, Izyaslav's great-grandson, somehow or other managed to wrest Turov and Pinsk from Yury Dolgorukiy's son Boris, the last of the Monomashichi to rule there. For the rest of the century the district remained the possession of Yury, his five sons and three grandsons. The inevitable happened. Turov splintered into a number of minor principalities: Pinsk, Kletsk, Dubrovitsa on the Goryn', Nesvezh', Slutsk and probably others too. To whom their rulers owed allegiance is not known – probably, at the turn of the century, Roman of Volynia and Galicia was their suzerain. In the thirteenth century the principality of Turov and Pinsk – if ever it existed as such – seems almost to have disappeared from the political map of southern Russia. Only twice more, before the Tatar invasion of 1223, do we hear of the princes of Turov and Pinsk: in 1207 they sided with the Ol'govichi against Ryurik of Kiev (see below, p. 31); and in 1212 they appear to have taken part in the campaign of the Rostislavichi against Kiev (see below, p. 42, n. 71).[36] After that they disappeared almost entirely from the scene. For all the chroniclers cared, they might not have existed. Like Polotsk, Turov was, later in the thirteenth century, to prove an easy victim of Lithuania.[37]

*   *   *   *

In striking contrast with all the above-described districts which made up the lands of Russia in the twelfth century was the principality of Polotsk, situated west of Smolensk and north of Turov. At no time a patrimony of any of the descendants of Yaroslav I, it never knew the umbilical cord which tied the other districts to the mother city of Kiev. However strongly the rulers of Kiev attempted to subjugate it, it somehow managed to remain aloof and independent for much of the eleventh and twelfth centuries. It had its own dynasty, springing from Vladimir I's second eldest son Izyaslav, sent there to rule together with his mother Rogneda some time at the end of the tenth century. And it was the only principality which bordered both with Lithuania and with the territory of the German Knights at the end of the twelfth century, being thus vulnerable to outside interference on the part of two potentially aggressive elements along its entire western frontier.

The land was, like the district of Turov, agriculturally poor and for the most part wooded and marshy, but from a commercial point of view it had one great advantage over most of the other principalities – through its centre ran the Western Dvina river, which provided a direct link with the Baltic, as did the upper waters of the Neman in the western region of the principality. There were also good river connections with the south: in the south-eastern corner of the district flowed the Dnepr as well as its two major tributaries, the Drut' and the Berezina.

The sources which provide information on Polotsk during the eleventh and twelfth centuries are fragmentary, confusing and totally inadequate for our needs. Even if a chronicle were kept in Polotsk – or Minsk, or Vitebsk, for that matter – few traces of it remained in the records of Kiev, Novgorod or Suzdalia. In the eleventh century Polotsk appears to have been relatively strong and undivided; for the entire hundred years we hear of only two princes on the throne, Izyaslav's warlike son Bryacheslav (1001–44) and his even more aggressive grandson Vseslav (1044–1101). In the twelfth century, however, the principality split into a number of minor districts – Polotsk, Minsk, Vitebsk, Drutsk, Izyaslavl', Logozhsk, perhaps more – amongst Vseslav's numerous sons and grandsons. Attempts were made to unite the country, under the aegis now of Minsk, now of Polotsk, but they failed. By the beginning of the thirteenth century even the sparse references to Polotsk in the chronicles began to dry up, a sure sign of the principality's enfeeblement. Pressure from the German crusaders along the Dvina and their enthralment of Polotsk's Lettish tributaries (in the early thirteenth century the outposts of Kukenois (Kokenhusen) and Gercike on the Dvina, hitherto held by Russian garrisons commanded by Polotsk princelings, fell to Bishop Albert of Uexküll and his Saxons),[38] pressure from Lithuania in the west and Smolensk in the east, the constant feudal conflicts of the twelfth century, the sporadic attempts of Kiev to control Polotsk and the disastrous fragmentation of the country – all took their toll. Although Henry of Livonia talks of one 'Prince Vladimir' as 'king of Polotsk' at the turn of the century,[39] and although the principality managed somehow to survive for a few decades more, nevertheless it was hopelessly weakened politically and militarily. It presented no threat to any of its neighbours, least of all to Suzdalia, and it was only a question of time before the most aggressive of them, Lithuania, absorbed it.[40]

* * * *

The only Russian district which was not a principality proper – i.e. one governed by the prince of a dynasty settled there or by one appointed from outside – but which nevertheless depended on an extraneous prince and his army to defend its frontiers and fight its wars was Novgorod. The centre of this city state (for it could not be called a principality and not yet a republic) was Lake Il'men', with the town itself situated just north of it on the Volkhov river. The land extended north to the Gulf of Finland, the Neva, the southern shores of Lake Ladoga and the River Svir'. In the east it flanked Suzdalia; in the south – Smolensk and Polotsk. The western frontier ran south along the Narova river, through the centre of Lake Peypus (Lake Chudskoe) and well west of the Velikaya river to the northernmost tip of Polotsk. All this area was administered centrally from Novgorod; only the western town of Pskov and its considerable dependent territory enjoyed self-government, though a self-government strictly supervised by Novgorod, which appointed its *posadnik*, or chief executive.

Novgorod itself was the second largest town in Russia after Kiev. Situated both on the north–south route from the Baltic (via the Neva, Lake Ladoga and the Volkhov) to the Black Sea (via the Lovat' and portage to the Dnepr) and on the east–west routes linking Novgorod with the Volga (via the Pola and Lake Seliger, and via the Msta and portage to the Tvertsa river), it was the great trading centre with the South, the East and the West, but especially with the West. Novgorod's wealth, however, came not only from its commerce, but also from its vast northern colonies. These stretched north to the Arctic and east to the Urals (Pechora and Yugra districts). In the rich central area known

17

as the Zavoloch'e ('Beyond the Portage'), that is the land in the Northern Dvina basin north-east of the portage between the White Lake and Lake Kubenskoe, Novgorod authority was already firmly established by the twelfth century, with administrators and governors appointed by the central authority. The remote outlying districts (Perm', Yugra, Pechora and the Kola peninsula) were under Novgorod control only in so far as they paid regular tribute and cannot in any way be considered to have been 'colonized' by Novgorod by the beginning of the thirteenth century – or by the end of it for that matter.

From an administrative point of view the city of Novgorod was split into two halves. On the west bank of the Volkhov was the so-called 'Cathedral Side' (*Sofiyskaya storona*) divided into three administrative districts or boroughs (*kontsy*) (Nerevskiy, Zagorodskiy and Lyudin, the latter two known as Prussian Street, *Prusskaya ulitsa*) and the *detinets* or kremlin, dominated by the cathedral of St Sofia; east of the river was the 'Trade Side' (*Torgovaya storona*) with two *kontsy* (Plotnitskiy and Slavenskiy). Each of the five *kontsy* was responsible for the administration of the five *volosti* or districts into which the central region of Novgorod land was divided.

From as early as the second half of the ninth century Novgorod was dependent on whoever was prince of Kiev. Later, princes were sent from Kiev to 'rule' in Novgorod. What that meant in the early days in terms of power – how much authority the prince wielded, how much land he owned, to what extent administrative, judicial and fiscal functionaries were appointed by him – we cannot say. But in the eleventh century and in the first half of the twelfth he was certainly more than just the military commander and defender of the frontiers, and his presence, though necessary in view of the Novgorodians' extraordinary inability to defend themselves militarily, was clearly irksome to them.

Early in the twelfth century, as Novgorod's urge for independence grew, so the prince's power began to erode: the office of *posadnik*, the annually elected 'mayor' or chief executive of the city, became elective – formerly he had been the appointee and right-hand man of the prince, now he was chosen by the town assembly (*veche*) from among the boyars of Novgorod, and was thus converted from an instrument of the prince's will to a potential check on his power. The *veche* acquired the right also to appoint the all-powerful bishop (archbishop from 1165) – the nominal head of state, the keeper of the treasury, the lord of the state lands, the supreme ecclesiastical judge, the future chairman of the ruling assembly – and, later, the *tysyatskiy* – the commander of the local militia and chief of police. But most important of all, Novgorod ceased to be dependent on Kiev for its supply of rulers. From 1136, when a civic uprising resulted in the ousting of a former prince of Kiev's son from the city, Novgorod enjoyed the prerogative of selecting its own prince from *any* princely dynasty. Of course, a strong prince of Vladimir, Kiev or Chernigov could still enforce his will on Novgorod and oblige the city to accept his nominee. But there was no longer a tradition or unwritten law according to which it was Kiev whose ruler automatically placed his son or close relative in Novgorod, and Novgorod was able to tack between the three main princely groupings: the senior branch of the Monomashichi (mainly the Rostislavichi, the princes of Smolensk), the cadet branch (Yury Dolgorukiy and his children) and their by now remote cousins, the Ol'govichi of Chernigov. All three families provided princes for Novgorod during the second half of the twelfth century.

It must not be imagined that Novgorod's newly-acquired right to select its own princes necessarily led to a diminution of the prince's power: this was only the case when a weak prince, or rather the appointee of a weak prince, was on the throne. It would appear that in general there was little or no limitation of princely authority in the second half of the twelfth century – or at any rate none that was recorded – except for the right to oust an unwanted incumbent, which the city exercised from time to time during this period without incurring serious reprisals from outside. The reasons for this inability to lessen princely power are not hard to find: in spite of the fact that the leading officials of the city were elected independently of the prince, there was no solidarity amongst those who constituted the main force behind their election, namely the boyars. For in the twelfth century the boyars themselves were divided in their allegiance to the purveyors of Novgorodian rulers. From 1136 onwards various sharply conflicting boyar groupings can be identified: there were those who supported the Ol'govichi and those who opposed them; later, the opponents of the Ol'govichi divided between the supporters of the Suzdalian princes and those of the Smolensk princes. It meant that whoever was prince could usually rely on support from one faction or another; but it also meant that no boyar party could retain power *without* the backing of whoever was prince at the time. Consequently, instead of forming a consolidated opposition to princely authority and privilege and elaborating some form of oligarchic republican rule, the boyars were bitterly divided amongst themselves by the very fact that the city state had the right to choose, or to influence the choice of, its own princes and also to get rid of them.[41]

Towards the end of the twelfth century the authority of Vsevolod III of Suzdalia began to make itself felt in Novgorod more and more. For much of the 1180s and 1190s the prince of Novgorod was his creature – one Yaroslav Vladimirovich, a distant relative (he was a grandson of Mstislav the Great) and remotely connected to him by marriage. Although his rule was interrupted for short periods by representatives of the Ol'govichi and the Rostislavichi, nevertheless it appeared that by the end of the century Novgorod was reconciled, for the time being at least, to a firm commitment to accept its rulers from Suzdalia. In 1199 it was Vsevolod III himself who removed Yaroslav from Novgorod and replaced him with his three-year-old son. It looked as though the city had temporarily lost even its right to choose its prince. In one more district Suzdalian influence was dominant.

* * * *

From this survey of the political organization of each of the territories of Russia at the end of the twelfth century and of their previous history it can be seen that by 1200 Kiev had lost what appeared a century earlier to be universally recognized control over most of the land of Russia – Volynia, Southern Pereyaslavl', Turov and Smolensk in the south, as well as Suzdalia and Novgorod in the north, in other words *all* Russian districts except Chernigov-Ryazan', Galicia and Polotsk; while Vsevolod III now had a firm grip not only on his patrimony of Suzdalia, but also on Southern Pereyaslavl', Murom-Ryazan' and Novgorod. It can also be seen why power had shifted, even if only temporarily, from the south to the north, and why the ruler of emergent Suzdalia had supplanted the prince of Kiev as the dominant ruler in Russia. It was not because Kiev had become in any way economically weakened – there is no evidence in the Russian sources to show that the slackening of Black Sea trade, for instance, significantly affected Kiev – or because there had been any noticeable migration from south to north in the twelfth century – again, there is no evidence to show that the population of Suzdalia or Novgorod increased at the expense of Kiev or of any other southern principality. The real reason for this momentous shift of influence must be sought first and foremost in the fact that there was no *one* dynasty which ruled Kiev throughout the twelfth century. As has been shown, control alternated first between Monomashichi and Ol'govichi, then later between senior and junior branches of the Monomashichi themselves, with, of course, accompanying bursts of disruptive civil war. In contrast, Suzdalia, for most of the twelfth century, was ruled by three strong princes, a father and two sons, all three intolerant of rivalry, conscious of their particular family unity and unwilling to let control over Rostov, Suzdal' and Vladimir slip into the hands of any other branch of the Monomashichi, still less of such outsiders as the Ol'govichi or the princes of Ryazan'. Furthermore, Suzdalia remained totally unfragmented during the twelfth century: authority was safely in the hands of the ruling prince, and there were no signs yet of the settling of sons or brothers in *otchiny* carved out of the territory of Suzdalia.

It is, therefore, in this singlemindedness and cohesiveness of Yury Dolgo-rukiy and his two sons, in their determination jealously to guard and systematically to expand their northern state, and in the inability of any *one* branch of the Ryurikovichi to control Kiev as Vladimir Monomakh and Mstislav the Great had done, that we must look for the main reason for what appears to be the temporary 'decline' of Kiev at the beginning of the thirteenth century and the emergence of a powerful and dominant Suzdalia.

REFERENCES AND NOTES

1. *NPL*, p. 160 (*s.a.* 989).
2. See Kuchkin, 'O marshrutakh'; Smirnov, *Volzhskie bolgary*, Ch. 2; Nasonov, *Russkaya zemlya*, Ch. 11.
3. Presnyakov, *Obrazovanie*, p. 27.
4. *PSRL*, vol. 2, cols 520, 521, *s.a.* (ultra-March) 6670.
5. Kuchkin, 'Rostovo-Suzdal'skaya zemlya', p. 87.
6. Ibid.
7. See Poppe, 'On the Title of Grand Prince', p. 685.
8. Zimin, 'Novgorod i Volokolamsk', pp. 103–4.
9. See Kuchkin, 'Rostovo-Suzdal'skaya zemlya', pp. 88 *et seq.*

10. See Tolochko, *Kiev i Kievskaya zemlya*, pp. 114–63.

11. According to Tatishchev, Rostislav was given Smolensk in 1125. *Istoriya*, vol. 2, p. 137.

12. For a detailed description of the boundàries of Smolensk, see Alekseev, *Smolenskaya zemlya*, pp. 53–4.

13. See Yanin, 'Mezhdunarodnye otnosheniya', p. 122.

14. See Alekseev, 'Nekotorye voprosy'.

15. *NPL*, p. 160.

16. *PSRL*, vol. 1, col. 257, note a.

17. Zaytsev, 'Chernigovskoe knyazhestvo', pp. 95 *et seq*.

18. Ibid, pp. 104–8.

19. See Kuchera, *Pereyaslavskoe knyazhestvo*, pp. 118–20, 136.

20. Gleb was in fact appointed to Kiev in 1169 by his nephew Mstislav Andreevich at Andrey Bogolyubskiy's instigation. He died in 1171, murdered, so his brother Andrey was told.

21. It is not clear from the sources when Yaroslav became prince of Pereyaslavl', but it seems likely that he succeeded his cousin Vladimir in 1187.

22. *PSRL*, vol. 1, col. 470.

23. Tatishchev, *Istoriya*, vol. 4, p. 326; Kuz'min, *Ryazanskoe letopisanie*, p. 127.

24. For an account of the political history of Ryazan' on the twelfth century, see Mongayt, *Ryazanskaya zemlya*, Ch. 29; Ilovaysky, *Istoriya*, Ch. 2.

25. See Pashuto, *Ocherki*, pp. 168 *et seq*.

26. See *Ocherki istorii SSSR IX-XIII vv.*, p. 365.

27. *PSRL*, vol. 1, col. 266.

28. Ibid., col. 263.

29. *PSRL*, vol. 2, col. 659.

30. Ibid., col. 660.

31. Ibid., col. 661.

32. Ibid., col. 667.

33. Ibid.

34. Ibid., cols 310 12.

35. Even before he was given Kiev in 1054. *PSRL*, vol. 2, col. 150.

36. According to Tatishchev, they also participated in the campaign of the Rostislav-ichi in 1221. See below, p. 38.

37. On Turov in the eleventh and twelfth centuries, see Lysenko, *Goroda Turovskoy zemli*, pp. 21–31.

38. Brundage, *The Chronicle of Henry of Livonia*, pp. 90–3.

39. Henry's *Chronicle of Livonia* was written between 1225 and 1229. Ibid , pp. 13, 26.

40. On Polotsk, see Alekseev, *Polotskaya zemlya* and a shortened version in *Drevnerusskie knyazhestva* ('Polotskaya zemlya', pp. 202–39).

41. See Yanin, *Novgorodskie posadniki*, Ch. 3.

CHAPTER TWO

South Russia 1200–1223

In 1194 Svyatoslav Vsevolodovich, the last of the Ol'govichi to occupy the throne of Kiev for any length of time, died. He was immediately succeeded by the powerful and energetic figure of Ryurik Rostislavich, equalled amongst his relatives in mobility and enterprise only by his nephew Mstislav the Daring. For the next forty-five years or so he and his sons, nephews and cousins – the Rostislavichi – were to dominate south-Russian politics together with the Ol'govichi of Chernigov and the princes of south-west Russia. The aim of all three warring factions was the same: the consolidation of power over the whole of the south of Russia under the control of a prince ruling in the mother city of Kiev. For however much the town and principality may have lost in political authority during the feudal wars of the twelfth century and however much the rulers of Suzdalia may have considered that over-all power now resided in their branch of the Monomashichi family and in their capital city of Vladimir in the north, Kiev was still the supreme prize and the powerful magnet and was still to remain the residence of the metropolitan, the head of the Russian Church, for a century to come.

In the main, the struggle which ensued was to be fought out, as it had been throughout much of the second half of the twelfth century, between the Rostislavichi and the Ol'govichi. Most of the time a state of simmering, sometimes open, warfare existed between them. Occasionally the two families would form an ephemeral alliance, but only with the aim of combating a common enemy in the shape of whoever controlled the west-Russian lands. In the background to this conflict were the rulers of Vladimir in the north-west, Vsevolod III and his sons, sometimes aloof, but always watchful, ready to intervene if the balance of power in the south needed redressing, and aware of their over-all military and economic superiority. From the great Kievan chronicle[1] – in its latter stages, the family chronicle of Ryurik Rostislavich – it is clear that Ryurik recognized this authority and was ready to acknowledge the suzerainty of Vsevolod III: in the delicate territorial negotiations with Roman Mstislavich and Vsevolod in 1195, negotiations which tottered on the brink of open war, Ryurik told Roman: 'We cannot exist without Vsevolod; we have placed in him the seniority amongst all [our] cousins in the tribe of Vladimir [Monomakh]'[2];

and to Vsevolod he declared: 'You, brother, are senior to us all in the tribe of Vladimir.'[3] Maybe this was nothing more than the language of diplomacy, but the Suzdalian (the so-called Lavrent'evskiy) Chronicle – biased though it may have been – points out that it was Vsevolod III who in fact 'sent his men to Kiev' when Svyatoslav died in 1194 'and put Ryurik Rostislavich on the throne of Kiev'.[4] In 1203 the same chronicle has Roman of Galicia talk of Vsevolod as 'my father and master (*otets i gospodin*)'.[5]

The crisis of 1195–96, which occurred almost immediately after Ryurik's assumption of power, is of importance in so far as it foreshadows much of the inter-princely discord of the first third of the thirteenth century. Any hope of a firm alliance between Ryurik and his powerful son-in-law Roman Mstislavich of Volynia was soon shattered when in the summer of 1195 Vsevolod III, perhaps in an attempt to disrupt the bond between the southern princes, demanded that Ryurik hand over to him the five towns in the south of the territory of Kiev (Torchesk, Trepol', Korsun', Boguslavl', Kanev) which he had previously donated to Roman. Rather than risk the hostility of Vsevolod, Ryurik complied. Roman immediately requested Yaroslav of Chernigov, Svyatoslav Vsevolodovich's brother and the new head of the Ol'govichi clan, to attack Kiev and himself tried to raise an army in Poland. But his efforts were in vain: he failed to get any assistance from the Poles, and the Ol'govichi were unwilling – or not yet ready – to attack Ryurik; indeed, in the autumn of 1195 the Ol'govichi, after considerable pushing on the part of Ryurik and the threat of armed intervention by Vsevolod III, agreed to a temporary truce with Ryurik.

And temporary it turned out to be. In March 1196 Yaroslav of Chernigov invaded the territory of Smolensk. The war that followed was fierce, disruptive, all-embracing and confusing. Fighting took place in the districts of Smolensk, Polotsk, Kiev and Chernigov and spread as far west as Peremil' in Volynia and Kamenets in Galicia; the Rostislavichi (Ryurik of Kiev, his brother David of Smolensk and his nephew Mstislav Romanovich) supported by Gleb Vladimirovich of Ryazan' and Vsevolod III of Suzdalia were ranged against the Ol'govichi of Chernigov (Yaroslav and his nephew Oleg Svyatoslavich), the princes of Polotsk and Roman of Volynia; detachments of Polovtsians, as was so often the case, fought on both sides. But the war led to no concrete results: no territory was seized or annexed, and none of the warring parties won decisive victories. It ended with an unsatisfactory peace in 1196, not between the Rostislavichi, the Ol'govichi and Roman of Volynia, but between Vsevolod III and Yaroslav of Chernigov. The terms of the peace, however, were as inconclusive as the war had been: the Ol'govichi agreed, it is true, to relinquish any attempts to wrest Kiev and Smolensk from the Rostislavichi; and they also agreed to release Ryurik's nephew, who had been captured in the early stages of the fighting. But they refused to break off relations with Roman of Volynia. Vsevolod, it seems, did not insist. It was indeed to his advantage that no lasting agreement between Kiev-Smolensk, Chernigov and Volynia had been reached. The relationship between the Rostislavichi and the Ol'govichi remained a fragile one, and it was only a question of time before a clash between Ryurik and Roman broke the brittle peace in the south.[6]

The clash when it came in 1200 could not have surprised anyone. On a purely personal level there had been antagonism between Ryurik and Roman ever since 1196 when Roman attempted to rid himself of his first wife, Ryurik's daughter Predslava. No reasons are given in the only source to mention the event (the Lavrent'evskiy Chronicle), only the method ('he wished to make her take the veil')[7]; and whether the separation or divorce was connected with the war of 1196 or with Roman's desire to make a politically more profitable marriage we do not know. At any rate poor Predslava seems somehow to have resisted forcible tonsure for the time being and to have escaped – or to have been sent back – to her father in Kiev,[8] and Roman, with little regard for the canons of the church or the feelings of his father-in-law, married a princess who was not only energetic and enterprising but also connected by birth with both Byzantium and Hungary. For the Anna, who emerges in the chronicle as the second wife of Roman and who bore him his two famous sons, Daniil and Vasil'ko, was in all probability none other than the daughter of the emperor Isaac II Angelus and the step-daughter of the sister of King Andrew II of Hungary. Her close links with Byzantium and Hungary, as well as her friendship with Poland and Lithuania,[9] stood her husband and her children in good stead. In 1199, unhampered by any interference from the Hungarians, who alone could have seriously obstructed his progress, Roman occupied Galich. The ancient but by now feeble dynasty of the descendants of Yaroslav I's eldest son, who had kept their hold – sporadic and precarious in the latter half of the twelfth century – on the lands of the upper Dnestr ever since the middle of the eleventh century, had come to an end. The two great south-west-Russian principalities of Volynia and Galicia were now linked under the capable and vigorous rule of Roman, 'Rex Russiae', as a French chronicler of the mid-thirteenth century called him, 'Romanus rex Ruthenorum', as he was known in Erfurt, and 'ever-memorable autocrat of all Rus'', according to the Ipat'evskiy Chronicle.[10]

Roman's seizure of Galich was sufficient to scare the other south-Russian princes. By supporting the previous ruler of Galicia, Vsevolod III had done what he could to keep the two western principalities politically apart[11]; but he had been unable in any way to hamper Roman's annexation of Galicia. Now it fell to him to form some sort of coalition in the south with the aim of building up resistance to Roman, if not of actively dislodging him from Galicia.

His first step was to send his son Yaroslav on 10 August 1200[12] to the most south-easterly principality of Pereyaslavl'. During the rule of its last two princes, Vladimir Glebovich and Yaroslav Mstislavich, Pereyaslavl' had been firmly under the control of Suzdalia (see above, p. 11). Both princes were nephews of Vsevolod III, and it was Vsevolod, and not the metropolitan or even the prince of Kiev, who despatched a bishop to the vacant see of Pereyaslavl' in 1197.[13] But Yaroslav Mstislavich had died in 1198,[14] and although the principality had shown no signs of disaffection or revolt the symbolic appointment of the ten-year-old son of the grand prince, accompanied no doubt by a sizeable detachment of troops and a bevy of administrators, was enough to secure the district at least for the time being.

Vsevolod's plan, however, went further than merely strengthening the southern boundaries. The princes of Chernigov, it will be remembered, had concluded a treaty with Vsevolod in 1196 and had agreed to renounce any claims on Kiev or Smolensk – in other words, to discontinue hostilities with the Rostislavichi – but at the same time they had refused to disrupt their friendship with Roman. Clearly the operative figure had been Vsevolod III, and it would appear that in 1200 it was again he who persuaded the Ol'govichi to break off relations with Roman. Persuasion perhaps was hardly necessary, for Yaroslav of Chernigov, who had signed the treaty of 1196, had died two years later and had been replaced by his cousin, Igor' Svyatoslavich, brother-in-law of the last independent prince of Galicia.[15] Ryurik needed even less persuasion: he was under no treaty obligation to Roman; it was Roman who had started the war of 1195 against him; and Roman had uncanonically divorced his (Ryurik's) daughter Predslava, who was now in Kiev to tell the sorry tale of her misfortunes to her father.

The momentous events of 1200 are described only in the Suzdalian (Lavrent'evskiy) Chronicle[16] and in later compilations deriving from it; the Novgorod and Galician chronicles[17] make no mention of them; while the contemporary Kievan chronicle – the family chronicle of Ryurik[18] – unfortunately ends in 1199. The narrative is dry, factual and unemotional and curiously enough reflects no obvious sympathy for any of the participants. Ryurik and Igor' of Chernigov were taken by surprise. Before they had time to set off west from Kiev, Roman had mobilized an army from Volynia and Galicia and was moving east. As he approached Kiev his army was joined not only by the *Chernye klobuki* – the 'Black Caps' (Karakalpak in Turkish), one of the Turkic tribes settled in the Ros' river area and normally loyal to whoever was prince of Kiev – but also by the 'descendants of Vladimir [Monomakh]' and 'the people of the towns of Rus''. Which of the 'descendants of Vladimir' in fact deserted Ryurik is not stated – perhaps it was just an expression of the chronicler to indicate the massive support his army enjoyed[19] – but clearly Ryurik was abandoned by any allies he may have had, and Roman met with no resistance. Even the Kievans were anxious to welcome the new ruler[20]: the gates of the large northern district of Kiev known as Podol, the trade and craftsmen's centre of the city, were opened, while Ryurik and whichever of the princes of Chernigov were still with him retreated to the comparative safety of 'the Hill' (*Gora*), the strongly defended 'fortress of Yaroslav' where the prince's palace was situated.[21] Once Roman's army had entered the city there was no hope of resistance. Ryurik and the Ol'govichi submitted without fighting and were sent off, Ryurik to the town of Vruchiy north-west of Kiev, a family possession of the Ryurikovichi during the last thirty years of the twelfth century (see above, p. 7), and the Ol'govichi to Chernigov.

What was to be done with Kiev? Clearly Roman could not remain in the city and control his difficult west-Russian possessions from there; after all, Galicia with its troublesome boyars and pro-Hungarian sympathizers had only been annexed by him in the previous year. On the throne of Kiev, therefore, he placed Ingvar' Yaroslavich of Lutsk in Volynia. It might appear that the appointment of so seemingly minor a prince to the supreme throne was an indication of Roman's contemptuous attitude towards Kiev – similar to Andrey Bogolyubskiy's appointment of his brother Gleb in 1169 (see above, p. 3). But whom else could he have appointed? Ingvar' was, after Roman, the senior of the princes of Volynia and indeed the second eldest surviving great-grandson of Mstislav the Great (see Genealogical Table 2) – and Roman was unlikely even to consider any other descendant of Vladimir Monomakh, and certainly not one of the Rostislavichi.

At any rate Kiev remained safely under Roman's control – for two years all was quiet in the south – and Roman was able to undertake a highly successful punitive raid against the Polovtsians in the winter of 1200/01, which resulted in the freeing of a number of Russian prisoners captured no doubt in the confused fighting in 1196.[22] But if the aim of the attack was to stun the Polovtsians into inactivity, it failed, for in 1203 the Polovtsians irrupted into south-Russian affairs, and with a vengeance.

It was too much to expect that the ebullient Ryurik would be satisfied with involuntary retirement and would sit quietly in Vruchiy. Nor was it likely that the numerous rulers of Chernigov would be prepared to watch Roman strengthening his authority in the south: his next move, after all, might well be a take-over of Pereyaslavl', after which Chernigov would be under pressure along the whole of its southern boundary. The unwonted lull which had lasted for two years came to a sudden end on 2 January 1203. Ryurik, the Ol'govichi and all the available Polovtsian khanates ('all the land of the Polovtsians'[23]) invaded and captured Kiev.

Even if we take into consideration the fact that the most detailed and vivid chronicle account of the capture of Kiev – that found in the chronicles of Suzdalia and Northern Pereyaslavl' – consists largely of 'disaster clichés' used both before and after 1203 to illustrate and enliven major calamities, it is clear that the damage inflicted on the city was savage and long to be remembered. The district of Podol was the first to be seized and burned – Ryurik had not forgotten how the citizens had opened the gates to Roman two years earlier. The citadel (the 'Fortress of Yaroslav') was next taken; the cathedral of St Sofia and the church of the Tithe (*Desyatinnaya tserkov'*) were sacked, as were 'all the monasteries'. Most of the looting, capturing and killing was evidently left to the Polovtsians, who led off their prisoners to the steppe.[24] The only people who escaped with their lives, but with the loss of half their goods, were the foreign merchants who had taken refuge in the churches.[25]

What precisely happened after the sack of Kiev is unclear. Ingvar' either was taken prisoner or managed to escape to Volynia.[26] The Ol'govichi went back to the district of Chernigov with their prisoners.[27] As for Ryurik, he seems to have preferred discretion to valour. Fearing reprisals in Kiev and opposition from Roman's previous allies – especially the Black Caps – he withdrew to his residence at Vruchiy, leaving no doubt a garrison in the city.[28] Strange as it may seem, it needed the intervention of Roman for Ryurik to be able to return to Kiev. Roman hastened to Vruchiy (16 February 1203) with the aim not of confronting Ryurik militarily or of recapturing Kiev, but simply of keeping him apart from the Ol'govichi and the Polovtsians; for this was where the danger lay for Roman — in a Rostislavichi–Ol'govichi coalition backed up by the Polovtsians.

But for all his authority as ruler of west Russia Roman could do no more than urge and persuade. True power, as always, lay in the hands of the grand prince of Suzdalia. Few agreements could be ratified without his blessing. Ryurik was obliged to 'kiss the cross' in allegiance to Vsevolod III and his sons. 'Send your man', said Roman, 'and I shall send my man to our father and master Grand Prince Vsevolod; do you beseech him, and I shall beseech him, that he give you back Kiev.'[29] It was a curious request for the conqueror of Kiev to have to make to Vsevolod. But he made it, and Kiev was indeed duly restored to him, no doubt at the price of an agreement never to participate on the side of the Ol'govichi in future wars. At the same time Roman persuaded Vsevolod to agree to a treaty with the Ol'govichi obliging them to remain at peace with their neighbours.[30]

Ryurik's capture of Kiev in 1203 restored south Russia to the status quo of the beginning of the century, with Roman controlling Volynia and Galicia, the Rostislavichi holding Smolensk and Kiev and the Ol'govichi sandwiched uncomfortably between Smolensk and Suzdalian-held Southern Pereyaslavl'. Few people could have believed that the 'peace' of 1203 engineered so energetically by Roman would hold for long. Not only was Roman anxious to reassert his authority in Kiev and remove his troublesome father-in-law Ryurik from the scene, or at any rate to guarantee the impotence of his neighbours in the east, but Ryurik himself could scarcely have felt at ease in Kiev, especially now that his alliance with the Ol'govichi had been broken; nor could Vsevolod III be certain that the Rostislavichi would not upset the balance by once again allying themselves with the Ol'govichi; and the position of his by now 13-year-old son Yaroslav may not have appeared as secure in remote and vulnerable Southern Pereyaslavl' as it did when he sent him there three years earlier.

But at first at any rate all went well, and the events of the late winter of 1203 or early spring of 1204 could only have reassured Vsevolod. Ryurik, Roman, Yaroslav Vsevolodovich of Pereyaslavl' and unspecified 'other princes' all undertook what turned out to be a highly successful combined operation against the Polovtsians which resulted in the capture of a number of prisoners.[31] Significantly enough, the Ol'govichi either were deliberately not invited to participate, or refused.[32]

The spirit of harmony and cooperation did not last for long, although it seems that an attempt was made to hammer out some sort of an agreement between Roman and Ryurik. On the way back from the Polovtsian campaign they conferred with Yaroslav — or rather with his advisers — in Pereyaslavl' and then moved on to Trepol' on the Dnepr, half way between Pereyaslavl' and Kiev. Here it was planned at least to discuss terms of an inter-princely treaty and to agree on what districts should come under the jurisdiction of which clan. What precisely happened in Trepol' is not recorded in the sources. But 'the devil caused great confusion' — a standard chronicle cliché denoting the beginning of yet another round of internecine strife. The upshot was that

Roman arrested Ryurik and sent him to Kiev where he had him, his wife and his daughter (Roman's ex-wife) forcibly tonsured. At the same time Ryurik's two sons, Rostislav and Vladimir, were led off to Galich as Roman's personal prisoners.[33] In all probability Ingvar' Yaroslavich was sent back to resume his role as prince of Kiev.[34]

Once again Vsevolod III stepped in to redress the balance and to hamper the consolidation of Roman's power over Volynia, Galicia and Kiev. He sent his envoys to Galich and somehow, by threats or cajoling, persuaded Roman to release the two sons of Ryurik. Rostislav Ryurikovich he placed on the throne of Kiev.[35]

It was not, however, the restoration of one of the Rostislavichi to the throne of Kiev that put an end to this particular phase of the civil war in the south, but the unexpected death of Roman in 1205. In despair, perhaps, of ever achieving his ends in Kiev as long as Vsevolod III was able to interfere and impose his will on the princes of Smolensk and Chernigov, he set off on a more ambitious venture than any he had undertaken so far. He invaded Poland. He planned firstly to defeat Leszek of Cracow, king of Little Poland, and then to advance north-west into Saxony.[36] The campaign came to a sudden end on 19 June 1205 at Zawichost on the Vistula, half way between Vladimir and Cracow. Leszek and his brother Conrad of Mazovia defeated and killed him. So great was the victory that Leszek and Conrad erected an altar in the cathedral of Cracow to commemorate it.

The death of Roman, to whom the chronicler of his son Daniil devoted a short but dazzling memorial,[37] signalled the end of an era. First and foremost, it meant that Galicia was now wide open to invasions. Roman's widow, Anna, for all her Byzantine craft and guile, was quite unable to cope with the intrigues of the Galician boyars. There was no question of her settling with her two infant sons, Daniil and Vasil'ko, in Galich, and indeed we find her concentrating her energies on Volynia; eventually, in 1219, she succeeded in establishing her authority over Vladimir and at least part of the old principality of Volynia. Galicia, during the fifteen years after Roman's death, was to remain prey to outside invaders – Hungarians, Poles, Russians – and external pressures – papal emissaries attempting a conversion of the Orthodox population to some sort of union with Rome, if not to pure Catholicism. Nor was it only the throwing open of Galicia and the disruption of the great south-western bloc of Volynia-Galicia that resulted from Roman's death: the struggle for mastery over south Russia intensified; it was no longer a three-cornered contest; it became an even more destructive fight to the death between the two seemingly irreconcilable enemies, the Rostislavichi and the Ol'govichi.

As we have seen, from 1195 to 1205 the main protagonists in the struggle for power had been Roman and Ryurik, and each in his quest for supremacy had enlisted the aid of the Ol'govichi. The Ol'govichi in these, for them lean, ten years had not shown themselves strong enough to play a leading part in the contest. Nor were they headed by princes of sufficient energy, leadership or stamina: Yaroslav (d. 1198), Igor' (d. 1202) and Oleg (d. 1204), the senior members of the family to occupy in turn the princely (or, as it was sometimes called even in those early days, the grand-princely) throne of Chernigov from 1194 to 1204, are never once mentioned in the chronicles as the 'leaders' of the Ol'govichi in the civil wars. But with Roman's death and with the emergence of a new and powerful figure on the scene in the person of Vsevolod Svyatoslavich Chermnyy ('the Red'), who succeeded his brother Oleg on the throne of Chernigov in 1204, the Ol'govichi began to play a new and altogether more decisive role in the affairs of south Russia.

*   *   *   *

It was civil war all over again. From 1205 to 1212 hardly a year passed without violent conflict breaking out between the Rostislavichi and the Ol'govichi. Again and again Kiev changed hands, see-sawing between the two, as did many of the towns in the south and south-west. But why the instability? The extraordinary frequency with which Ryurik and Vsevolod of Chernigov dislodged one another on the throne of Kiev can perhaps best be explained by Vsevolod III's readiness to let his squabbling cousins fight it out amongst themselves this time. So long as neither side assumed too great a supremacy over the other, he was prepared not to intervene. Furthermore, as will be seen below, for much of this period his hands were tied by Ryazan'. On the one occasion on which he actually set out with the intention of dealing with Chernigov (in 1207), he was deflected by certain of the princes of Ryazan' who had 'taken council with the Ol'govichi against him'.[38] There can be little doubt that this deflection was engineered by Vsevolod Chermnyy himself: the princes of Ryazan', even though they were not Ol'govichi themselves, were closer to them genealogically than to any other branch of the descendants of Yaroslav I (see above, p. 11).

So for seven years the Rostislavichi and the Ol'govichi fought one another for possession of Kiev and for mastery over south Russia. Only once did they form anything like an alliance with each other, and that only in the hope of a swift take-over of Galicia, if not of all south-west Russia. As soon as the news of Roman's death reached them, Vsevolod Chermnyy and Ryurik, who had by now unfrocked himself and was once more in the saddle as prince of Kiev, decided to patch up their old enmity[39] and sweep into Galicia. But the campaign of 1205 was a failure, and the Suzdalian chronicler, who had no love for the Ol'govichi, reported, not without a certain malicious delight, that they failed in their venture 'and returned home with great shame'.[40] They set off again in the following year. This time it was a full-scale invasion: all the available Ol'govichi and Rostislavichi[41] took part, as did the Polovtsians, the Berendei and other Turkic auxiliaries settled near Kiev.[42]

The invasion of 1206 turned into what amounted to an international conflict. Apart from the south-Russian troops and their Turkic allies, the Hungarians, the Poles and even Vsevolod III's son Yaroslav of Pereyaslavl' were involved: the Hungarians were called in by a section of the Galician boyars in the name of Anna and her infant sons; the Poles – by Ryurik and Vsevolod Chermnyy; and Yaroslav, who arrived too late to have the slightest impact – curiously enough by the Hungarians. The advancing, the retreating and the few clashes that actually took place are reported with singular lack of lucidity in the chronicles.[43] One thing, however, emerges from these confused accounts: the Rostislavichi fared poorly (as too did the Poles, who were put in their place by the Hungarians), while the Ol'govichi achieved what must have appeared at the time to be a resounding success. All we hear of Ryurik's exploits is that having brushed aside a force from Vladimir and Galich ('Vladimir and Galich boyars') at Mikulin on the Seret, he marched on Galich but was unable to dislodge the Hungarian garrison and returned to Kiev 'having achieved nothing',[44] a term employed by the chroniclers to denote total failure. As for the Ol'govichi, the sons of Igor' Svyatoslavich (the cadet branch of the family) somehow managed – more by guile and the intrigues of the anti-Hungarian boyars of Galicia, it seems, than by military skill[45] – to install themselves in the key cities: Vladimir in Galich, Roman in Zvenigorod (in the north of Galicia) and Svyatoslav in Vladimir.[46]

The control exercised by the Igorevichi over Galicia and Volynia lasted off and on for five years. It was highly precarious, and not surprisingly so, in view of the determined efforts of the Hungarians, the Poles, the pro-Hungarian Galician boyars and Roman's widow Anna to be rid of these importunate outsiders from Chernigov. The three brothers had anything but a quiet time and never looked like establishing themselves permanently in the south-west: they suffered indignities at the hands of the boyars and the Hungarians – one, Roman, had the doubtful distinction of being the only ruling Russian prince ever to have been arrested while taking a bath–[47] and eventually, in 1211, after uncovering a boyar plot against them and putting five hundred conspirators to death, they were hanged.[48]

Shaky as the hold of the Igorevichi over Volynia and Galicia may have been in 1206, the campaign itself ended in something of a triumph for the Ol'govichi. Acting as if according to a concerted plan with his cousins, Vsevolod Chermnyy hastened back to Kiev and seized the city – not too difficult an operation in view of the fact that his brother Gleb held the key fortress of Belgorod, which Ryurik had injudiciously given him in 1205 (see n. 39). At the same time he demanded that Yaroslav quit the principality of Southern Pereyaslavl' and return to his father Vsevolod III in Suzdalia. Yaroslav had no alternative but to obey, and Vsevolod Chermnyy put his son Mikhail in his place. So for a short time at least the Ol'govichi could be said to have held sway over the whole of south Russia: from Volynia in the west to Pereyaslavl' in the east.[49] No ruler of Chernigov had ever been in nominal control over so vast a territory.

Vsevolod Chermnyy, however, had reckoned without two things: the resilience and strength of the Rostislavichi and the fury of Vsevolod III, who was not one to suffer lightly such high-handed treatment of his children. The seizure of Kiev could have one result only – a fresh outbreak of civil war. It was one thing to occupy the capital itself, but it was quite another to gain control over the outlying towns and districts of the principality of Kiev. The Rostislavichi had struck roots in the provincial Kievan towns of Vruchiy, Vyshgorod and Belgorod as early as the sixties and the seventies of the twelfth century.

These were vital strategic centres: Vruchiy in the north, situated between Kiev and Turov, was the old capital of the land of the Drevlyane in the tenth century and was strongly fortified; Belgorod, 23 kilometres to the south-west of Kiev, a military stronghold and a diocesan centre, was key to the possession of the capital[50]; while the economic centre of Vyshgorod, fifteen kilometres north of Kiev, commanded the approaches to the capital from the north.[51]

No sooner had Vsevolod Chermnyy taken Kiev than the Rostislavichi occupied all three towns: Ryurik – Vruchiy, his son Rostislav – Vyshgorod, and his nephew Mstislav Romanovich of Smolensk – Belgorod.[52] To complete the encirclement of Kiev, yet another of Ryurik's nephews, Mstislav Mstislavich (nicknamed the Daring, *udaloy*), held the southern garrison town of Torchesk,[53] the headquarters of the various Turkic auxiliaries in the service of the prince of Kiev and a vital defence centre against the Polovtsians.

Ryurik had not long to wait. Before the year was over he and all the Rostislavichi he could muster pushed Vsevolod out of Kiev and his son out of Pereyaslavl'.[54] The Ol'govichi tried to recapture Kiev in that same winter of 1206–7, but they were forced to withdraw to Chernigov after besieging Ryurik for three weeks.[55] The first year of the war between the Rostislavichi and the Ol'govichi ended much as it had started, with the latter in Chernigov and the former in Kiev, the only difference being that the Rostislavichi now held Pereyaslavl', while the Ol'govichi controlled Volynia and Galicia.

The pattern of 1206 was repeated in 1207 with the Ol'govichi taking Kiev, only to be ousted again by the Rostislavichi in the winter. But this time Vsevolod Chermnyy did not make the same mistakes as before. The troops he collected were clearly more numerous than those with which he had taken Kiev in 1206 – apart from 'all his brothers and nephews' (a standard cliché to denote a full turn-out) and the almost statutory 'pagans' (i.e. Polovtsians), he had with him an army from Turov and Pinsk[56] as well as reinforcements from Galicia under the command of Vladimir Igorevich. More significant was the systematic manner in which he mopped up the strategic centres of resistance and disposed of the Rostislavichi. He marched through Pereyaslavl' territory, crossed the Dnepr south of Kiev and first took the fortress town of Trepol' commanding the main approaches to Kiev along the Dnepr from the south. Kiev surrendered without a fight. Outnumbered, Ryurik fled north to his residence-stronghold of Vruchiy. Next Belgorod was surrounded and attacked: Mstislav Romanovich was obliged to request a safe-conduct to enable him to retreat to Smolensk. Finally the army moved south and besieged Torchesk on the Ros', forcing Ryurik's other nephew, Mstislav Mstislavich, to surrender. What happened to Vyshgorod is not mentioned in the chronicle account, but presumably it fell at the same time as Kiev surrendered and Rostislav fled with his father Ryurik to Vruchiy.[57] By August 1207 Vsevolod Chermnyy was ensconced in Kiev.

For all his meticulous elimination of one nest of Rostislavichi after another, Vsevolod Chermnyy was by no means secure. If the immediate threat of yet another incursion by Ryurik seemed remote at the end of the summer of 1207, there was still the danger of Vsevolod III in the north. He had not forgotten the 'insult' to his son, and if he had not taken immediate reprisals in 1206 it was because Ryurik had done it for him. But now, in August 1207, he decided that it was time to strike. 'Is the land of Rus' *their* patrimony alone and not ours?' he is made by his chronicler to utter on hearing of the military successes of the Ol'govichi; 'whatever God may propose for me [in my struggle] with them, I shall march on Chernigov'.[58] For once the chronicler put words into his mouth which truly reflected his views; the ousting of Yaroslav and the seizure of the 'land of Rus'' without his approval were enough to stir him at last to action. But Vsevolod III's great punitive expedition of 1207, which set off with the express intention of removing his troublesome namesake from Kiev, turned, quite unexpectedly, into a major invasion of Ryazan'.

It was the first clash of the thirteenth century between the Suzdalians and what for the last thirty years had been their passive neighbours to the south. The Ryazanites, as has been shown above, had been reduced to a state of virtual vassaldom by Vsevolod III (see above, p. 12); their old close links with Chernigov had been broken; they had shown no resistance to any of Vsevolod's demands and had acted with complete obedience, if not servility, as though they recognized him as their suzerain. But in the large and diffuse princely family of Ryazan' there were restless elements which resented the overlordship of Vsevolod and which hankered after their old subservience to Chernigov.

Vsevolod set off south in August 1207 with a large army consisting of the *druzhiny* of four of his sons as well as detachments from all the major Novgorod districts. But he also reckoned on support from Ryazan' and Murom, whose princes were summoned to join the main army at its rendezvous in Moscow. It was here that Vsevolod realized that he could no longer rely on Ryazan' as an ally: he was informed that some of the princes were planning treachery, having 'taken council with the Ol'govichi'.

Vsevolod's reaction was swift and decisive. A number of Ryazanite princes, their wives and their retainers were immediately arrested and sent to Vladimir; the Suzdalian army invaded Ryazan' territory, captured the second largest city, Pronsk, and only spared Ryazan' on the condition that all the disloyal princes who had not yet been arrested as well as the local bishop proceed as prisoners to Vladimir. Murom, whose ruler had wisely cooperated with the Suzdalians, was left untouched.[59]

Once again Ryazan' was cowed — temporarily at any rate. It is true that it was not what Vsevolod had set out to do, but his initial purpose, the removal of Vsevolod Chermnyy from Kiev, was none the less achieved as an indirect result of the quelling of Ryazan'. Hearing that both Vsevolod III and Chernigov's most likely allies were safely out of the way in Ryazan', Ryurik did the job for him. By the end of the year he had ejected Vsevolod Chermnyy from Kiev and ascended the throne for no less than the seventh and last time in his life.[60]

He lasted for nearly three years. Apart from an abortive attack by the Ol'govichi in early 1208,[61] there were no more attempts to dislodge him militarily. Instead Vsevolod Chermnyy used diplomacy. The ground was prepared for him by the irruption of Ryurik's nephew Mstislav Mstislavich into Novgorod affairs. In the winter of 1208/9 Mstislav, who after his surrender in

Torchesk in 1207 had moved to Toropets, the northernmost city of the principality of Smolensk, unexpectedly occupied Torzhok on the eastern borders of Novgorod territory. Having arrested the respresentatives of Vsevolod III's son Svyatoslav (prince of Novgorod since early 1208), Mstislav marched into Novgorod and removed Svyatoslav (see below, p. 54). Whether this was a deliberate move to spread the influence of the Rostislavichi into territory which by now the grand prince of Vladimir considered to lie within his own sphere of influence, or whether it was merely an irresponsible act on the part of the ebullient Mstislav, it was enough to incense Vsevolod III: once again one of his sons had been summarily dealt with. Unable to dislodge Mstislav by force, he was prepared to, and indeed had little choice but to, listen to proposals from the other side – from the Ol'govichi. They came at the end of 1210.

The fortunes of the Ol'govichi were at a low ebb in that year. They had been unable to remove Ryurik from Kiev or to establish themselves there by military strength alone; they had suffered setbacks in south-west Russia: Vladimir Igorevich had been ousted from Galicia in 1209, and Ryurik's son Rostislav had – only temporarily, it is true – replaced Roman Igorevich there in early 1210[62]; and in the east their former appendage Ryazan' had been militarily crushed by Vsevolod III and many of its senior citizens, including the bishop, were being held under duress in Vladimir. The only hope of restoring their fortunes lay in soliciting Vsevolod III's aid.

It was done with some subtlety. In December 1210 Vsevolod Chermnyy managed to persuade the metropolitan of Kiev, Matfey, to undertake a mission to Vladimir-on-the-Klyaz'ma. The chronicles merely state that 'Vsevolod Chermnyy and all the Ol'govichi sent [him] to Grand Prince Vsevolod . . . asking for peace and submitting in all things' and that Vsevolod III, 'seeing their submission . . . kissed the cross' – in other words, concluded a treaty with the Ol'govichi.[63] The aim of the mission was twofold: to have Ryurik removed from Kiev – no doubt Metropolitan Matfey only too willingly agreed to this request of Vsevolod Chermnyy: the head of the Russian Church could hardly have welcomed an unfrocked monk on the throne of Kiev; and secondly, to beg for clemency for the Ryazanites held in Vladimir – again, Vsevolod Chermnyy had only to remind the metropolitan that one of his bishops was being kept in Vladimir under duress.

The terms of the treaty are not mentioned in any of the sources, but we can reconstruct them from subsequent events. Clearly Vsevolod Chermnyy made some concessions. In all probability he agreed to bring pressure to bear on the Ryazanites, for we hear of no more eruptions of anti-Suzdalian hostility in the principality during the last two years of Vsevolod III's reign. As for the metropolitan's requests, he was partially successful in one: Vsevolod III agreed to release the wives of the Ryazan' princes whom he held in captivity,[64] but the bishop of Ryazan' and the princes remained in Vladimir. In the other he achieved all that Vsevolod Chermnyy could have desired: Vsevolod was given Kiev. To cement the treaty a marriage was arranged between the two houses: Vsevolod Chermnyy's daughter Agafia was married to Yury, Vsevolod III's son, on 10 April 1211.[65]

As for Ryurik's fate, the chronicles are suspiciously abrupt, laconic and enigmatic. All they say is that he 'sat (*sede*) in Chernigov' and that he died later, 'ruling (*knyazha*) in Chernigov'. Both verbs used (*sede, knyazha*) are those normally denoting princely rule; yet it would be difficult to imagine Vsevolod Chermnyy placing his arch-enemy on his patrimonial throne. We know, too, that in 1212, when Ryurik was probably still alive, Gleb Svyatoslavich, Vsevolod Chermnyy's eldest surviving brother, was ruling Chernigov.[66] In all likelihood then, Ryurik was held prisoner in Chernigov until his death in 1215, and in fact the chronicler's use of 'rule' was little more than a euphemism to disguise the fact that the Ol'govichi were keeping him well out of harm's way.[67]

None of the contemporary sources mourned his death, none echoed the dazzling eulogy written by his own chronicler at the turn of the century. Only Tatishchev had a few sour words to say, which, if based on fact, might explain his unpopularity:

he ruled for 37 years. Four times he was driven out [of Kiev], and he was tonsured, suffering much at the hands of his son-in-law [Roman Mstislavich]. He had no peace from any direction, for he himself was much addicted to drink and was manipulated by women (*zhenami vodim be*); he paid little attention to the ruling of the land, and his administrators (*tiuny*) did much evil. For this reason the Kievans had little love for him.[68]

For two years Vsevolod Chermnyy held on to Kiev, and the peace treaty signed by Vsevolod III remained in force. All was quiet in southern Russia: Ryurik's relatives made no move either to recapture Kiev or to rescue him from the indignity of his 'rule' in Chernigov. But no one, least of all Vsevolod III, could have been under any illusions about the latent power of the Rostislavichi, for Mstislav Mstislavich remained obdurately immovable in Novgorod.

* * * *

In 1212 Vsevolod III died, having ruled north-east Russia with skill, tact and patience for thirty-two years and having effectively manipulated political power in the south for much of his long reign as grand prince of Vladimir. Far-reaching changes in the political fortunes of all the Russian principalities occurred soon after – and undoubtedly as a direct result of – his death. The ten years before the first invasion of the Tatars in 1223 saw fierce in-fighting in Suzdalia amongst his numerous sons and a complete change in the balance of power in the south: 1212–23 witnessed the apogee of the authority of the Rostislavichi and what looks like the eclipse of the Ol'govichi, who, though for much of the time they must have enjoyed the support of Vsevolod Chermnyy's son-in-law, nevertheless remained stubbornly in the background, or so it appears from the chronicles, and played little part in the unabating internecine conflicts.

Of course the relative silence of the sources on the activities of the Ol'govichi in this period may well be explained by the fact that the chronicle closest to the events reported (the Suzdalian Lavrent'evskiy) reflects for most of the years between 1212 and 1237 the private chronicle of Grand Prince Yury, who may have had little desire to see the involvement of his father-in-law's family in the inter-princely squabbles publicized: hence the forbearance even to mention the removal of Vsevolod Chermnyy from Kiev in 1212[69] and the perplexing entry on Ryurik's 'rule' in Chernigov.

The ousting of Vsevolod Chermnyy was a major triumph for the Rostislavichi. At the beginning of 1212 the Rostislavichi had a military success in the north-west. Troops from Novgorod (under Mstislav Mstislavich), Pskov (under the prince of Smolensk's son Vsevolod) and Toropets (under Mstislav's brother David) invaded the land of the Estonian Chud' on the Baltic Sea coast, succeeded in levying tribute on them and took a number of prisoners.[70] This was followed, in the summer of 1212, by a massive campaign against the Ol'govichi.

It started in Novgorod. Mstislav Mstislavich, now in full control of the north-west, set off with a Novgorodian army to Smolensk where he was joined by the senior prince of the Rostislavichi, Mstislav Romanovich, known as 'Mstislav the Old' (*Mstislav Staryy*), the two sons of Ryurik, two of David Rostislavich's sons (Konstantin and Mstislav) and curiously enough Ingvar' Yaroslavich, the west-Russian prince of Lutsk who had been placed on the throne of Kiev twelve years earlier by Roman Mstislavich.[71] Although the Novgorodian detachments showed at first some reluctance to go beyond Smolensk, they were eventually persuaded to continue the campaign by the eloquent *posadnik* of Novgorod, Tverdislav ('Brother Novgorodians! Our fathers and grandfathers suffered for the land of Rus'; let us therefore, brothers, follow our prince.'[72]).

The army's route lay along the Dnepr. The town of Rechitsa and 'many other Chernigov towns' were taken before they reached Kievan territory. Vyshgorod, just north of Kiev, fell and two of Vsevolod Chermnyy's cousins, who were defending it, were taken prisoner. With the Rostislavichi at the gates of Kiev Vsevolod Chermnyy could offer no resistance: he fled with his troops to Chernigov, pursued by the Rostislavichi, who besieged him and his brother Gleb for two to three weeks until an armistice was concluded. Meanwhile Ingvar' Yaroslavich was left temporarily in charge of Kiev, while Mstislav Romanovich of Smolensk restored order in Vyshgorod. Eventually Mstislav assumed control of Kiev, and Ingvar' returned once more from the capital to Lutsk, just as he had done twelve years earlier.

The fall of Vsevolod Chermnyy in 1212 and his subsequent death in the same year ushered in a new era in the political history of south Russia. This time it was an age of relative stability. Little or nothing is heard of the activities of the Ol'govichi: flanked on their western and north-western boundaries by the territories of the Rostislavichi, there was seemingly little they could do but lick their wounds, wait quietly in their splintered principality and argue about who was to rule in which of the numerous little districts that now made up Chernigov. There was no question of their combating the authority of the Rostislavichi, and indeed we even find them assisting Mstislav Mstislavich in his two Galician campaigns of 1218 and 1221 (see below, pp. 37–8). The Rostislavichi were secure. No one, not even Vsevolod III's sons, challenged their right to rule Kiev – and indeed there was always a member of the clan on the throne of Kiev for the next twenty-three years. The territory controlled by the family for much of the period 1212–23 was huge. Apart from Kiev and Smolensk, they held Novgorod (until 1221, that is) and Pskov; the town of Polotsk was captured by them in 1221 or 1222 (see below, p. 38); Turov and Pinsk may well have been under their authority; and, in the last years before the first Tatar invasion of 1223, even Galicia succumbed to one of the Rostislavichi.

The south was untroubled for two reasons: first, because there was no one strong enough to match the Rostislavichi militarily; and second, because the whole power struggle had shifted from a Rostislavichi–Ol'govichi conflict to one between the Rostislavichi and the majority of the sons of Vsevolod III. It was not that Yury and Yaroslav Vsevolodovichi, their two major Suzdalian opponents, were able to make any attempt to dislodge Mstislav Romanovich from Kiev; it was rather that the area of conflict had moved from south to north – and especially to the north-west. For the main struggle was to be over Novgorod: who was to be prince – a son of the grand prince of Vladimir, as had been the practice for most of Vsevolod III's reign, or a representative of the Smolensk dynasty?

The north–south struggle was curiously uneven, and for the first time the authority of the grand prince of Vladimir was threatened. The days of Vsevolod III's unquestioned supremacy and control were over, disrupted by the disastrous split between his sons during the first five years after his death (see below, pp. 46 *et seq.*). Yury and Yaroslav cast around for allies, but to little effect. In 1214 Yaroslav himself married Mstislav Mstislavich's daughter, but the marriage did nothing to promote friendship between him and his father-in-law: indeed in 1215 there was open conflict over Novgorod (see below, p. 55), and in the following year Mstislav played a leading role in the defeat of Yaroslav and his brothers at the battle on the Lipitsa river (see below, pp. 48 *et seq.*). The marriage was swiftly dissolved. The only other allies they could look to were the Ol'govichi, to whom indeed they planned to hand over Kiev should they win the war of 1216 against their brother Konstantin and his allies (see below, p. 49); perhaps too the marriage of their younger brother Vladimir to the daughter of Gleb of Chernigov in 1215[73] could be considered as an attempt to link the two clans. But again nothing came of it, and the Ol'govichi were conspicuous for their absence in Yury's and Yaroslav's clashes with the Rostislavichi.

It was only at the beginning of the 1220s that Yury, undisputed grand prince of Vladimir since 1217, managed to redress the balance by replacing the Rostislavichi in Novgorod first with his son and then, in 1222, with his brother Yaroslav. But if the Rostislavichi lost ground in Novgorod, they gained it in the south-west, for in 1221 Mstislav Mstislavich, who by now had renounced all claims on Novgorod, was master of Galicia.

Ever since the battle of Zawichost and the death of Roman in 1205, south-west Russia had been in a state of ferment and civil war – only too well reflected in the chaotic, confused and often mystifying reporting and dating of events in the local (Ipat'evskiy) chronicle. The ineffectual intervention of the Ol'govichi in Galicia, which culminated in the hanging of the three sons of

Igor' Svyatoslavich (see above, p. 30), was followed by an intensification of the struggle between the various interested parties – the Hungarians, the Poles, the Galician boyars, Roman's widow Anna with her two young sons, as well as the nephews and cousins of Roman – and those descendants of Mstislav the Great who had settled in Volynia. None seemed capable of holding more than a small part of either principality for more than a very limited period of time. Even the carve-up of south-west Russia between the Hungarians and the Poles at the treaty of Spisz in 1214 led to no consolidation of power, but to further fragmentation, with eastern Galicia, including Galich, falling to Hungary, western Galicia and many of the border towns of Volynia – to Poland, and Vladimir, the capital of Volynia – to Anna.[74]

The treaty of Spisz and the subsequent ensconcement of the king of Hungary's son on the throne of Galich probably stirred Mstislav Mstislavich's imagination and indignation. And if the thought of the Hungarians in full control of what was after all a Russian patrimony was not enough to move him, then news of anti-Orthodox persecution and attempts to install Latin priests in the churches of Galicia[75] certainly did. In the winter of 1214/1215 he went to Galich via Kiev 'to ask the king for Galich for himself'. Whether this implied a military invasion of Galicia is not certain. Probably not, for there is no mention of it in either the Novgorod or the Suzdalian chronicles, nor is there any evidence that military operations took place; it was more likely an attempt to reconnoitre the situation in the south-west and to gauge the strength of the Hungarians and the mood of the boyars.[76]

Evidently the time was not ripe for a major invasion of Galicia; indeed Mstislav's restraint was justified when the Hungarians in 1215 or 1216 seized those parts of western Galicia (Peremyshl' and Lyubachev) which had been granted to Leszek of Cracow at Spisz.[77] And in any case Mstislav was fully occupied in Novgorod in the years 1215–17.

Mstislav Mstislavich's eventual irruption into Galician affairs is, like so much of the history of south-west Russia in this period, reported confusingly in a number of sources. The chronology of events is especially hard to establish. At the end of 1216 or the beginning of 1217 Mstislav, alerted by a message from Leszek of Cracow asking for help against the Hungarians,[78] went to Kiev, in all probability to consult with Mstislav Romanovich on the possibility of a combined Rostislavichi operation in Galicia.[79] The embassy resulted in the first invasion of Galicia in 1218, which he undertook with his cousin Vladimir Ryurikovich and with troops from Polotsk.[80] It was completely successful. Kálmán, the son of King Andrew of Hungary, who had been placed there by his father after the treaty of Spisz, was arrested with his wife and sent back to Hungary, and Mstislav installed himself as prince of Galich.[81] But it was not for long. In the following year he married off his daughter Anna to the 18-year-old Daniil, Roman's eldest son, now prince of Vladimir-in-Volynia. It was an auspicious start to his rule in Galicia: the union of the two families looked as though it might lead to the union of Volynia and Galicia. But it was not to be. A curious misunderstanding between Mstislav, Daniil and Leszek – Mstislav in fact refused to help his son-in-law drive the Poles out of Volynia, but Leszek was nevertheless convinced that he had advised him to do so – led to Mstislav's expulsion. In 1219 the Hungarians, summoned by Leszek, ousted him. Once again Kálmán was sent to rule Galicia.[82]

Mstislav had clearly underestimated the strength and determination of the Hungarians, the danger of a Polish-Hungarian coalition and the opposition of the pro-Hungarian boyars in Galich, who were later to cause him so much trouble. In the following year he returned to Galicia, this time with a more powerful army under the command of the prince of Kiev himself, as well as with unspecified 'other princes' and a contingent of Polovtsians. Their activities, however, were limited to besieging Kálmán in Galich and ravaging the countryside.[83] It was only in 1221 that Mstislav mounted his third – and by far his most serious – campaign against Galicia.

The chronicles have practically nothing to say about this momentous event in the history of south-west Russia: the Suzdalian chronicler is at his most irritatingly laconic – perhaps because after all now that Novgorod was nearly rid of the Rostislavichi there was little need to bother with the antics of Mstislav Mstislavich, who merely 'fought with the Hungarians, slaughtered many of them and seized the king's son'[84]; the Galician chronicle is characteristically muddled and obscure, though under the year 1219 it does relate in some detail what would appear to have been Mstislav's campaign of 1221. Only Tatishchev gives a remarkably clear and very detailed account of what happened, basing himself not, it would seem, on his imagination, but on some source which has disappeared.

The south-Russian army was under joint command of Mstislav Romanovich of Kiev and Mstislav Mstislavich: it consisted mainly of detachments under various Rostislavichi, but troops from Chernigov (commanded by the senior prince of the Ol'govichi, Mstislav Syatoslavich), Turov, Lutsk in Volynia and even Suzdalia ('Yaroslav [Vsevolodovich] of [Northern] Pereyaslavl'' is mentioned as participating) also took part, as well as a considerable number of Polovtsians. There were two battles: the first on the river Seret, east of Galich, in which the Hungarian outposts were defeated; the second close to Galich in which the combined Russian army shattered the Hungarians, the pro-Hungarian Galicians and the Poles under Leszek, who had been called in to help. After a 17-day siege Galich surrendered. Kálmán was taken prisoner and Mstislav Mstislavich reinstated himself in Galich, where he was to remain for the next six years.[85] Kálmán and his wife were eventually despatched to Hungary. The period of Hungarian domination was over – at least for the time being.

Thus by 1223 the Rostislavichi had consolidated their control over most of southern Russia. They held Galicia, Kiev and Smolensk. Whoever ruled the old principality of Turov seems to have been at the beck and call of the prince of Kiev. Smolensk's western neighbour, the crumbling fragmented principality of Polotsk, about which remarkably little is known for the first quarter of the thirteenth century, was clearly coming more and more under the political and economic influence of Smolensk, and indeed in 1221 or 1222 the capital Polotsk itself was captured by troops from Smolensk.[86] We can assume then that most of the principality, with the exception of the western Baltic districts, which were lost to the German Knights by 1220 and which were under constant pressure both from the Germans and from the Lithuanians in the early thirteenth century, was in the hands of the prince of Smolensk at the beginning of the 1220s. As for Southern Pereyaslavl', again the sources give very little information. All we know is that Vladimir, Vsevolod III's fourth eldest son, ruled there from 1213 to 1215 when the Polovtsians raided Pereyaslavl' and took him prisoner, and that when he was released in 1217 he was given a district in the north to rule and not Pereyaslavl'.[87] We hear little more of Southern Pereyaslavl' until 1227 when Grand Prince Yury sent his nephew Vsevolod Konstantinovich to rule there. Who held the territory between 1215 and 1227? In view of the close matrimonial and military links between the Rostislavichi and the Polovtsians,[88] it is not improbable that the Rostislavichi – no doubt with the connivance of the Polovtsians – extended their authority eastwards from Kiev into the territory which the rulers of Suzdal' had long considered to lie within their purview. Indeed Vladimir Vsevolodovich was probably replaced by Ryurik's son Vladimir, for a reliable source reports that 'Vladimir Ryurikovich *from Pereyaslavl'*' assisted Mstislav Mstislavich in his campaign against Yaroslav Vsevolodovich in 1215.[89]

Only three south-Russian districts were immune from Rostislavichi control, the three which made up the old heritage of Svyatoslav Yaroslavich – Chernigov, Ryazan' and Murom. Ever since the death of Vsevolod Chermnyy in 1212 the Ol'govichi had kept a low profile, showing no signs of aggressiveness towards either the Rostislavichi or Suzdalia. The Ryazanites, by 1223, were in no fit state effectively to oppose any external enemies. It is true that there had been some fight left in them after the débâcle of 1207: in 1208 they had attempted to overthrow Vsevolod III's son Yaroslav, who had been sent to govern Ryazan', and for their pains had seen Ryazan' and Belgorod burned to the ground and their inhabitants bodily removed and resettled in Suzdalia[90]; in the following year two of the princes who had managed to escape deportation even mounted an invasion of Suzdalia, but it was easily and efficiently crushed by Vsevolod's son Yury.[91] Ryazan' by now was militarily and morally exhausted. Two events, however, helped to lift it from the bottom of the pit: in 1212 Yury, the new grand prince of Vladimir, granted an amnesty to all deported Ryazanites;[92] and in 1217 Gleb Vladimirovich, the ringleader of the conspiracy of 1208, and his brother Konstantin, by murdering, in a vain attempt to gain power, more Ryazanite princes (a brother and five cousins) than were to perish during Baty's capture of Ryazan' in 1237, paradoxically enough solved for the time being the problem of fragmentation in the principality and thus somewhat strengthened the authority of the two surviving members of the family, Ingvar' and Yury Igorevichi.[93] Yury of Suzdal' neither intervened in their internal affairs nor did he summon them to take part in his campaigns: no Ryazan' troops were present either in the major expedition against the Volga Bulgars in 1220 (see below, p. 51) or in the Russo-Polovtsian army which met the first Tatar invasion of 1223. As for Murom, the senior prince, David Yur'evich, remained the firm ally of the grand prince of Vladimir and caused him no headaches.

It might appear that at the beginning of the third decade of the thirteenth century, in spite of the virtual dependence of Ryazan' and Murom on Suzdalia, the balance of power was now strongly in favour of the Rostislavichi. It was, however, significantly redressed in the early 1220s by events in the northwest, for, as will be seen in the following chapter, control over Novgorod once again slipped into the hands of the descendants of Vsevolod III, and the Rostislavichi were deprived of their greatest economic asset.

REFERENCES AND NOTES

1. That is, *Ipat* up to 1199.
2. *PSRL*, vol. 2, cols 685–6.
3. Ibid., col. 686.
4. *PSRL*, vol. 1, col. 412.
5. Ibid., col. 419.
6. *PSRL*, vol. 2, cols 681–702.
7. *PSRL*, vol. 1, col. 413.
8. *PSRL*, vol. 2, cols 708, 711.
9. Pashuto, *Ocherki*, p. 72.
10. *PSRL*, vol. 2, col. 715.
11. See Pashuto, *Vneshnyaya politika*, p. 162.
12. *PSRL*, vol. 1, col. 416 (*s.a.* 1201, but see Berezhkov, *Khronologiya*, p. 86).
13. *PSRL*, vol. 1, col. 414 (*s.a.* 1198, but see Berezhkov, op. cit., p. 86).
14. *PSRL*, vol. 1, col. 415 (*s.a.* 1199, but see Berezhkov, op. cit.. p. 86).
15. Igor', the leading character of *The Tale of Igor''s Campaign* (a work describing his foolish expedition against the Polovtsians in 1185), was married to the sister of Vladimir Yaroslavich of Galicia.
16. *PSRL*, vol. 1, cols 417–18 (*s. a.* 1202, but see Berezhkov, op. cit., pp. 86–7).
17. That is, *N1* and the *svod* of 1200–92 in *Ipat* (*NPL* and *PSRL*, vol. 2.).
18. That is, *Ipat* up to 1199 (*PSRL*, vol. 2).
19. The phrase *a Volodimertsi lishasya Ryurika* was not understood by the compiler of *M*, who omitted it in his otherwise close rendering of the version found in *L* (*PSRL*, vol. 25, p. 100).
20. See Tolochko, *Kiev*, p. 110.
21. For the location of Podol and *Gora*, see Tikhomirov, *Drevnerusskie goroda*, pp. 187–9, 194.
22. *PSRL*, vol. 1, col. 418 (*s.a.* 1202, but see Berezhkov, op. cit., p. 87).
23. Led by Konchak, the father-in-law of Vladimir Igorevich of Putivl' (in Chernigov), and Daniil Kobyakovich. *NPL*, pp. 45, 240. Note that Konchak had fought against Igor' Svyatoslavich in the latter's unfortunate 'campaign' of 1185, while Daniil's father Kobyak had been taken prisoner by Svyatoslav Vsevolodovich of Kiev in 1183 together with his sons. of whom 'Daniil' had evidently been converted to Christianity in Kiev.
24. 'As many monks and nuns and priests and priests' wives and Kievans and their daughters and their sons [as survived the initial slaughter] were all led off by the foreigners to their tents [i.e. HQ in the steppe].' *PSRL*, vol. 1, col. 419.
25. Only in *NPL*, pp. 45, 240.

26. According to *Ipat* he was active in Volynia in 1208–9 and in 1212 was even put on the throne of Kiev for a short time (see above, p. 35 and *PSRL*, vol. 25, p. 109).
27. *PSRL*, vol. 1, col. 419.
28. According to *N4*. Vsevolod Chermnyy of Chernigov 'sat upon the throne' after Ryurik's capture of Kiev (*PSRL*, vol. 4, p. 180), probably an error taken from a later entry; it is not mentioned in any other source.
29. *PSRL*, vol. 1, col. 419.
30. Ibid., col. 420. Cf. col. 421 where the treaty is reported a second time with the date 6 February (1203?). Tatishchev (second redaction only) motivates Roman's peace move by his plans to invade Poland and his desire to secure the isolation of Ryurik from the Ol'govichi. *Istoriya*, vol. 3, p. 169.
31. *PSRL*, vol. 1, col. 420 (*s.a.* 1205); *TL*, p. 286; *NPL*, p. 240.
32. It is possible that they were at the time engaged in operations against the Lithuanians (*NPL*, p. 45; *PSRL*, vol. 1, col. 421, *s.a.* 1205), although this may have been in the previous year.
33. *PSRL*, vol. 1, col. 420 (*s.a.* 1205); *TL*, p. 286. Cf. *N1*, which states that Roman sent one Vyacheslav to Kiev 'ordering him to tonsure Ryurik' (*NPL*, p. 240).
34. Mentioned only in Tatishchev (second redaction only). *Istoriya*, vol. 3, p. 170.
35. *PSRL*, vol. 1, cols. 420–1 (*s.a.* 1205).
36. 'Romanus, a finibus suis egressus et per Poloniam transire volens in Saxoniam'. *Chronica Alberici Monachi Triumfontium*, in *MGH* (Scriptores), vol. 23, p. 885.
37. 'Ever-memorable autocrat of all Rus', who overcame all the pagan tribes by the wisdom of his mind, who walked in the commandments of the Lord, who fought against the pagans like a lion, was wrathful like a lynx and destructive like a crocodile, who passed over the land like an eagle and was as brave as an aurox . . .' (*PSRL*, vol. 2, cols 715–16).
38. *PSRL*, vol. 1, col. 430.
39. To mark the occasion Ryurik gave Belgorod to Vsevolod's brother Gleb. *PSRL*, vol. 25, p. 104.
40. *PSRL*, vol. 1, col. 426. No mention is made of Ryurik's role in this venture, though the Rostislavichi clearly took part.
41. 'Vsevolod Chermnyy and his brothers, Vladimir Igorevich [son of Igor' Svyatoslavich] and his brothers and Mstislav Romanovich from Smolensk . . . Ryurik and Rostislav and Vladimir [his sons] and his nephews'. *PSRL*, vol. 1, col. 426.
42. *PSRL*, vol. 10, p. 5.
43. The main sources are *L* (*s.a.* 1206) and *Ipat* (*s.a.* 1202): *PSRL*, vol. 1, cols 426–7, and vol. 2, cols 717–18.
44. *PSRL*, vol. 2, col. 717.
45. 'Vladimir . . . stealing away . . . from his brothers, galloped to Galich. . . .' *PSRL*, vol. 1, col. 427.
46. *PSRL*, vol. 2, col. 718.
47. *i ya Romana v bani myyushchasya*. Ibid., col. 722.
48. Ibid., cols 723–4, 727. *Ipat* gives the names of the three Igorevichi as Roman, Svyatoslav and Rostislav. According to *M*, the three Igorevichi hanged were 'Roman and his two brothers' (*PSRL*, vol. 25, p. 108). It looks as though Rostislav, who is not mentioned elsewhere, may have been one of Igor''s sons and that Vladimir either was dead or had left the country: the seventeenth-century Gustinskiy Chronicle (*s.a.* 1209) states that Roman drove his brother Vladimir

out of Galich with Hungarian aid and took over the throne himself, while Vladimir 'returned to his patrimony of Putivl'' (*PSRL*, vol. 2 (1843 edn), p. 330. Cf. M (*s.a.* 1208): *PSPL*, vol. 25, p. 107).

49 The principality of Turov may also have been allied, or subordinate, to the Ol'govichi at the time. In 1207 they joined Vsevolod Chermnyy's campaign against Kiev. See below, n. 56.

50. 'The loss of Belgorod by the prince of Kiev meant the loss of Kiev.' Tolochko, 'Kievskaya zemlya', p. 27.

51. For a detailed description of all three towns, see ibid., pp. 51–2, 27–8, 23–4; Tikhomirov, *Drevnerusskie goroda*, pp. 304–5, 298–300, 294–8. On Vyshgorod, see Nasonov, '*Russkaya zemlya*', Ch. IV and Tolochko, *Kiev*, pp. 132–6.

52. *PSRL*, vol. 1, col. 427.

53. Torchesk had been handed over to Vsevolod III in 1195 (see above, p. 23); presumably Mstislav was sent there by Ryurik in 1206 or earlier.

54. *PSRL*, vol. 1, col. 428.

55. Ibid.

56. 'The Svyatopolchichi from Turov and from Pinsk' (PSRL, vol. 1, col. 429) – presumably Vladimir and Rostislav of Pinsk, the sons of Svyatopolk of Turov. See Baumgarten, *Généalogies* (1), p. 10.

57. *PSRL*, vol. 1, col. 429.

58. Ibid., cols 429–30.

59. The basic version of the Ryazan' campaign of 1207 is that found in L (*PSRL*, vol. 1, cols 429–33). Terse, factual and written by an eye-witness, it served as the main source for most later versions. For a detailed discussion of the sources, see Kuz'min, *Ryazanskoe letopisanie*, pp. 130–40.

60. *PSRL*, vol. 1, cols 432–3. The brief report of Ryurik's return to Kiev is clearly an interpolation in the account of Vsevolod III's Ryazan' campaign, but not necessarily of later origin.

61. *PSRL*, vol. 1, col. 434.

62. *PSRL*, vol. 25, p. 108. Not in *L*.

63. *PSRL*, vol. 1, col. 435; vol. 25, p. 108.

64. Only in *M. PSRL*, vol. 25, p. 108.

65. *PSRL*, vol. 1. col. 135: vol. 25, p. 108 (date only in *M*).

66. *PSRL*, vol. 25, p. 109 (not in *L* or other chronicles).

67. On Ryurik's fate, see Fennell, 'The Last Years'.

68. Tatishchev, *Istoriya*, vol. 4, p. 341.

69. *NPL.*, pp. 53, 251–2 (*s.a.* 1214, but see Berezhkov, *Khronologiya*, pp. 257–8); *PSRL*, vol. 25, p. 109. Tatishchev's account is basically the same, although he adds considerable detail. *Istoriya*, vol. 4, pp. 344–5; cf. vol. 3, pp. 189–90.

70. *NPL*, pp. 52, 251.

71. See above, pp. 25–6. Pashuto explains Ingvar''s participation in the campaign by his hostility to the sons of Roman of Galicia (Daniil and Vasil'ko) and by the latter's friendship with Vsevolod Chermnyy. *Ocherki*, pp. 48–9. According to Tatishchev, Mstislav Romanovich, coming 'from Turov', joined Mstislav Mstislavich's army later, at the mouth of the Pripyat' river, i.e. just inside Kiev territory. This would indicate that Turov and Pinsk were under the control of the Rostislavichi at the time and that Turov troops took part in the campaign. *Istoriya*, vol. 4, p. 345.

72. *NPL*, pp. 53, 251–2.

73. *PSRL*, vol. 1, col. 438.

74. *PSRL*, vol. 2, cols 730–1. On the treaty of Spisz, see Pashuto, *Ocherki*, p. 200; *The Hypatian Codex*, (ed. Perfecky) pp. 132–4; Rhode, *Die Ostgrenze Polens*, p. 106.

75. 'The king of Hungary put his son in Galich and drove the bishop and priests from the church and brought their own Latin priests to serve.' *PSRL*, vol. 25, p. 110 (also in *E*, *L'v*, and *Nik*, but not in *L*).

76. *PSRL*, vol. 25, p. 110 (also in *E*, *L'v* and *Nik* (*s.a.* 1214 and 1215)).

77. *PSRL*, vol. 2, col. 731.

78. '. . . Leszek sent to Novgorod for Mstislav saying "You are my brother. Come and rule in Galich."' Ibid., col. 731 – erroneously dated 6720/1212.

79. *NPL*, pp. 57, 257 (for dating, see Berezhkov, *Khronologiya*, p. 259). He returned to Novgorod in the early spring of 1217. No mention is made of the purpose of his visit.

80. Perhaps with a detachment from Chernigov? There were still Chernigov troops with him in 1219. See *PSRL*, vol. 2, col. 733.

81. *NPL*, pp. 59, 260–1. *S1*, *N4* and *M* repeat *N1*. The entry in *Ipat s.a.* 6720/1212 may refer to Mstislav's first occupation of Galich (*PSRL*, vol. 2, cols 731–2). Only Tatishchev (*Istoriya*, vol. 4, pp. 356–7) mentions the troops from Polotsk under 'Vasil'ko of Polotsk'.

82. Mstislav's first rule in Galicia and the subsequent events up to his expulsion in 1219 are described in some detail in *Ipat*, where Daniil is made to play an important role (PSRL, vol. 2, cols 731–5). Mstislav's expulsion is briefly reported in *M* and derivative chronicles (*E*, *L'v*, *Tv.sb.*), but not in *L* or *N1*. (*PSRL*, vol. 25, p. 116).

83. Only in *M* and derivative chronicles (*E*, *L'v* and *Tv.sb.*). *PSRL*, vol. 25, p. 118.

84. *PSRL*, vol. 1, col. 445. *M*, *E* and *L'v* add 'and sat [as prince] in Galich'. See ibid., vol. 25, p. 118.

85. Tatishchev, *Istoriya*, vol. 4, pp. 359–60; *PSRL*, vol. 2, cols 737–8.

86. 'The Yaroslavtsy [descendants of Yaroslav the Wise?] of Smolensk took Polotsk on 17 January from Princes Boris and Gleb'. *NPL*, p. 263 (N.B. not in the early recension of *N1* or in any derivative chronicle, e.g. *S1*, *N4*). Cf. Tatishchev, *Istoriya*, vol. 4, p. 360: 'The prince of Smolensk with Yaroslav [Vsevolodovich?] of [Northern?] Pereyaslavl' marched against Polotsk and took the town on 17 January from Boris and Gleb . . .'

87. *PSRL*, vol. 1, col. 442.

88. Ryurik Rostislavich and two of his nephews were married to Polovtsian princesses.

89. *PSRL*, vol. 25, pp. 110–11. Lyaskoronsky (*Istoriya Pereyaslavskoy zemli*, pp. 445–7) thinks that Vladimir Ryurikovich was soon replaced in Pereyaslavl' by an Ol'govich – this is based on a misunderstanding of Tatishchev, according to whom 'Yaroslav Mstislavich of Pereyaslavl'' took part in the Galician campaign of 1221. The earlier version of Tatishchev (vol. 4), however, omits the patronymic and clearly refers to Yaroslav Vsevolodovich of *Northern* Pereyaslavl'. In any case there is no evidence of any 'Yaroslav Mstislavich' among the known princes of Chernigov alive at this period.

90. *PSRL*, vol. 1, col. 434; vol. 25, p. 105 (and in *E* and *L'v*); *LPS*, p. 109 (*s.a.* 1209); *NPL*, pp. 51, 249 (*s.a.* 1210). Tatishchev (second redaction only) adds that the two main conspirators, Gleb and Izyaslav Vladimirovichi, who had shown themselves loyal to Vsevolod III in 1207, were in touch with the Ol'govichi, who even promised them military aid (*Istoriya*, vol. 3, p. 182).

91. *PSRL*, vol. 25. pp. 107–8 (*E*, *L'v* and *Nik* similar); vol. 1, col. 434; *LPS*, p. 109. On chronology, see Berezhkov, *Khronologiya*, pp. 101–3.

92. *PSRL*, vol. 1, col. 437; vol. 25, p. 109; *LPS*, p. 111 (*s.a.* 1213).

93. Gleb and Konstantin were driven out by Ingvar' and Yury Igorevichi. In 1219 they attempted an invasion of Ryazan' with a Polovtsian army but were repelled by Ingvar' (*PSRL*, vol. 1, col. 444; vol. 25, p. 116) and were never mentioned again in the chronicles.

   For the tale of the massacre of the six princes in 1217, see *PSPL*, vol. 1, cols 440–1: vol. 25, p. 115; *NPL*, p. 58 (*s.a.* 1218, old recension only). The versions of *L* and *N1* are very close and perhaps derive from a non-extant Ryazan' chronicle (see Lur'e, *Obshcherusskie letopisi*, p. 34). Those of *M* and similar *E* and *L'v* omit the moralizing passages of *L* and *N1* and add that Gleb fled to the Polovtsians after the murder (cf. Tatishchev, *Istoriya*, vol. 4, p. 352). See also Nazarov ('"Dvor" i "dvoryane"'), who considers that the *N1* version was borrowed directly from Yury's chronicle (i.e. *L*).

CHAPTER THREE

North Russia 1200–1223

SUZDALIA

At the beginning of the thirteenth century the 46-year-old grand prince of Vladimir Vsevolod III was at the peak of his career. Six of his eight sons were still alive: Konstantin (15), Yury (12), Yaroslav (10), Vladimir (7), Svyatoslav (4) and Ivan (2).[1] His rule extended over the whole of Vladimir-Suzdalia. As has been seen in the previous chapter, during the last twelve years of his life (1200–12), he maintained his position of supremacy, as *primus inter pares* amongst all the numerous descendants of Vladimir Monomakh and of Oleg of Chernigov, that is he was recognized by all as overlord. In Ryazan' he kept the distant relatives of the Ol'govichi under the strictest control by vigorously interfering in their affairs and by keeping them at arm's length from their cousins and western neighbours in Chernigov. Somehow or other he managed to maintain a delicate balance between the warring factions in the south and in the south-west: between Roman of Volynia and Galicia, the powerful Rostislavichi of Smolensk and the at times potentially dangerous Ol'govichi, playing off one against the other with what looks like consummate skill and never allowing too great a concentration of power in the hands of one ruler. In this he could be compared to the great khans of the Golden Horde in the early fourteenth century, who were to keep a stable equilibrium between Moscow, Tver' and Lithuania. The only two setbacks in his inter-princely policy occurred in the last years of his life: in 1206 his son Yaroslav was forced to quit Southern Pereyaslavl', which he had held since 1200, and to abandon this the most southerly of all the principalities of the old Kievan realm to the Ol'govichi and later to the Rostislavichi; more serious, he lost control over Novgorod in the winter of 1208–9 when Mstislav the Daring took over the city for the Rostislavichi.

Prior to the year before his death he suffered no reverses in his own territory. His sons, who treated him with singular respect and obedience and whom he never failed to exploit when he required their military assistance, caused him no anxiety or unrest. But the trouble that was to come after his death – the fratricidal conflict between his sons – was already foreshadowed in 1211. Hitherto only Konstantin, the eldest son, had been allocated a district within Suzdalia as his patrimony – 'Rostov and five other [unspecified] towns in addition' –

in 1208.[2] In 1211, however, Vsevolod, feeling that the end of his life was at hand and realizing perhaps that his children were merely waiting for him to die before emulating their countless ancestors and launching into bloody internecine war, decided to try to forestall the chaos by drawing up a settlement for his two eldest sons: on his death Konstantin was to rule in Vladimir, while Yury was to take over Rostov[3] and presumably Konstantin's five other towns as well. It looked like a perfectly equitable solution, but Konstantin, who by now had struck roots in Rostov, had other plans: his aim was to have the best of both worlds and to rule as grand prince not in Vladimir but in his northern city and yet to have Vladimir attached to Rostov as his own family possession. Twice Vsevolod sent for him, but each time he refused to budge. Eventually Vsevolod assembled what looks like a precursor of the great *zemskie sobory* (national councils) of the sixteenth and seventeenth centuries – a congress in Vladimir embracing all the estates at which 'all his boyars from his towns and districts, Bishop Ioann [of Rostov and Vladimir], the abbots, priests, merchants, service-men (*dvoryane*) and all the people' were present. At the congress he bestowed Vladimir on his second eldest son Yury, 'entrusting all his brothers to him', in other words granting him the grand principality and seniority within the family. The third eldest son, Yaroslav, was given the third most important district in Suzdalia, that of Northern Pereyaslavl'. The contemporary account of the congress[4] – excluded from the Suzdalian Lavrent'evskiy Chronicle, which at the time was devoted almost entirely to Konstantin's interests and indeed was mainly redacted in Rostov – ends with a traditional and vivid expression of Konstantin's fury: 'hearing this he raised his eyebrows in wrath at his brothers, especially at Yury'.

On 13 April 1212 Vsevolod III died. He was given a long but entirely impersonal obituary in the local chronicle, chock-a-block with fulsome praise and clichés.[5] All his sons except Konstantin dutifully attended the funeral in Vladimir. No sooner was he buried than, as was only to be expected, fratricidal strife broke out. Accounts of this the first conflict between the brothers differ according to the origins of the sources: the strongly pro-Konstantin Lavrent'evskiy Chronicle passes over the incident in strict silence, mentioning only the peaceful outcome; the fragments of a Vladimir chronicle, which have survived in a late-fifteenth-century codex[6] and which here clearly reflect elements of Grand Prince Yury's private chronicle, give the viewpoint of Yury and Yaroslav, while the latter's family chronicle – that of Suzdalian Pereyaslavl'– is much the same but more detailed. In fact it turned out to be something of a non-event. What happened in 1212 was merely a prelude to what was to come. Konstantin set about raising an army with his brother Svyatoslav, who had fled to him, 'in anger at Yury'[7] – no doubt as a result of what he considered to be the latter's unfair distribution of territory among his brothers; while Yury and Yaroslav, after concluding a mutual pact directed against Konstantin, marched on Rostov. According to the indubitably biased chronicle of Suzdalian Pereyaslavl', negotiations were initiated by Yury, who magnanimously offered to exchange Vladimir for Rostov, but, needless to say, were flatly rejected by Konstantin, who demanded Vladimir for himself and Rostov for his son, and suggested that Yury content himself with the town of Suzdal'.[8] But 'because it was extremely muddy', so says the chronicler, but more probably because neither side was yet willing to risk a set-to without being sure of victory, there was little fighting, and after four weeks of needless shilly-shallying a temporary truce was concluded.[9]

The situation, however, was still confused. To complicate matters Vladimir and Svyatoslav in 1213 changed sides: the former, dissatisfied with the domain of Yur'ev Pol'skiy given him by Yury (no doubt he considered that, as the fourth son of the old grand prince, he had a right to a better patrimony, say Suzdal'), defected in a huff to Konstantin, who, in an attempt to gain a foothold in the south-west of Yury's lands, sent him off to capture the town of Moscow;[10] while the latter defected once again, this time from Konstantin back to Yury, who gave him the now vacant Yur'ev Pol'skiy for his troubles.[11] But Vladimir and Svyatoslav were small fry, they merely muddied the waters and their switch of allegiance made no difference to the over-all balance of power. Both were still in their teens, had had little or no experience of the rough and tumble of inter-princely warfare and had hardly had time to build up effective *druzhiny*. Konstantin, however, still unable to reconcile himself to his loss of seniority, territory and power, had behind him the support of all the northern lands of Suzdalia.

The second clash between the two brothers was as inconclusive and wasteful of effort as the first. It took place in 1213. This time the initiative came from Konstantin, or at least it was he who was the first to make a move, so the sources ill-disposed to him tell us. Neither brother, however, seemed capable of taking decisive action which might lead to a solution of the festering crisis. Konstantin confined his activities to the Kostroma area of Yury's domain,[12] while his new ally Vladimir set off north from Moscow in a feeble attempt to take one of Yaroslav's towns, Dmitrov, only to be ignominiously forced to scamper back to Moscow.[13] Yury and Yaroslav at least took a step in the right direction by setting off towards Rostov. But again both sides showed no enthusiasm whatsoever when it came to the actual fighting, and the three brothers once more agreed to call it a day. Even Vladimir, skulking in Yury's outpost of Moscow, was let off the hook. Yury winkled him out and sent him off to distant Southern Pereyaslavl' where he remained out of harm's way for the time being.[14]

So the position at the end of 1213 was much the same as before. For three years there was a curious and unnatural lull. All was calm, at any rate on the surface. The chroniclers of Vladimir and Rostov, always ready to jump to the defence of their respective masters or to accuse their opponents of initiating 'devilish strife', make no mention of any acts of hostility between the sons of Vsevolod.[15] This strange reluctance to resolve the crisis by force may this time have been the result of a fierce fire in Vladimir in 1213 (200 houses and 4 churches burned) and a calamitous famine which swept Suzdalia in the same year.[16] But it may also bear witness to the fact that both sides were busily building up their forces and preparing for what must have seemed to all an inevitable and bloody conflict.

47

The third and final confrontation between Konstantin and his brothers took place in 1216. This time it was full-scale war, complicated by the participation of outside forces: Konstantin had on his side the Rostislavichi and the Novgorodians, while Yury, Yaroslav and Svyatoslav were aided by troops from Murom and frontiersmen from the Polovtsian steppes known as Brodniki (see below, n. 22 to chapter 4). The whole course of the fighting and the complex negotiations between the two sides was meticulously recorded – in all likelihood by a participant – in a long and detailed narrative which originated in Smolensk.[17]

It all started not as a direct confrontation between the brothers but as it were indirectly, almost by accident, in Novgorod. One thing led to another. As will be seen (see below, p. 55), the initiative in fact came from one of the Rostislavichi, the mettlesome Mstislav Mstislavich. He had just reoccupied Novgorod after his reconnaissance of Galicia and was faced with the danger of his son-in-law Yaroslav on his doorstep. For Yaroslav, after his brief occupancy of the princely palace in Novgorod during Mstislav's absence, had not only rounded up a number of Mstislav's supporters, but had taken over Novgorod's outposts of Torzhok and Volok Lamskiy, had cut off supplies to the city and had arrested as many Novgorodian merchants in Torzhok as he could lay hands on. War between him and Mstislav was inevitable. Mstislav's first aim was to dislodge him from Torzhok and to force him to release his hostages. At first it was merely border skirmishes on the frontiers of Novgorod, Smolensk and Suzdalia. But little by little the various detachments on either side coalesced, their numbers swollen with reinforcements: Yaroslav linked up with the superior forces of his brother Yury, while Mstislav not only enlisted the support of his relatives (his brother Vladimir, then prince of Pskov, his cousin Vladimir Ryurikovich of Smolensk and Vsevolod the son of the prince of Kiev, Mstislav Romanovich) but, realizing that there was no love lost between the brothers, shewdly alerted Konstantin to the state of affairs on the western borders of Suzdalia.

Eventually the two opposing armies faced each other on the Lipitsa river in the neighbourhood of Yur'ev Pol'skiy. As was so often the case before a major battle, attempts were made to avoid actually fighting and to settle matters amicably – the initiative coming, so the biased sources, all of which favour the Rostislavichi, tell us, from the side of Konstantin and his allies. Again and again it was stressed that the allies' quarrel was not so much with Yury as with Yaroslav, and the constant demand was that Yaroslav release his Novgorodian hostages and remove his forces from Volok Lamskiy. When these demands were contemptuously rejected by both Yury and Yaroslav, the question of land distribution was raised: 'We are all members of the same family', so Konstantin's envoy is reported as saying; 'Let us give seniority to Prince Konstantin. Put him [on the throne] in Vladimir, and all [the rest of] the land of Suzdal' will be given to you.'[18] Again the overtures were dismissed.

Before the battle began Yury and Yaroslav, utterly confident of victory, agreed between themselves on the future carve-up of Russia. In spite of the tendentious nature of the chronicle versions, there is no reason to doubt the veracity of the account of this particular incident,[19] for the author explicitly states that a copy of the pact, written and agreed to by the princes, 'was captured in Yaroslav's headquarters by the men of Smolensk after the battle and given to the princes [of Smolensk]'. According to the agreement, Yury was to get 'the land of Vladimir and Rostov'; Yaroslav was to be given Novgorod; Svyatoslav – Smolensk. Kiev was to go to 'the princes of Chernigov',[20] and Galicia – to Yury and Yaroslav between them.[21] Needless to say, the Rostislavichi were to be left empty-handed.

The battle, which was fought on 21 April, ended not surprisingly in total victory for Konstantin and his allies. As is usual in medieval Russian battle descriptions, it is hard to gauge the numbers involved or the losses sustained owing to the gross hyperbole with which such statistics are given. According to the Smolensk accounts – the only early version to give any figures – Yury and Yaroslav lost 9,233 killed and 60 prisoners, while the casualties of Konstantin and the Rostislavichi amounted to 6 (5 killed from Novgorod and 1 from Smolensk).[22] Even allowing for exaggeration, it was clearly a major setto: in the regiments of Yury and Yaroslav there were thirty banners (*styagi*) and a hundred 'trumpets and drums' (*truby i bubny*),[23] all falling to the enemy. Yury and Yaroslav both fled, Yury precipitously to Vladimir ('on his fourth horse, having exhausted three; wearing only a shirt'), Yaroslav, still more so, to Pereyaslavl' ('on his fifth horse, having exhausted four').

The situation in Vladimir was hopeless. Yury tried to rally the few stragglers from his army who managed to escape and reach the capital, 'some wounded, some naked', but it was obvious that resistance was out of the question, and when the Novgorod and Smolensk troops reached Vladimir and set it on fire, Yury surrendered quietly. Mstislav gave him safe-conduct to what amounted to exile in the town of Gorodets Radilov on the easternmost reaches of the Volga in Suzdalian territory. As for Yaroslav, portrayed as the villain of the piece in both Novgorod and Smolensk sources, his first action on arrival in Pereyaslavl' was to round up all the merchants from Novgorod and Smolensk he could find in his district and throw them into cellars. Those from Novgorod, 150 in all, died of suffocation; those from Smolensk, 15 in number, were imprisoned elsewhere and managed to survive.[24] As the allies approached Pereyaslavl', Yaroslav sent messengers to Konstantin begging him not to hand him over to his father-in-law. But there were no recriminations. Yaroslav showered gifts on the allied princes and was allowed to remain in Pereyaslavl', but only after Mstislav had extricated his daughter, all the Novgorodians and anyone else who had fought in Yaroslav's army.[25]

The war was over. Mstislav returned to Novgorod and his brother Vladimir to Pskov. Konstantin took up office in Vladimir as grand prince and spent the last two years of his life between the capital and Rostov. Yaroslav, after pleading in vain for the return of his wife, resigned himself to a period of political eclipse in Pereyaslavl'. As for Yury, it is doubtful whether he planned to remain for long in obscurity in his distant place of exile. The problem was how to dislodge his elder brother; armed intervention was out of the question in view of Konstantin's alliance with the Rostislavichi and he could hope for no assistance from Yaroslav. He had, however, one trump card: Simon, bishop of Suzdal'and Vladimir, had followed him into exile, thus creating an awkward ecclesiastical hiatus in the capital.[26] Konstantin had little alternative but to make his peace with him. The agreement reached between the two brothers in 1217 was the obvious one: after Konstantin's death Yury was to reassume the title of grand prince; meanwhile he was to rule in the town of Suzdal'.[27] At the same time Konstantin appointed his two sons Vasil'ko and Vsevolod to Rostov and Yaroslavl' respectively, entrusting them after his death 'to God, to the most pure Mother of God and to [his] brother . . . Yury'.[28]

Yury did not have long to wait in Suzdal'. On 2 February 1218, five months after his pact with Yury, Konstantin died in Vladimir. His personal chronicler in Rostov composed a lengthy obituary, followed by a traditional description of the lamentations of the population and all his brothers and an account of the burial.[29] As is almost invariably the case with such medieval Russian effusions, we learn nothing about the man himself – the virtues of humility, charity, piety, love of the clergy, etc., are purely stereotyped – except that he 'built many churches', decorating them with ikons and 'filling them with books', and that he 'often read [sacred] books'.[30] As for the reaction of the mourners, too much credence should not be given to the description of the lamentations of his brothers ('they wept with great weeping as for a father and a beloved brother, for all held him in the place of a father . . . for they all loved him beyond measure' (!)); but it is interesting to note that the annalist has his boyars weep for him 'as the defender of their lands' and his servicemen (*slugy*) as their 'provider (*kormitelya*) and master'.

Yury assumed the grand principality once again and installed himself in Vladimir, where he was to remain until his death at the battle on the Sit' river in 1238. The first five years of his reign – up to the first Tatar invasion of 1223 – were calm and undisturbed by fratricidal war. His brothers and nephews lived in amity with him and obeyed his commands: Yaroslav showed no signs of dissatisfaction with his principality of Suzdalian Pereyaslavl', and took over Novgorod at Yury's behest when the latter's son fled the city in 1223 (see below, n. 78); Vladimir, who in 1217 had managed to escape from, or was released by, the Polovtsians[31] and had been given the minor district of Starodub on the Klyaz'ma east of Vladimir, remained there quietly and peacefully until he died in 1228; Svyatoslav kept Yur'ev Pol'skiy, which Yury had given him in 1213 (see above, p. 47); the two eldest sons of Konstantin ruled Rostov and Yaroslavl'. Novgorod, as will be shown below, returned to the Suzdalian fold in 1221, having dismissed the last of the Rostislavichi to rule there. As for the south, there is no record of any clashes, or indeed of any contact, with the Rostislavichi in the five years 1218–23.

Yury's major concern during this period of his rule was with the Volga Bulgars. Since the beginning of the thirteenth century there had been practically no relations between the Bulgars and Suzdalia; the only recorded events were a successful raid by Vsevolod III's troops in 1205 against the Volga and Kama Bulgars,[32] a Bulgar attack on Ryazan' in 1209 and a counter-attack organized by Vsevolod in the following year.[33] In 1218, however, the Bulgars raided and seized the most north-easterly possession of the prince of Rostov – Ustyug on the Sukhona river – and then proceeded south along the Unzha river as far as the town of Unzha.[34] Although they failed to take Unzha and although Ustyug was soon restored to Vasil'ko of Rostov, the Bulgar menace was not to be ignored. Hitherto raids had been mainly concentrated on Ryazan' and Murom. Now Suzdalian territory was threatened. Yury took decisive steps to discourage the Bulgars from further aggression. In 1220 he mounted a major campaign: troops were sent under Svyatoslav of Yur'ev Pol'skiy; he was joined by detachments from Pereyaslavl', Rostov, Ustyug and Murom. The bulk of the army gathered at the junction of the Volga and Oka rivers and sailed downstream to Oshel' in Bulgar territory. The town was taken (15 June), the Bulgars were defeated and much of the land on the lower reaches of the Kama was ravaged by troops from Rostov and Ustyug. So effective was the campaign that in the winter of the same year the Bulgars sent three separate embassies to Yury begging for peace. But Yury was planning yet another expedition down the Volga, and it was only the third Bulgar embassy, which met him at Gorodets Radilov, that had any effect. Yury agreed to peace terms 'such as had been made under his father Vsevolod and his grandfather Yury'.[35] To crown his vital campaign and to secure his eastern frontiers from any further attacks, Yury in 1221 founded the city of Nizhniy Novgorod at the confluence of the Volga and Oka rivers.[36]

There were to be no more Bulgar raids on Ryazan', Murom or Suzdalia. Indeed in 1229, in view of the Tatar threat to Bulgar territory (see below, p. 76), the Bulgars concluded yet another peace, this time to last for six years, with Yury. Not only were prisoners exchanged, but the Bulgars even alleviated a famine in north-east Russia, which resulted from a poor rye harvest, by shipping grain along the Volga and Oka.[37] From then on the Russians were to hear little more of the Bulgars until at last the news reached them of the sack of the town of Bulgar by the Tatars in 1236.

NOVGOROD

The turbulent events in south, south-west and north-east Russia during the first quarter of the thirteenth century are clearly reflected in the history of Novgorod. As has been seen in Chapter 1, during the second half of the twelfth century the three leading princely families – the princes of Suzdal', the Rostislavichi of Smolensk and the Ol'govichi of Chernigov – had all contended for control over Novgorod, while the various boyar groupings in the city aligned themselves for the most part with this or that clan. The same struggle was to continue throughout the first quarter of the thirteenth century, although by now the Ol'govichi, for all their temporary successes in the south, no longer succeeded in placing their own princes in Novgorod. From the beginning of the century up to 1224 the only contestants were members of Vsevolod's family, supported in the main by boyar representatives from the 'Prussian Street'

(*Prusskaya ulitsa*: i.e. the Zagorodskiy and Lyudin *kontsy*), and the Rostislavichi, backed by boyars from the Nerevskiy *konets* and the 'Trade Side' (mainly the Slavenskiy *konets* (see above, p. 18)).

On 1 January 1200 Vsevolod III's 3-year-old son, Svyatoslav, arrived in Novgorod, replacing Yaroslav Vladimirovich, Vsevolod's brother-in-law,[38] who had ruled off and on for eighteen unpopular years, hampered for much of the time by an obstreperous anti-Suzdalian *posadnik*, Miroshka Nezdilich.

The five years of Svyatoslav's stay (one can hardly call it 'rule') in Novgorod were uneventful, calm on the surface and curiously unaffected by the momentous happenings in the south and the south-east. There were, it is true, invasions of Novgorod territory – by the Lithuanians from the west in 1200 and by the Swedes from the north-west in 1201[39] – but these were successfully dealt with and no serious losses were sustained. The calm was illusory, however. Even though Miroshka was replaced at his death in 1203 by a pro-Suzdalian *posadnik* (Mikhalko Stepanovich), who no doubt protected the interests of the infant prince, Vsevolod III was uneasy. Realizing that sooner or later troops from the north-west would be needed to help Suzdalian forces control affairs in the south and that in the event of a serious war something more impressive was needed than a merely symbolical representative of the grand prince in the person of a small boy, he recalled Svyatoslav and replaced him in March 1205 by his eldest son, 19-year-old Konstantin.[40] The Novgorodians countered by appointing an anti-Suzdalian posadnik, Dmitr Miroshkinich.[41]

The combination of a strong Suzdalian prince in Novgorod and a representative of the anti-Suzdalian faction holding the senior administrative office presaged trouble. It came two years later. The Novgorod chronicle, reticent and elliptical though it may be concerning the events of 1207–8, nevertheless shows clearly how closely the question of which princely clan was to provide Novgorod with a ruler was linked with the internal vicissitudes of the boyar parties. Clearly Konstantin was not having things all his own way, for in March 1207 one Lazar' was sent by Vsevolod to Novgorod. Described by the chronicler as 'Vsevolod's man' (*Vsevolozh' muzh*), his task was evidently to stir up trouble against the *posadnik*.[42] If this was the case, he was eminently successful, as subsequent events were to show.

In the late summer of 1207 Konstantin was ordered by his father to join him on his great punitive expedition against Chernigov – the expedition that was to be deflected to Ryazan' (see above, p. 32). He took what looks like a numerous army consisting of troops from Novgorod, Pskov, Ladoga and Torzhok.[43] And with him went the *posadnik* Dmitr. After the surrender of Pronsk (October 1207) Vsevolod sent the Novgorod soldiers home, having liberally rewarded them for their participation in the campaign and having granted them "full freedom', not to choose their own prince, but to settle their inter-boyar conflicts without princely consent and to sanction any reprisals a *veche* might recommend against Dmitr Miroshkinich and his family.[44] 'Love him who does good for you, but punish the evil ones' were his enigmatic farewell words.[4] If this was an invitation to violence, it was seized upon with alacrity. Konstantin and Dmitr, who had been wounded at the battle of

Pronsk, as well as seven 'senior men' (*vyatshikh muzh*) – presumably close political associates of Dmitr – returned with Vsevolod to Vladimir. The Novgorodians found themselves without a prince and without a *posadnik*.

Vsevolod had done his work well; he and Konstantin had won over the Novgorod army to their side, at any rate the majority of them. As soon as the troops returned home, they summoned a *veche* (November 1207) 'against *Posadnik* Dmitr and his family', stirred up the people and urged them to recoup their losses caused by what were evidently Dmitr's stringent financial measures.[46] The populace went about its business in a manner peculiar to Novgorodians on the rampage – sacking and burning the houses and estates of Dmitr and his family, seizing their serfs and confiscating their possessions. And when the corpse of Dmitr, who had died in Vladimir from his wounds, arrived in the city, they attempted to inflict the ultimate indignity on it and throw it into the river Volkhov, only to be stopped by the archbishop.[47]

So confident was Vsevolod III of support in Novgorod that no sooner had he learned of the appointment of Mikhalko Stepanovich's son, the pro-Suzdalian Tverdislav, to the office *posadnik*,[48] then he sent his son Svyatoslav, by now 11 years old, to rule there once again. Svyatoslav arrived in Novgorod on 9 February 1208. More arrests of Dmitr's relatives and adherents followed – they were sent to Vladimir to be dealt with by the grand prince. It looked as though the pro-Suzdalian party amongst the boyars had gained the upper hand and that Svyatoslav's rule would be a peaceful one. But Vsevolod had reckoned without the Rostislavichi – and without the remnants of the anti-Suzdalian party; for in spite of all the reprisals taken against the followers and kinsmen of Dmitr, the representatives of the boyar faction from the Nerevskiy and Slavenskiy *kontsy* – the supporters of Dmitr and the opponents of Tverdislav and the pro-Suzdalian party – were still active and influential. Furthermore, a new, powerful, dashing and imaginitive member of the Rostislavichi clan was soon to appear in the north-west and to put paid to Vsevolod's plans to control Novgorod for many years to come.

Mstislav Mstislavich, known to his contemporaries as 'the Daring' (*udaloy*), was born sometime before 1176, the son of Mstislav Rostislavich 'the Brave' (*Khrabryy*). Little is known of his early years except that in 1193 he held the Kievan fortress town of Trepol' on the Dnepr. In 1207 he was stationed in the southern outpost of Torchesk on the Ros' river when he was driven out during the course of Vsevolod Chermnyy's victorious Kievan campaign (see above, p. 31). He fled to the principality of Smolensk. There he took over the north-ernmost town and district of Toropets, the ideal jumping-off place for any attack on Novgorod.

Mstislav chose his time well. While Vsevolod III and his sons were engaged in the second punitive campaign against Ryazan' in late 1208 (see above, p. 39), he invaded Novgorod territory. He took the eastern outpost of Torzhok, the most important of Novgorod's possessions and the key fortress near the borders of Suzdalia. There he arrested Svyatoslav's representatives and the local *posadnik*, and sent the following message to Novgorod: 'I greet St Sofia [the cathedral church of Novgorod] and the tomb of my father[49]; I have come to you, in sorrow for my patrimony, having heard of the violence done by your princes.' The message was undoubtedly addressed to the opponents of Suzdal' rule and the 'violence' was a reference to the measures taken against Dmitr's family and the pro-Rostislavichi boyars. It met with immediate success. Tverdislav was unable to save his patron, and Mstislav was invited to Novgorod where he was 'placed upon his father's throne'. Svyatoslav was summarily arrested and confined to the archbishop's palace.[50]

Vsevolod's action was swift and it can hardly have come as a surprise to Mstislav: he had all the Novgorodian merchants he could lay hands on seized and their wares confiscated.[51] Thus both sides held trump cards. It looked like an impasse, unless of course Mstislav, whose military prowess had yet to be tested, could be forcibly ejected. Vsevolod and Mstislav both put up a show of strength: in early 1209 Vsevolod sent an army under Konstantin to Tver', just east of Torzhok, but on the Suzdalian side of the border; Mstislav marched east, presumably with his own *druzhina* and as many troops as his supporters in Novgorod could muster. But it turned out to be nothing more than an exercise in sabre-rattling; both sides had far too much to lose for them to risk military defeat. So an agreement was reached: Svyatoslav was sent back to his father and the merchants were released.[52]

Mstislav Mstislavich was now firmly established in Novgorod. There was nothing to dislodge him. Before the year 1209 was out he had busied himself with the southern and eastern fortifications of Novgorod territory, strengthening Velikie Luki in the south as an outpost against growing Lithuanian attacks and personally supervising the defences of Torzhok[53]; he had replaced Tverdislav with a creature of his own, Dmitr Yakunich[54]; he had with impunity ignored Vsevolod III's ominous expression of overlordship and seniority in a message conveyed to him by Konstantin ('you are a son to me and I am a father to you').[55] Not even the disastrous fire of 1209, which took place during Mstislav's absence destroying 4,300 houses and 15 churches[56] and which may well have been the work of arsonists from the pro-Suzdalian camp, nor the fire of 1217, in which another 15 churches were burned,[57] could undermine his authority.

For nine years he managed Novgorod's affairs with a firm and skilful hand. During all of this period only two raids into Novgorod territory from the west are recorded, while Mstislav or his relatives constantly hammered Novgorod's western neighbours, the Chud' (Estonians): at least five campaigns were undertaken,[58] some of them relatively small with the aim of capturing prisoners, horses and cattle or levying tribute on the natives, others more ambitious reaching as far as Vorob'ino ('castrum Warbole' in Henry of Livonia's Chronicle) in northern Estonia ($41\frac{1}{2}$ km south-west of Revel' (Tallin)) (1212) and Riga in the west (August 1216). The ultimate aim of Mstislav's western policy was clearly not to establish bases in Estonia or to convert the Estonians to Christianity, or to expand the frontiers of Novgorod and Pskov westwards, but rather to act as a deterrent and to discourage the Chud' from invading Novgorod territory, to maintain a system of tribute, which had been in force since the middle of the twelfth century,[59] and above all to afford some sort of bulwark against the ever-encroaching forces of the German Knights.[60] Pskov was kept under strict control by the Rostislavichi: from 1208 until at least their final exit from Novgorod in 1221 there was always a close relative of Mstislav in Pskov – most of the time it was his brother Vladimir, who seems even to have survived the take-over of Novgorod by Yury of Vladimir in 1221.[61] As for Novgorod itself, it was only when Mstislav left the city in the winter of 1214/1215 to reconnoitre Galicia (see above, p. 37) that his enemies took advantage of his absence[62] – and no doubt of the words he is alleged to have uttered before leaving: 'you are free to choose your own prince' – and sent for a Suzdalian, Yaroslav, Vsevolod's third eldest son and Mstislav's son-in-law.[63] But this, Yaroslav's first sojourn in Novgorod, was short-lived. He did what he could to round up Mstislav's supporters, but the opposition to his rule was too strong, and when he heard that Mstislav, having returned from Galicia, was amassing an army in Smolensk,[64] he moved to Torzhok. From there every possible pressure was brought to bear on Novgorod: after a crop failure in all Novgorodian districts except Torzhok, he did what so many would-be subjugators of Novgorod were to do in the fourteenth and fifteenth centuries and cut off the vital east–west flow of supplies to the city by blocking the Tvertsa river; Novgorodian envoys, who begged him to return and lift the blockade, were summarily arrested, as were numerous Novgorodian merchants who happened to be in Torzhok at the time[65]; auxiliary forces sent from Suzdalia to aid Yaroslav raided Toropets.[66] The way was open for Mstislav to retake Novgorod. On 11 February he returned to the hard-pressed city, arrested the governor left there by Yaroslav, ordered his son-in-law to release all Novgorodian prisoners and quit Torzhok, and, when this was refused, set off east with a Novgorodian army (1 March 1216). Within two months the fighting was over (see above, pp. 48–9): Yaroslav and his brothers were defeated and Mstislav was back, once more in sole and undisputed command of Novgorod.

The extent of Mstislav's authority – and popularity – in Novgorod during his ten years of rule is shown perhaps best of all by his ability to manage the boyars, or rather to maintain amicable relations with the anti-Rostislavichi faction. For approximately half of the time of his rule pro-Rostislavichi boyars were *posadniki*; but for the rest of the time it was Tverdislav, son of the firm supporter of Suzdalian rule, Mikhalko Stepanovich (see above, p. 52), who held office, and it was he who stood by Mstislav in a moment of crisis – in 1212, when the Novgorodian army, in spite of Mstislav's pleadings, refused to march beyond Smolensk in the campaign of the Rostislavichi against the Ol'govichi, Tverdislav managed to persuade the troops to follow their prince (see above, p. 35).

There *was* of course some opposition to Mstislav in Novgorod which even the servile chronicler – only too ready to laud any of Mstislav's actions – was unable to conceal. In 1210, for instance, his firm supporter Mitrofan the archbishop of Novgorod[67] was for some reason or other deposed and sent to Toropets in Rostislavichi territory.[68] Nor must it be forgotten that in 1215 his enemies succeeded in acquiring a Suzdalian prince during his temporary absence (see above). But still, his authority was great, so great indeed that in 1212 he had only to summon a *veche* and put his proposals before it in order to persuade the Novgorodians to march with him and his relations on a campaign which in no way concerned them or touched their interests (see above, p. 35) and to utter the age-old formula of consent: 'Whithersoever, O Prince, you cast your eyes, there shall we lay down our heads.'[69]

Mstislav's final departure from Novgorod did not mean the end of Rostislavichi rule in the city – indeed, it was to continue for four more years – but it signified the end of Rostislavichi stability there. When he announced his intention of seeking fresh conquests in Galicia in July 1217, the Novgorodians begged him to stay.[70] But he was inflexible. Before leaving, however, he assured the continuance of Rostislavichi control over the city: Archbishop Mitrofan was allowed to return, and the eldest son of Mstislav Romanovich of Kiev, Svyatoslav, was sent for from Smolensk.[71]

It was soon after Svyatoslav's arrival that trouble began. The first crisis occurred in January 1218, when fighting between the main rival factions broke out. From the confused account given in the local chronicle one thing emerges clearly: it was an attempt on the part of the representatives of the Trade Side (*Torgovaya storona*) and the Nerevskiy *konets* – both pro-Rostislavichi strongholds – to oust the pro-Suzdalian *posadnik* Tverdislav. Svyatoslav tried to influence the stormy *veche*, which was in session for a week, and demanded that Tverdislav be dismissed from office. But the representatives of the pro-Suzdalian Lyudin *konets* won the day: Tverdislav remained *posadnik*, and a shaky peace was patched up between the two sides.[72]

No doubt in view of Svyatoslav's inability to ride the storm in Novgorod and deplete the opposition, Mstislav of Kiev replaced him with his second eldest son Vsevolod, who at least had had some experience of ruling Pskov (see below, n. 61). At first he enjoyed an element of success. Shortly after he arrived in February 1218 rumours were spread in the city to the effect that Tverdislav had been in touch with Yury and Yaroslav of Suzdalia and had urged them to prevent a Novgorodian expedition to the Northern Dvina district from crossing Suzdalian territory. This time, whether or not there was any truth in the accusations, Tverdislav was obliged to hand over the office of *posadnik* to his rivals.[73] Later in the year Archbishop Antony, who had replaced the pro-Rostislavichi Mitrofan in 1210, was ousted, no doubt as a result of the fall of Tverdislav. He decamped to Torzhok and his rival, Mitrofan, was again acclaimed archbishop. But Antony too had his supporters. Towards the end of 1218 or the beginning of 1219 he returned to Novgorod – at the same time as Tverdislav once more was made *posadnik*[74] – and contested Mitrofan's right to the archbishopric. This time Vsevolod and the Novgorodians had no alternative but to solve the embarrassing question of two archbishops in the city by placing the matter in the hands of the metropolitan. Mitrofan and Antony were sent off to Kiev; the metropolitan, not surprisingly in view of the proximity to his court, and no doubt the influence, of the prince of Kiev, the senior member of the Rostislavichi family, decided in favour of Mitrofan, Antony being fobbed off with the Galician eparchy of Peremyshl'.[75]

The third post-Mstislavian crisis to hit Novgorod occurred in 1219. Again

Tverdislav was in the centre of the storm. For reasons undisclosed by the chronicler Vsevolod vented his anger on the *posadnik*. The town was in uproar; the supporters of both sides even put on their armour, and fighting was only avoided by Archbishop Mitrofan, who managed to persuade the allegedly sick Tverdislav to relinquish his office and take the monastic tonsure. Once again the *posadnichestvo* changed hands.

The chronicles give no indication as to which boyar group the new *posadnik*, Ivanko Dmitrievich, belonged to, nor do they provide any clue as to what happened in Novgorod between 1219 and 1221.[76] However, a radical change in public opinion must have taken place, for in 1221 the Novgorodians, for no given reason, suddenly requested Vsevolod to leave: 'We do not want you; go wherever you wish.'[77] It was the end of Smolensk hegemony in Novgorod; never again was a member of the Rostislavichi dynasty to sit upon the throne in the 'court of Yaroslav'. Mitrofan and *posadnik* Ivanko were despatched with a delegation of senior citizens to Vladimir to ask Yury for a prince. From now on – with the exception of brief spells of Ol'govichi rule (Mikhail of Chernigov and his son Rostislav) – Novgorod was to receive princes only from Suzdalia. True, these princes changed often with alarming rapidity,[78] but at first at any rate it was not so much the result of a clash of boyar interests or the reflexion of conflict between Novgorod and Vladimir as an expression of the will of the grand prince: 'If it is not pleasing to you to hold Novgorod by means of your son', a Novgorod embassy said to Yury when his son fled the city soon after being sent there in 1221, 'then do you, Prince, give us your brother'.[79]

* * * *

What light do the events of the first two decades of the thirteenth century in Novgorod throw on the peculiar relationship between boyar authority and princely power? Is there any evidence of a change from the conditions of the twelfth century, any signs of a move towards Novgorodian independence, towards the initiation of those elements of republicanism which were to become so manifest in the fourteenth century? It is hard to form any valid conclusions owing to the confused nature of the events reported in the sources, most of which, however, bear the stamp of contemporaneity and were probably little tampered with by later redactors.[80] There are too many paradoxes, contradictions and unanswered questions. The Novgorodians clearly retained a certain freedom to get rid of their princes and to request external rulers (of Vladimir and Kiev) to send them princes. On the other hand, strong princes, both inside and outside Novgorod, were able to impose their own terms, often independently of which boyar group was in the ascendant at the time,[81] and indeed to influence the power-struggle between the various boyar groupings – in 1207, for example, Vsevolod III incited the Novgorodians to take reprisals against the anti-Suzdalian faction (see above, pp. 52–3). Furthermore, it is difficult, if not impossible, to tell what degree if any of limitation of princely power this might have implied. Was there any attempt by any *posadnik*, Tverdislav, say, or Ivanko Dmitrievich, to compromise in order to achieve some sort of boyar solidarity in face of princely authority? Indeed, was there any element of

57

'succession' in the alternation of *posadniki*? In other words, did the replacement of a pro-Suzdalian by a pro-Rostislavichi *posadnik* necessarily entail the overthrow of the former, or had some system of rotation been evolved which might indicate a consolidation of boyar opposition to the prince?

One can only arrive at some tentative, and, unfortunately, somewhat negative, conclusions. Firstly, it would appear that the events of 1200–23 show no signs whatsoever of the slackening or erosion of the authority of the prince – or indeed of the *posadnik* for that matter. Secondly, no new relationship between the boyars as a whole and the prince were evolved during this period: elements of contractual links between prince and Novgorod become evident only at a later date.

So the conclusion one must reach is that no perceptible change occurred and that the pattern of relationships between prince and Novgorod were much the same in the first quarter of the thirteenth century as they had been in the last half of the twelfth. Novgorod had still a long way to go before being able to advance towards true independence and republicanism.

REFERENCES AND NOTES

1. Boris died in 1188, Gleb in 1189.
2. *PSRL*, vol. 1, col. 434.
3. *PSRL*, vol. 25, p. 108. According to Tatishchev's unlikely account, Yaroslav, Vladimir, Svyatoslav and Ivan were to receive Pereyaslavl', Suzdal', Yur'ev Pol'skiy and Starodub respectively (*Istoriya*, vol. 4, p. 342); according to *LPS* (p. 110, *s.a.* 1213), Yaroslav was to receive Pereyaslavl', Vladimir – Yur'ev Pol'skiy, while Svyatoslav and Ivan were to be entrusted to *Yury* as grand prince.
4. *PSRL*, vol. 25, p. 108 (also in *E, L'v* and N*ik*).
5. *PSRL*, vol. 1, cols 436–7
6. Called by Nasonov the 'Vladimir Fragments' (*Istoriya*, pp. 201 *et seq.*). These Vladimir elements (1207–20) found in *M* (and often in *E, L'v* and N*ik*) clearly originated in a Vladimir *svod* of the early thirteenth century (see Lur'e, *Obshcherusskie letopisi*, p. 57); they reached *M* and the other later chronicles via the hypothetical *svod* of 1472–79. See Appendix A.
7. *LPS*, p. 110.
8. Ibid., pp. 110–11.
9. Ibid., p. 111; *PSRL*, vol. 1, col. 437.
10. *LPS*, p. 111; cf. *M*, which gives a slightly different account of the incident (*PSRL*, vol. 25, p. 109).
11. *PSRL*, vol. 25, p. 109.
12. Kostroma was burned, Sol' Velikaya (south-west of Kostroma? Perhaps the main supplier of salt to Suzdalia) was captured, both part of Yury's territory. He also took Nerekhta, south of Kostroma, which was part of the district of Pereyaslavl'. *LPS*, p. 111; *PSRL*, vol. 25, p. 109. Not in *L*.
13. *LPS*, pp. 111–12.
14. Ibid., p. 112; *PSRL*, vol. 25, p. 110; vol. 1, cols 437–8.
15. Indeed, in 1215 Konstantin actually sent reinforcements to assist Yaroslav in his war with Mstislav Mstislavich over Novgorod. *PSRL*, vol. 25, p. 111.

16. Ibid., p. 110; *LPS*, p. 112.
17. The full account is found only in *S1* and *N4* (*PSRL*, vol. 5 (1925 ed), pp. 193–201; vol. 4, pp. 186–97); in other words it formed part of the hypo-thetical '*svod* of 1448'. The main source for this long and remarkable *povest'* was clearly a non-extant Smolensk chronicle or a tale of the exploits of the Rostislavichi (the author twice talks of 'our princes' when referring to the princes of Smolensk, and once mentions documents recording Yury's discussion with Yaroslav before the final battle which were 'captured by the men of Smolensk'). *N1* contains a shorter, but clearly contemporary, version (*NPL*, pp. 55–7, 254–8), while *M*, *E*, *L'v* and *Nik* are close to much of the version found in *S1* and *N4*, but omit most of the pro-Rostislavichi bias (*PSRL*, vol. 25, pp. 111–14). *L* has only the briefest summary of the outcome (*PSRL*, vol. 1, cols 439–40). For a detailed anal-ysis of the source problems of the 'Tale of the Battle on the River Lipitsa', see Lur'e, 'Povest' o bitve'.
18. *PSRL*, vol. 5, p. 195; vol. 4, p. 189; vol. 25, p. 112.
19. Cf., however, Lur'e, 'Povest' o bitve', p. 113.
20. In 1215 their brother Vladimir had married Gleb of Chernigov's daughter in Southern Pereyaslavl' — a sign perhaps of their readiness to seek anti-Rostislavichi allies. See above, p. 36.
21. *PSRL*, vol. 5, p. 196; vol. 4, p. 190.
22. *PSRL*, vol. 5, pp. 198–9; vol. 4, pp. 193–4 (repeated in *M*). Tatishchev gives the numbers as 17,250 and 2,500 respectively (*Istoriya*, vol. 4, p. 350). Cf. *Nik*: 17,200 and 550 (*PSRL*, vol. 10, p. 75).
23. *PSRL*, vol. 5, pp. 198–9.
24. Ibid., pp. 199–200; vol. 4, p. 195. Cf. *Nik*, where the numbers are swollen to 315 and 90 (*PSRL*, vol. 10, p. 75). No numbers are given in *N1*.
25. *PSRL*, vol. 5, p. 201; vol. 4, p. 196; vol. 25, p. 114; *NPL*, pp. 56, 257.
26. At the retirement of Ioann, bishop of Vladimir, Suzdal' and Rostov in 1214, Yury appointed Simon, abbot of the Monastery of the Nativity of the Virgin in Vla-dimir, to the see of Vladimir and Suzdal', while Konstantin, then prince of Rostov, had his spiritual father Pakhomy consecrated bishop of Rostov. Pakhomy died in 1216 and was replaced by Kirill I as bishop of Rostov. See *PSRL*, vol. 1, cols 438, 439.
27. Reported only in *M*, *E*, *L'v* and *Nik* (i.e. fragments presumably of Yury's chron-icle), but not in Konstantin's chronicle (*L*). See *PSRL*, vol. 25, p. 115. According to Tatishchev, Yury agreed that on *his* death Vladimir should pass to Konstantin's eldest son. (*Istoriya*, vol. 4, p. 352).
28. *PSRL*, vol. 1, col. 442? Tatishchev adds that the youngest son Vladimir was to get Beloozero when he grew up (*Istoriya*, vol. 4, p. 356).
29. *PSRL*, vol. 1, cols 442–4.
30. Cf. Tatishchev's account of the arrival in Vladimir of Bishop Vladimir of Polotsk in 1218 (in error for 1217: see dating in *L*): 'he brought him [Konstantin] many Greek books by ancient teachers, for he knew that the prince loved them more than all possessions'. *Istoriya*, vol. 4, p. 354. He also says that he bought many Greek books which he had translated and that his library consisted of over 1000 Greek books alone (ibid., p. 356).
31. He had been taken prisoner by the Polovtsians in 1215.
32. Only in *T* and *Nik*. *TL*, p. 291; *PSRL*, vol. 10, p. 50.
33. See Tatishchev, *Istoriya*, vol. 4, pp. 340, 341; *PSRL*, vol. 10, p. 60.
34. *PSRL*, vol. 25, p. 116 (*s.a.* 1219); vol. 5, p. 201; vol. 4, p. 199. Cf. Tatish-

chev's version, according to which the *'Yugry'* (i.e. the inhabitants of Ustyug) barely beat them off, but Unzha was captured by them (*Istoriya*, vol. 4, p. 357). On Unzha, see Kuchkin, 'Nizhniy Novgorod', p. 235.

35. For a very detailed account of the Bulgar campaign of 1220 and the subsequent embassies to Yury, see *M* (*PSRL*, vol. 25, pp. 116–17) (also in *E* and *L'v*). *L* (*PSRL*, vol. 1, cols 444–5) has only a short version. See Kuchkin, 'O marshrutakh', pp. 42–4 for a description of the geography of the campaign.

36. *PSRL*, vol. 1, col. 445. See Kuchkin, 'Nizhniy Novgorod', pp. 236 *et seq.*

37. Tatishchev, *Istoriya*, vol. 4, p. 369; *PSRL*, vol. 10, p. 98; see also Kargalov, *VFR*, pp. 69–70; Noonan, 'Suzdalia's Eastern Trade', p. 375.

38. Yaroslav was a grandson of Mstislav the Great and was married to an Ossetian princess, the sister of Vsevolod III's first wife. See Genealogical Table 2.

39. *NPL*, pp. 45, 239, 240. The Swedes (or Danes or Norwegians?) are described as 'Varangians' (*Varyagi*).

40. *NPL*, pp. 49–50, 246. Vsevolod told the Novgorodians that in view of the forthcoming military operations (*v zemli vashei rat khodit*), Svyatoslav was too young (. . . *Svyatoslav mal*).

41. *NPL*, pp. 50, 246.

42. *NPL*, pp. 50, 247. Yanin (*Novgorodskie posadniki*, p. 118) considers that the execution of one Aleksa Sbyslavich, 'ordered' by Dmitr Miroshkinich's brother, was somehow engineered by Lazar' to arouse opposition to the Miroshkinichi faction.

43. *PSRL*, vol. 1, col. 430.

44. Yanin, *Novgorodskie posadniki*, pp. 117–18.

45. *NPL*, pp. 50, 248 (*s.a.* 1209).

46. *Yanin, op. cit.,* p. 117.

47. *NPL*, pp. 51, 248.

48. According to *N1*, Tverdislav was appointed when Vsevolod sent Svyatoslav to Novgorod (February 1208) (*NPL*, pp. 51, 248, *s.a.* 1209). However, it seems more likely that he became *posadnik* immediately after the *veche* of November 1207.

49. Mstislav's father died and was buried in Novgorod in 1180, having ruled there just over six months. *NPL*, pp. 36, 226.

50. *NPL*, pp. 51, 249 (*s.a.* 1210–11, but see Berezhkov, *Khronologiya*, pp. 255–6).

51. Tatishchev, *Istoriya*, vol. 4, p. 340. See also Vsevolod's subsequent message to Mstislav (*NPL*, pp. 51, 249).

52. The events of the winter of 1208/1209 are confusingly and contradictorily reported in three different accounts: *N1*; *LPS* (*s.a.* 1212) and *M* (*s.a.* 1208); and *L* (*s.a.* 1209). See *NPL*, pp. 51–2, 249; *LPS*, p. 69; *PSRL*, vol. 25, p. 107; vol. 1, col. 435. See also Tatishchev, *Istoriya*, vol. 4, pp. 340–1.

53. *NPL*, pp. 52, 249 (*s.a.* 1211, but see Berezhkov, *Khronologiya*, p. 256).

54. *NPL*, p. 52. 'Dmitr Yakunich came from Rus' [Smolensk?] and Tverdislav yielded the office of *posadnik* of his own will to one senior to himself.' Yanin, taking the date to be 1211, considers this to be evidence of a new order of seniority amongst the boyar groupings, a sign of boyar cohesion (*Novgorodskie posadniki*, pp. 124–5). The dating, however, is more likely 1209 (the entry following immediately after the description of the agreement between Mstislav and Konstantin), and Tverdislav's removal was a logical first step for Mstislav to take.

55. *NPL*, pp. 51, 249.

56. Ibid., pp. 52, 250.

57. Ibid., pp. 57, 258.

58. Two in 1210 (*NPL*, pp. 52, 250, *s.a.* 1212), one in 1212 (*NPL*, pp. 52–3, 251, *s.a.* 1214), one in 1216 (*PSRL*, vol. 5, p. 201; also in *N4*, *M* and *Nik*, but not in *N1*), and one in 1217 (*NPL*, pp. 57, 258).

59. See Shaskol'sky, *Bor'ba*, p. 4.

60. During the combined Novgorod-Pskov campaign of Vladimir Mstislavich of Pskov and Tverdislav against Medvezh'ya Golova (Otenpää, Odenpäh), 120 km west of Pskov (1217), the Estonians asked the Germans for help: in the ensuing clash the Novgorodians killed two German *voevody* (knights?) and took one prisoner (*NPL*, pp. 57, 258).

61. In 1225 or early 1226 he helped defend Torzhok against a Lithuanian attack: he may well have still been in Pskov at the time (*NPL*, pp. 64, 269. But see Rapov, *Knyazheskie vladeniya*, p. 182). In 1212 he had been temporarily replaced in Pskov by Vsevolod, the son of Mstislav Romanovich of Kiev, but was back again in 1216 (*NPL*, pp. 52, 53, 55, 250, 251, 255).

62. Ibid., pp. 53, 252. Cf. *Nik*, according to which the 'Novgorodians wished to oust their prince', as he was 'too bold and clever' for them (*PSRL*, vol. 10, p. 67).

63. Yaroslav married Rostislava, Mstislav's daughter, in 1214 in Northern Pereyaslavl'. *LPS*, p. 111.

64. Only in *M* (repeated in *E*, *L'v* and *Nik*), according to which Mstislav brought his cousins, Vladimir Ryurikovich 'from [Southern] Pereyaslavl' and Vsevolod Mstislavich 'from Kiev', to help him recapture Novgorod from Yaroslav. See *PSRL*, vol. 25, pp. 110–11.

65. *NPL*, pp. 53–5, 252–4; 'more than 2,000' were arrested altogether.

66. Only in *M* (repeated in *E* and *L'v*). Yury sent his brother Svyatoslav and his *voevoda* Mikhail Borisovich, and Konstantin sent his son Vsevolod. *PSRL*, vol. 25, p. 111.

67. That Mitrofan favoured the pro-Rostislavichi faction can be seen from the events of 1207 — it was he who prevented the Novgorodians from throwing the corpse of the ex-*posadnik* Dmitr Miroshkinich into the Volkhov (see above, p. 53). Note too that when the pro-Suzdalian Tverdislav lost office in 1218, Mitrofan was reinstated. See *NPL*, pp. 57–9, 259–60.

68. 'In that year [1210], in the winter, on 22 January, . . . the evil one, who from the beginning did not wish men well, put envy into people's hearts against Archbishop Mitrofan and Prince Mstislav; and they did not allow him to conduct his business and led him off to Toropets. . . . At that time, before the expulsion of Archbishop Mitrofan, Dobrynya Yadreykovich had arrived from Constantinople . . . he took the tonsure in the Khutin' Monastery . . . and was sent to Rus' [i.e. to Kiev] for consecration, and when he arrived back was installed as Archbishop Antony . . .' *NPL*, pp. 52, 250.

69. *NPL*, pp. 53, 251.

70. Ibid., pp. 57, 258–9.

71. Ibid., pp. 58, 259.

72. Ibid., pp. 58–9, 259–60.

73. Ibid., pp. 59, 260.

74. Ibid., pp. 60, 261. No explanation of this change of fortune is given in the chronicle.

75. Ibid., pp. 60, 261. On Mitrofan and Antony, see Khoroshev, *Tserkov'*, pp. 41 *et seq.*

76. The items in *N1.s.a.* 6728 (1220–1) cover events in 1219 (except for Tverdislav's tonsure 8 February 1220); the one item *s.a.* 6729 (1221–2), Vsevolod's dismissal,

refers to 1221. See Berezhkov, *Khronologiya*, pp. 260–1.

77. *NPL*, pp. 60, 262.
78. In 1221 Yury's 7-year-old son Vsevolod was sent; in the winter of 1222/3 he 'fled secretly by night with all his retinue' and was replaced by Yaroslav, Yury's brother. In 1223 Yaroslav quit Novgorod and Vsevolod was sent back again, only to flee once more in the same year. See *N1*, *s.a.* 1222/3.
79. *NPL*, pp. 61, 263.
80. This is especially the case with *N1*, which provides most of the information on the period. Some items have been rescinded, of course, but the majority of Novgorodian 'crises' are described with the vividness of an eye-witness.
81. For example in 1207 Konstantin had no difficulty in getting the Novgorodians to march against Chernigov during the *posadnichestvo* of Dmitr (see above, p. 52); and Mstislav persuaded them to join him, again in a campaign against Chernigov, when Tverdislav was *posadnik* (see above, p. 35).

CHAPTER FOUR

The Tatar Invasions

THE FIRST INVASION (1223)

The vast Tatar-Mongol[1] empire of Chinghis Khan was created in a remarkably short period. At the beginning of the thirteenth century the nomadic tribes inhabiting the north of what is now Mongolia and the lands around Lake Baykal lacked any form of political cohesion. In 1206, however, a *kuriltai*, or gathering of the leaders of the clans, appointed as supreme ruler the head of one of the Mongol tribes, Temuchin, who had brought under his control the dominant tribes of the Tatars, the Keraits, and the Naimans. He was given the name and title of Chinghis Khan. After a period of consolidation and military organization Chinghis Khan began his great campaign against Northern China. Although the war was to continue off and on for twenty years, by 1215 Peking was already in Mongol hands and most of northern China and Manchuria was under Mongol rule. After conquering the Central Asian kingdom of Kara Khitay, the Mongols proceeded to overcome the huge but disunified empire of Muhammed II of Khorezmia comprising the present-day Uzbek, Tadzhik and Turkmen republics, as well as Afghanistan and the greater part of Iran. On reaching Azerbaijan, the westernmost district of Khorezmia, Chinghis's generals, Jebe and Subetey, asked the supreme khan's permission to proceed north and reconnoitre the 'Western lands'. While Chinghis and his three sons, Juchi, Chaghatay and Ogedey, rounded off their conquest of Khorezmia, Jebe and Subetey crushed Azerbaijan and Georgia and moved into the north Caucasian plain. There, in the second half of 1222, they came up against the 'Alans' (i.e. Ossetians) and 'Kipchaks' (i.e. nomadic Polovtsians). According to the Arab historian Ibn al Athir (1160–1233), although the Ossetians and Polovtsians united to resist the Mongols, they were disunited by a trick – a trick repeated later in 1223 in an unsuccessful attempt to alienate the Russians from the Polovtsians (see below, p. 65): envoys were sent to the Polovtsians bribing them and urging them to abandon the Ossetians on the grounds that the Mongols and Polovtsians were 'of the same blood', whereas the Ossetians were of alien stock. It worked, and the Mongols proceeded to rout first the Ossetians and then their 'blood brothers' the Polovtsians.[2] After taking Sudak (Surozh) on the south coast of the Crimea in early 1223, the Mongols appear to have regrouped in the south-Russian steppes – the Desht-i-Kipchak – before con-

63

tinuing their 'reconnaissance' in the 'Western lands'.

The Russians, it seems, had no intelligence of the campaigns and conquests of the armies of Chinghis Khan, or if they had they either ignored it or left it unrecorded. The information that a new enemy had appeared in the southern steppes was brought to Mstislav Mstislavich in Western Galich by his father-in-law Khan Kotyan, whose nomadic territory was probably close to the easternmost bend of the Dnepr.[3] Within a short time the Russians had suffered their first defeat at the hands of the Tatars.

The Russian sources which describe what happened in 1223 are many.[4] Some of them are detailed, factual and accurate; others are founded more on hearsay. The chronicles which reproduce these sources are often based on two or more of them – local chronicles which have not survived in their original forms – and although they may contradict one another in certain details and although they frequently contain signs of parochial bias, nevertheless they provide us with clear evidence of the local sources of those districts which were involved in the events of 1223.

Altogether there are four extant chronicles which reflect the original descriptions. Thinnest of the four is the Suzdalian Lavrent'evskiy Chronicle, which reproduces in a watered-down version the non-extant princely chronicle of Kiev and at the same time faintly reflects the attitudes of the chroniclers of Vladimir and Rostov to the events which really hardly concerned them, or so they thought. The Novgorod First Chronicle reproduces a much fuller version of the Kievan chronicle, but not surprisingly it gives no indication of the attitude of the Novgorodians, for they played no part in the allied march eastwards; the tone of the main narrative, too, is quite alien to the spirit of Novgorod: the sense of apocalyptical resignation, the total absence of anti-Tatar hostility, indeed the stressing of God's purpose in sending the Tatars ('they came *sent by God*') and the bitter anti-Polovtsian tone[5] are more suited to catastrophe-ridden steppe-adjoining Kiev than to thriving commercial Novgorod. The south-west-Russian Ipat'evskiy Chronicle gives a mixture of accounts revealing the points of view of the principality of Chernigov and of the district of Volynia, the exploits of whose princes, Daniil and Vasil'ko, were to form the basis of the second half of the chronicle;[6] the heroic deeds of Daniil and his west-Russian compatriots (especially the valiant Mstislav Yaroslavich of Lutsk) may have been for all we know figments of the chronicler's imagination; but the stressing of the role of Mstislav Svyatoslavich, who had succeeded his brother Gleb as prince of Chernigov, and the considerable attention paid to the principality of Chernigov and its minor princelings leave us in no doubt that the Ipat'evskiy Chronicle account was based primarily on yet another missing chronicle, that of Chernigov. Furthermore, there is no feeling of Christian resignation or of impending apocalyptic disaster which one associates more with Kiev and its literature. There is no attempt to exculpate the Tatars (they are called 'godless Moabites' in the opening words and their 'deceit' is heavily emphasized in the final episodes) or to blacken the Polovtsians – their 'great prince Basty', whoever he may have been, is even portrayed as accepting Christianity during the pre-battle preparations. Such was the typical attitude of the west-Russian chronicler. The remoteness of Volynia and Galicia inspired him with no bitter animosity towards the Polovtsians; and although their geographical position did not protect the west Russians from being overrun seventeen years later, nevertheless it did much to absolve their churchmen from the need to fawn on the Tatars.

The fourth chronicle to reflect an original description of the events of 1223 is the Sofiyskiy First, which together with the somewhat shorter version of the Novgorod Fourth derived from the hypothetical *svod* of 1448. As can be seen from the stemma (see Appendix A), this relatively late codex derived in its turn from all the above sources. However, it also was based on yet another non-extant chronicle, that of Smolensk, for, like the account of the battle on the Lipitsa river in 1216 (see above, pp. 48–9), it concentrates primarily on the Rostislavichi, both before, during and after the campaign.

Thus we have at our disposition evidence from all the major centres involved: Kiev, Chernigov, Volynia/Galicia, Smolensk and perhaps Vladimir and Rostov as well.[7] It must be remembered, of course, that these accounts were all produced in the first place by private princely chroniclers and that they reflect the passions, the enmities and the bias of each. However, from all this tangled evidence a clear picture of what actually happened emerges.

* * * *

As soon as the news of the steppe-invaders reached Western Galich, Mstislav Mstislavich, impressed by his father-in-law's lavish gifts ('horses and camels and buffaloes and girls'[8]) and predictions of disaster, summoned a council of war in Kiev, the natural gathering-point for the southern princes. The decision taken by the three leading princes (Mstislav Mstislavich of Galicia, Mstislav Romanovich of Kiev and Mstislav Svyatoslavich of Chernigov) was that the Russians and Polovtsians should move east into the steppe and attack the enemy wherever they might find them rather than wait for them to cross the Dnepr and invade ('It were better for us to meet them in foreign territory than in our own'[9]). The main army moved south to Zarub on the west bank of the Dnepr just opposite Pereyaslavl'.[10] Here they were met by Tatar envoys, who attempted to dissuade them from fighting and persuade them that the enemies of the Tatars were not the Russians but the Polovtsians. The words put into their mouths by the Novgorodian chronicler are largely fictitious and little more than the expression of a viewpoint only too familiar in early Russian chronicles (national disasters are the result of divine wrath; heathen invaders are 'God's scourge'), but nevertheless they express the desire of the Tatars not to engage in a major war with the Russians and not to invade the lands west of the Dnepr: 'We have heard that you are marching against us, having hearkened to the Polovtsians; but we have not attacked your land or your villages, nor have we marched against you; but we have come, sent by God, against our serfs and our grooms, the pagan Polovtsians. Make peace with us. Should [the Polovtsians] escape to you, then drive them off and take their goods for yourselves. We have heard that they have done much evil to you, and for this reason we are fighting them.'[11] The envoys were put to death and the army, joined

65

by reinforcements from Smolensk, Chernigov and Galicia, moved further south to the main fording-place in the easternmost bend in the Dnepr at Protolochi, where they were met by a second party of Tatar envoys. They were reminded once again that the Russians were not the enemies of the Tatars and were given an elliptical warning: 'You have hearkened to the Polovtsians and have killed our envoys and are marching against us. March on, then. But we have not attacked you. May God [be judge] of all men.'[12] This time the Russians let the messengers go.

The crossing of the Dnepr, the various skirmishes and encounters with Tatar outposts, the nine-day[13] march east across the steppe, the major encounter on the Kalka (probably a tributary of the Kalmius river, which flows into the Sea of Azov west of the Don) on 31 May, the heroic last stand and slaughter of Mstislav Romanovich and two other princes who refused to budge when the position of the defeated Russian and Polovtsian forces became evident, the treachery of the Brodniki (see below, n. 22), who betrayed Mstislav Romanovich, the retreat of the Russian army pursued by the Tatars as far as the Dnepr, the sack of Novgorod Svyatopolch (or Svyatopolch-grad) on the west bank of the Dnepr and the withdrawal of the Tatars eastwards – all are narrated with varying degrees of accuracy, clarity and coherence in the four major chronicle accounts. In spite of the initial successes won by Russian advance detachments, it was clearly a major defeat for the Russo-Polovtsian army. The losses were almost entirely in manpower. There is no evidence of towns or villages being destroyed in the principality of Southern Pereyaslavl', across which the Tatars must have pursued the fleeing Russians. And at the only point at which the Tatars actually crossed the Dnepr – at the ford near Novgorod Svyatopolch south of Kiev[14] – only the inhabitants of the town were killed, the Tatars making no attempt to occupy the fortress.

* * * *

What was the scale of the operation? Why were the Russians defeated? Was it due to superior tactics on the part of the Tatars? The element of surprise? Russian and Polovtsian unreadiness? Inferior numbers? The sources unfortunately give us little or no help with the answers to these questions. The battle descriptions are for the most part entirely conventional. Set phrases are used to describe the fighting and practically no details are provided – indeed all four versions are couched in much the same bleak style – unemotional, unadorned, deadpan – as is used throughout the early Russian chronicles to describe military episodes. Numbers too are purely conventional and often exaggerated: 500 from Smolensk join the main force,[15] 1,000 cross the Dnepr initially with Mstislav Mstislavich,[16] 10,000 Kievans perish,[17] only 'one in ten' of the Russians escape with their lives.[18] So from these one learns nothing of the scale of the operations.

Some clues, however, are provided. We know, for example, how many princes took part and which districts sent troops: the three Mstislavs, of Galicia, Kiev and Chernigov, presumably provided the major contingents; apart from them Vladimir Ryurikovich of Smolensk, Daniil Romanovich of Volynia,

Mstislav of Kiev's son Vsevolod, Mstislav Yaroslavich of Lutsk all participated and provided detachments. The smaller districts of Chernigov (Kursk, Trubetsk and Putivl') sent troops, as did Galich — independently of Mstislav Mstislavich —, Turov-Pinsk and others probably as well. In other words it would appear that most of, if not all, the southern and western principalities played their part, to say nothing of the Polovtsians themselves, who bore the brunt of the initial Tatar attack. Conspicuous for their absence were Novgorod and Pskov, not mentioned in any of the sources, and above all — Suzdalia. One version, that of the Ipat'evskiy Chronicle, pointedly remarks that 'Grand Prince Yury of Suzdal' was not present'[19] at the council of war in Kiev. True, the local chronicler of Suzdalia states that an appeal was made to the grand prince of Vladimir and that Yury sent a token force south under Vasil'ko Konstantinovich of Rostov. This, however, may well have been a figment of his imagination and nothing more than an attempt to salve the honour of the Vsevolodovichi and to cancel the impression of total inactivity, for Vasil'ko's 'force' failed to make contact with the allies and 'returned from Chernigov' — the furthest point south reached — 'protected by God and the strength of the holy cross and the prayers of his [late] father Konstantin and his uncle Yury',[20] as soon as he learned of the disaster. Needless to say, no other version mentions the Suzdalian 'contribution'.

Only one clue to the failure of the Russian effort is given, and this by the Ipat'evskiy Chronicle account, which mentions a 'great feud' between the three leading Mstislavs. Just before the final encounter on the Kalka, Mstislav Mstislavich ordered Daniil of Volynia to cross the river and reconnoitre the Tatar positions. When he gave the order to take up arms, 'Mstislav [Romanovich of Kiev] and the other Mstislav [Svyatoslavich of Chernigov], who were at headquarters, knew nothing of this: Mstislav [Mstislavich] had not told them through jealousy, for there was a great feud between them.'[21] Even allowing for the anti-Mstislav Mstislavich bias of this section of the Volynian-Galician chronicle — after all, Mstislav's control over Galich from 1219 to 1227 was little short of disastrous in the eyes of those who supported Daniil and Vasil'ko Romanovichi — it is clear that there must have been a fatal lack of unity among the three leading commanders. Add to this disintegration of command, the disaffection of the Brodniki,[22] the inability of the Polovtsians to stand up to the Tatars,[23] the general unpreparedness of the Russians and the diffuse nature of so many of the contingents involved, and it will be realized, partially at least, why the Russians suffered defeat.

Casualties are hard to estimate with any degree of accuracy. The report of the decimation of the Russian army in the Novgorod First Chronicle is obviously an exaggeration and can be ignored; so too can the rumour ('they say that . . .') of 10,000 Kievans killed in the battle (see above, p. 66). However, one of the sources, the Novgorod First Chronicle, gives some idea of casualties by listing the names of all the princes killed. There were nine altogether: two from the Rostislavichi clan (Mstislav Romanovich, prince of Kiev, and Svyatoslav of Kanev,[24] possibly the son of Rostislav Ryurikovich[25]), two Ol'govichi (Mstislav Svyatoslavich of Chernigov and his son Dmitry), two west-

Russian princes (Izyaslav Ingvarevich and Svyatoslav of Shumsk, perhaps the son or grandson of Ingvar' Yaroslavich[26]), two probably from the district of Turov and Pinsk (Aleksandr of Dubrovitsa, killed together with Mstislav of Kiev, and Yury of Nesvezh'[27]), and one of unknown place of origin, the son-in-law of Mstislav of Kiev, Andrey. As this amounted to half the number of princes who are said to have participated,[28] we can assume that the number of Russian casualties altogether was not far below half of the total.

As for the Polovtsians, the first Tatar invasion and the battle on the Kalka virtually put paid to them as a force to be reckoned with on the southern and south-eastern borders of Russia. Khan Kotyan, it is true, is reported as taking part in west-Russian military operations in 1225 and 1228, aiding first Mstislav Mstislavich and then Daniil,[29] and the Polovtsians helped the Ol' govichi in their take-over of Kiev in 1235 (see below, pp. 74–5). But these were two isolated incidents and by the middle of the 1230s the control of the Polovtsians over the south-Russian steppe seems to have been as good as over.[30]

*　　*　　*　　*

To judge from all the available sources, the impact of the first Tatar invasion on the Russians appears to have been remarkably small. Suzdalia was totally unaffected, so too were Novgorod and Pskov. The balance of power in the south remained exactly the same as before: Mstislav of Kiev and Mstislav of Chernigov were replaced by Vladimir Ryurikovich of Smolensk and Mikhail Vsevolodovich respectively. Mstislav Mstislavich and Daniil Romanovich remained firmly ensconsed in Galicia and Volynia.

Most remarkable of all, however, is the lack of concern shown by the contemporary annalists. After all, this was a new enemy, the first new enemy to appear on the southern steppes for over a century and a half. True, the Suzdalian and Novgorodian chronicles preface their accounts of the events of 1223 with a rhetorical introduction, in which the author expressed his bewilderment as to the origins of the invaders and quotes from the so-called Revelation of Methodius of Patara ('For thus did Methodius say: at the end of time those people would appear whom Gideon put to flight and would conquer all the earth from the East to the Euphrates and from the Tigris to the Pontic Sea with the exception of Ethiopia'[31]), but this had been used before by one of the compilers of the early-Kievan Primary Chronicle,[32] and the aim of the chroniclers in their introduction was to draw attention to the godlessness of the *Polovtsians* ('For these accursed Polovtsians had done much harm to the Russian land, and for this reason all-merciful God wished to destroy and to punish the godless Cumans [Polovtsians], the sons of Ishmael . . .') rather than to warn the Russian princes of the new steppe danger.

As far as the Russians knew, the Tatars faded away into the steppe: 'They returned from the river Dnepr, and we know not whence they came and whither they went. Only God knows whence they came against us for our sins.'[33] For the Russians it was just another steppe invasion, which at least had the merit of neutralizing the Polovtsians. They had fourteen years to wait before the new enemy appeared again at their gates.

PERIOD OF RESPITE 1223–1237

In Russia the period between the two Tatar invasions was in many ways similar to the first twenty-three years of the century. It could hardly be called an age of growth or prosperity, certainly not one of peaceful consolidation, except in the north-east where there were few of the conflicts which marked the years following the death of Vsevolod III: Vladimir, Rostov, Yaroslavl', Yur'ev Pol'skiy, all were undisturbed by civil war. True, Kiev remained in the hands of one of the Rostislavichi clan, Vladimir Ryurikovich, from the time he took over his uncle's throne in 1223 until 1235; and true, Ryazan' was untouched by civil war or external intervention. But Novgorod was still a bone of contention between princely families; the boyar factions there still struggled for power; and most of the period was marked by the feuding of Grand Prince Yury's brother Yaroslav of Northern Pereyaslavl' and the emergent champion of a resuscitated Chernigov, Mikhail Vsevolodovich. Eventually, in the few years before the second Tatar invasion, many of the princes and most of the southern principalities – Chernigov, Kiev and Galicia in particular – were involved in bitter unremitting civil strife which was to weaken them politically and make two of them, Chernigov and Kiev, easy targets for any invader.

The sources present us with more difficulties than they do for the previous period. The two major ones, those of Suzdalia and Novgorod, tend as usual to be highly parochial and to reflect either the princely interests of Vladimir and Rostov on the one hand, or the local outlook of Novgorod on the other. It is true, there are glimpses in them, and in the later chronicles too, of the interests of other centres: Northern Pereyaslavl', for instance (the local chronicle of which had come to an end in 1214), and occasionally Chernigov and Kiev. But there are no relics of the chronicle-writing of Ryazan', Smolensk or Southern Pereyaslavl' for this period, and for their history we can only rely on chance or oblique remarks passed by the contemporary annalists of Suzdalia and Novgorod and must carefully accept everything in the spirit of their particular political bias. As for the south west, the Ipat'evskiy Chronicle presents us for most of the time with an incoherent and strongly prejudiced picture of the struggle for power between Russians, Hungarians and Poles and the gradual emergence of the chronicler's two heroes, Daniil and Vasil'ko Romanovichi, towards leadership of Volynia and Galicia.

*   *   *   *

Suzdalia, in the years 1223–37, certainly presents a picture of greater political solidarity than do any of the other principalities. Perhaps this was due to the fact that it had played no role in the events of 1223 and had suffered no losses in men or rulers, and that it was faced with relatively insignificant external military pressures – the only enemy were the Mordvinians, who inhabited the area between the Volga and the lower reaches of the Oka east of Murom and Ryazan' and against whom Yury sporadically took minor punitive action;[34] or perhaps Suzdalia owed its stability to the policy, or the good fortune, of its grand prince. For Yury kept himself firmly in the saddle throughout the whole period. There was no one – except perhaps his brother Yaroslav for a short time – to contest the leadership. Yury's three nephews in the north, Vasil'ko of Rostov, Vsevolod of Yaroslavl' and Vladimir of Uglich, gave him little trouble and unhesitatingly obeyed his commands, marching with him or his brother Yaroslav on their campaigns,[35] submitting to dynastic marriages designed to further the political ends of the grand prince,[36] and on one occasion taking over command of a distant principality.[37] His brothers caused him little concern. All we hear of the youngest Ivan is that he took part in a campaign against the Mordvinians in 1226 with his elder brother Svyatoslav.[38] The latter ruled his patrimony of Yur'ev Pol'skiy throughout the period except for a year or so spent in Southern Pereyaslavl' where Yury sent him in 1228.[39] only on one occasion did Yury have any trouble, and that was with his brother Yaroslav in 1229. Yaroslav, 'doubting [the intentions] of his brother Yury, having hearkened to the falsehoods of certain people', won over to his side the three princes of Rostov with the intention of 'opposing Yury'. As the only information we have of this internal crisis comes from Yury's own chronicle, it is impossible to tell what caused it or what form the 'opposition' took. It was, however, soon settled. Yury summoned a council (*snem*) in Suzdal', at which Yaroslav and his three nephews 'kissed the cross' in allegiance to Yury, recognizing him as their 'father and master'[40] – the same words as those used in 1203 by Roman of Volynia and Galicia in respect of Vsevolod III (see above, pp. 22–3).

Yury's contacts with Novgorod were confined to the early part of the period under consideration. They are only reported in the Novgorod Chronicle – Yury's own chronicle, the Lavrent'evskiy, is silent on the matter – and so elliptically that one can only guess at what in fact happened and at the causes of the events. It will be remembered that in the winter of 1222/23 Yury's eight-year-old son Vsevolod, who had been sent to Novgorod as prince the year before, 'fled secretly by night with all his retinue' (see above, Ch. 3, n. 78). He was replaced by his experienced brother Yaroslav, who, presumably as the result of a quarrel with the city officials, also left at the end of 1223. Once again Vsevolod was sent and once again he fled 'by night, in secret, with all his retinue'.[41] This time Yury took firmer steps to deal with the recalcitrant city. He joined his son in Torzhok; with him came his brother Yaroslav, his nephew Vasil'ko of Rostov and his brother-in-law Mikhail Vsevolodovich of Chernigov.[42] As Yury, Vasil'ko and Mikhail were all accompanied by troops, they were in a formidable bargaining position. Yury demanded the handover of a number of Novgorodian boyars – those, presumably, who had opposed Vsevolod and Yaroslav. The Novgorodians refused, stating that they were prepared to 'die for St Sofia [the cathedral of Novgorod] and *Posadnik* Ivanko Dmitrievich'. Eventually a compromise was reached. No boyars were handed over and the Novgorodians agreed to pay a fine and to accept Mikhail as their prince.[43] From then on Yury ceased to have any dealings with Novgorod. For the next nine years the conflict over the city was to be between Yaroslav of Northern Pereyaslavl' and Mikhail of Chernigov. Yury, or so it appears from his chronicle, had no further interest in settling a son in Novgorod.

Yury's relations with the princes of southern Russia were peaceful. His friendly links with the Ol'govichi of Chernigov can be traced back to the treaty of 1210 between his father Vsevolod III and the prince of Chernigov Vsevolod Chermnyy and to his marriage with Vsevolod Chermnyy's daughter in 1211 (see below, n. 42). Since then nothing disrupted the alliance with his wife's family. It was cemented not only by further dynastic marriages[44] but also by military and diplomatic intervention on behalf of his brother-in-law.[45] On no occasion does Yury's chronicle – or any other chronicle for that matter – record a hostile act committed by Yury against Mikhail[46] or by Mikhail against Yury.

As far as can be seen, Yury's relations with the Rostislavichi were just as friendly as those with the Ol'govichi. Indeed, until the outbreak of civil war in 1235 the Rostislavichi showed few signs of hostility against any of the Russian princes and no inclination towards territorial aggrandizement. The only act of aggression on the part of a member of the family during the whole of this period was committed within the clan itself and occurred in 1232 when Svyatoslav Mstislavich took Smolensk by force from whoever had succeeded Mstislav Davidovich in 1230.[47] They appear amicably to have relinquished Southern Pereyaslavl' to Yury when he sent his nephew Vsevolod Konstantinovich to rule there in 1227.[48] Three years later the friendship between Yury and Vladimir was strengthened by the marriage of the former's son to the latter's daughter.[49] When needed the Rostislavichi cooperated militarily against external enemies.[50] On two separate occasions Vladimir of Kiev sent Metropolitan Kirill on peace-making missions: once to assist Yury patch up a truce between Mikhail of Chernigov and Oleg of Kursk in 1226 (see n. 45), and once in 1230 to try to prevent a war between Mikhail and Yaroslav.[51] Even between Vladimir and Mikhail friendly relations existed: in 1228, for example, Vladimir joined Mikhail in an expedition against Daniil of Volynia, an expedition which ended in a pact being concluded between all three princes.[52] Only on one occasion was there any sign of conflict, and that was in 1231 when Mikhail, having been thwarted by Yaroslav in his attempts to hold Novgorod, planned an attack on Kiev. Vladimir appealed to Daniil for help: 'Mikhail is marching against me. Help me, cousin!' Daniil acted as peacemaker and there was no war.[53] A grandiose council was held in Kiev in the same year attended by three Rostislavichi and three Ol'govichi, at which, presumably, Daniil's peace was confirmed.[54]

*   *   *   *

The true source of inter-princely contention during the period between the Tatar invasions was once again Novgorod. But the situation was different from before. Again the boyar groupings were split between two contenders for control over Novgorod, this time Yaroslav of Northern Pereyaslavl' and Mikhail of Chernigov; yet in spite of the internal inter-boyar conflicts there were signs of a concerted attempt to limit the power of the prince and to strengthen the influence of the purely Novgorodian appointments, such as those of *posadnik* and *tysyatskiy*. The Novgorodians could not, of course, and knew they could not, dispense with the prince, for it was he who provided Novgorod's defence against all potential Western enemies – the Germans, the Swedes, the Lithuanians, the Chud' (Estonians) and the Em' (Finns). Novgorod was somehow unable to provide itself with an army sufficiently strong to ward off attacks on its borders, let alone to counter-attack in enemy territory. And precisely in this period Western aggression was intensifying: in the ten years between 1224 and 1234 there were numerous raids – some deep into Novgorod territory – and Russian counter-attacks. The prince and his army were an essential part of Novgorod's defence. And the more the prince was required to fight, the less attractive Novgorod became as a place to rule in. The financial, seigniorial and commercial benefits, of which unfortunately we know no details, were clearly still a lure; but the amount of defence work required of the prince and the increasing opposition of the boyars as a whole were enough to make him hesitant. So we find the prince tending to reside in his patrimony, leaving a son as a token ruler in his absence and returning to Novgorod only when the military situation required his presence. At the same time we find the boyars *demanding* that the prince attend to his military duties: in 1230, for example, Mikhail's son Rostislav was required to leave Novgorod territory because Mikhail, absent in distant Chernigov, had failed to carry out his obligations. 'Your father', Rostislav was told, 'said he would mount his horse for war from the festival of the Exaltation of the Cross [14 September] and he kissed the cross [i.e. swore to do this]; but now it is already St Nicholas' day [19 December] . . . go away – we will find [another] prince for ourselves.'[55]

From 1224, when Yury obliged Novgorod to accept Mikhail, until 1233, when Yaroslav finally rounded up Mikhail's Novgorodian supporters, 'Yaroslavl' dvor', the princely residence of Novgorod, was occupied by no less than five different princes (Mikhail and his son Rostislav, Yaroslav and his two sons, Fedor and Aleksandr). This see-sawing between the two families can of course be explained largely by the state of near-war which existed between Yaroslav and Mikhail for most of the period: for example, in 1229 when Mikhail, having been installed for the second time as prince in Novgorod and having departed almost immediately for Chernigov leaving his son in command, demanded that Yaroslav quit the Novgorodian territory of Volok Lamskiy, a demand which was peremptorily refused;[56] or in 1231, when Yaroslav, once more reinstated in Novgorod, marched with his own and Novgorodian troops against the towns of Serensk and Mosal'sk in northern Chernigov.[57]

But it was the inter-boyar conflicts in Novgorod, the internal squabbles between two seemingly quite distinct factions, which were the major causes of the restless alternation of princes in the city. On the one side was the group led firstly by Ivanko Dmitrievich, who took office as *posadnik* in 1219 (see above, p. 57), and then by Stepan Tverdislavich, the son of the old pro-Suzdalian *posadnik* Tverdislav; this group firmly supported Yaroslav and his sons. On the other side were ranged Vnezd Vodovik, who succeeded Ivanko Dmitrievich as *posadnik* when the latter fled to Yaroslav in 1229, his brothers Mikhail and Danislav, his son Gleb and Boris Negochevich, who became *tysyatskiy* in 1229; these were the leading supporters of Mikhail.

Their quarrels (*rospri* is the word used by the chroniclers) exploded in a series of urban upheavals (*myatezhi*), the last and most serious of which led directly to the replacement of Mikhail's son by Yaroslav. The story of this *myatezh*, recorded in detail in the Novgorod First Chronicle, illustrates only too well the correlation between inter-boyar conflicts and the feud between Yaroslav and the Ol'govichi. In 1229 Mikhail, after a number of incidents in Novgorod following a clumsy attempt by Yaroslav to urge both Novgorod and Pskov to join him in an expedition against Riga, was requested to take over the city. He arrived in the spring of 1229 and within a short time the office of *posadnik* changed hands – from Ivanko Dmitrievich, who promptly fled to Yaroslav, to Vnezd Vodovik.[58] In the late summer of 1230, however, after Mikhail had performed his customary act of departing to Chernigov immediately after arrival[59] and had left his five-year-old son Rostislav 'in charge' so to speak, the opposing boyar party summoned a *veche* in opposition to Vodovik and his adherents. They in turn stirred up trouble against the followers of Yaroslav. The town was in uproar. Houses were plundered; one of Yaroslav's supporters fled the city and took refuge with Yaroslav; two were put to death. To make matters worse an early frost destroyed the crops and Novgorod suffered severe famine. Towards the end of the year Rostislav and Vodovik left for Torzhok, compelled to flee by the state of unrest in Novgorod. Trouble broke out immediately. This time it was Vodovik's associates whose houses were plundered. The outcome was predictable: Vodovik and the *tysyatskiy* Boris Negochevich fled from Torzhok to Chernigov. By the end of the year Rostislav had been given his marching orders, and Yaroslav was once again prince of Novgorod.[60] Mikhail and his son were never again to regain control of the city, but two years later the ex-*tysyatskiy* Boris Negochevich and those of his followers who were still alive in Chernigov – Vodovik had died there in 1231 – set out in an attempt to return to Novgorod and to prepare the ground for yet another take-over by Mikhail. But it was a forlorn venture. Headed at first by an Ol'govich princeling from Trubetsk, who abandoned them halfway through realizing that he had led them astray, they somehow managed to gain control of Pskov. The Pskovites were ready to support them, but when Yaroslav put pressure on Pskov by blocking supplies to the town they gave in. Boris and his party were shown off the premises. They fled to Medvezh'ya Golova (Otenpää, Odenpäh) across the border. In the following year, 1233, with German aid they captured Izborsk, southwest of Pskov, but were forced to surrender and were sent off in captivity to Pereyaslavl'.[61]

It was the end of the struggle for Novgorod between Yaroslav and Mikhail. From then on – indeed, from 1230 on – there was never a question as to who was to be prince in Novgorod. The internal support for the Ol'govichi was gone. Yaroslav and his descendants were to be the defenders of Novgorod's frontiers for the rest of the thirteenth century.

If a reason for Yaroslav's success is to be sought, then it will be found firstly in his ingenuity and military skill, and secondly – and perhaps as important – in the fact that his patrimony of Pereyaslavl' was close to Novgorod and that its westernmost outpost of Tver' was just across the border from Torzhok, whereas Mikhail's capital of Chernigov was almost as far removed as Kiev was from Novgorod.

* * * *

The relative peace in southern Russia was shattered in 1235 when civil war broke out again. 'The accursed, ever-destructive devil,' wrote the Novgorod chronicler in a stream of clichés customarily used to introduce internecine crises, 'who wishes no good for the human race, raised up sedition (*kramola*) amongst the princes of Rus', so that men might not live in peace; for the evil one rejoices in the shedding of Christian blood.'[62] During the next five years between 1235 and 1240 Kiev changed hands no less than seven times: three times it was held by Rostislavichi, twice by Ol'govichi, once by Yaroslav of Northern Pereyaslavl' and once by Daniil of Galicia. Princes moved with their armies hither and thither over the districts of Kiev, Chernigov and Galicia, fighting each other, making and breaking alliances. None, it seemed, was capable of holding the capital city for more than a few months. The complex manoeuvres, the battles, the alliances, the promises, the treacheries, the deceptions – all are reported with the utmost confusion in the only two sources to mention what looks like the disintegration of the south, the Novgorod First and the Ipat'evskiy Chronicles. The first of these laconically and dispassionately describes the events of 1235 and 1236; the second gives a longer but rambling account of events ranging from Kiev to Galicia, often confused, invariably misdated, once even misleadingly transposing events from the description of one episode to that of an entirely different one[63] – and all this viewed from the standpoint of Daniil of Galicia, who in the welter of conflict between the Romanovichi, Hungarians, Poles and pro-Hungarian boyars, was at last beginning to assert his authority over Galicia. The staid Suzdalian chronicler (Lavrent'evskiy) makes no mention of the clashes in the south, and indeed reports that all was 'peaceful' in 1235. Kiev, Chernigov and Galicia might have been a foreign country as far as he was concerned.

From the tangle of events recorded in the Novgorod and Ipat'evskiy Chronicles one can, however, discern a certain logical sequence and a pattern of behaviour. Even a brief reconstruction of these events will amply illustrate the disintegration of political life in the south and will help to explain the enfeeblement of the southern princes at the end of the 1230s.

The first hint of trouble came in 1234 or early 1235 when Vladimir Ryurikovich of Kiev approached Daniil of Galicia for military assistance, just as he had done three years previously (see above, p. 71). The reason for his request was again the aggressive attitude of Mikhail of Chernigov, aided this time by his cousin Izyaslav Vladimirovich.[64] The two Ol'govichi, who evidently besieging Kiev at the time, withdrew when Daniil's troops appeared. Vladimir and Daniil then took the initiative and marched against the Ol'govichi in Chernigov, an operation which had mixed results: Izyaslav 'fled', according to the Novgorod chronicle, to the Polovtsians, but in fact went to the steppe in order to recruit reinforcements; while Mikhail somehow managed to trick Daniil in a skirmish from which he, Daniil, only just escaped. Vladimir Ryurikovich, however, emerged safely from the fighting and returned to Kiev.

The war was by no means over. Izyaslav soon reappeared with a Polovtsian detachment, and he and Mikhail threatened Kiev once more. The decisive battle took place south of Kiev in Torchesk and ended in victory for the Ol'govichi. Vladimir was taken prisoner by the Polovtsians and Daniil went back to Galich, only to be tricked once again, this time by the pro-Hungarian boyars, into fleeing the country. After the victory Mikhail placed his cousin Izyaslav on the throne of Kiev.[65] For himself he had more ambitious plans – the conquest of Galicia. This he eventually achieved in the latter part of 1235. The Poles, who had occupied Galich after Daniil's departure, quit the capital, and Mikhail and his son Rostislav occupied it, encountering little resistance.[66]

Izyaslav did not last for long as prince of Kiev, for it appears that Vladimir ousted him after ransoming himself from Polovtsian captivity. But he too was ousted in turn by Yaroslav in 1236. The Novgorod chronicle describes how Yaroslav, leaving his son Aleksandr in Novgorod, took with him 'senior Novgorodians' and a hundred men from Torzhok and 'sat in Kiev upon the throne'.[67] Again it was a short tenure. For reasons undisclosed by the chronicler ('he was unable to hold it'),[68] he abandoned Kiev and returned to Suzdalia. This time it was Mikhail who occupied Kiev, having left his son Rostislav in charge of Galich. It was, however, a rash move, for while Rostislav was away on a campaign against the Lithuanians in 1238, Daniil had had no difficulty in taking over his old capital.[69] As for Kiev, it was twice more to be taken – briefly by Rostislav Mstislavich of Smolensk (at the end of 1239, or the beginning of 1240) and by Daniil – before finally falling to the Tatars in 1240.

*   *   *   *

One may well ask what drove the princes of Smolensk, Chernigov and Galicia to such frenetic and seemingly pointless activity. Was it greed? Was it desire to emulate their predecessors and control the whole of the south of Russia? Or was it merely the urge to acquire prestige by occupying what was still considered the mother of all Russian cities? Whatever the cause, the results were only too obvious: by 1239–40, the years of the final assault of the Tatars on Russia, even by 1237, the Ol'govichi and the Rostislavichi had exhausted themselves and their military resources. Even Daniil, who emerged strongest, with eventual control over Galicia and Kiev, needed time to recoup his losses in men and material. The princes of the south were no longer capable of concerted action as they had been earlier in the century, or of forming a firm alliance against any external enemy.

While the southern princes thus disastrously enfeebled themselves, the northerners, as has been shown above, enjoyed relative calm and stability; indeed, during the fourteen years between the Tatar invasions the entries in the Suzdalian chronicle mostly reflect family affairs (births, marriages) and art and architecture (churches decorated, churches built), evidence of a certain degree of political equilibrium and lack of friction amongst the princes. By 1233 the struggle for Novgorod was at an end and Novgorod was under the strict surveillance of Yaroslav and his son Aleksandr.

Yet for all their apparent stability the northern princes were living in a state of false security. With the exception of Yaroslav Vsevolodovich they were virtually isolated from the south. Yury's authority was confined to Suzdalia. The days had passed when the grand prince of Vladimir could command respect and obedience in Kiev, Chernigov and Smolensk, and even Volynia and Galicia. Now his word no longer sufficed to bring the feuding princes of the south to heel.

But most fatal of all for the land of Russia was the fact that all the princes, northern and southern, seemed blissfully to ignore the military danger in the east. It was as though they believed that the Tatars were just another nomadic tribe, like the Pechenegs or the Polovtsians, sent by God, as their chroniclers said, to punish them for their sins.

THE GREAT INVASION 1237–1240

Far from fading away into the steppe and disappearing, as the Russians no doubt hoped and assumed the Tatars had done after their investigatory probe into Russia in 1223, the Tatars in fact moved east into the territory of the Volga Bulgars. Here for the first time they came up against tougher resistance than they had met before: the Arab historian Ibn el-Athir describes how on several occasions they were ambushed by the Bulgars and lost considerable numbers of their troops. They withdrew from the area seemingly in some disarray, for Ibn el-Athir states that there were only a few survivors. They then moved south to Saksin[70] on the mouth of the Volga and thence to join the main armies of Chinghis Khan,[71] which were returning to Mongolia after defeating Jalal ad-Din, Muhammed II's son and successor in Khorezmia, and capturing the capital city Urgenj, south of the Sea of Aral.

Chinghis Khan died in 1227 and was succeeded by his son Ogedey as Khakan, Kaan or Great Khan. Projects for a major invasion of Eastern Europe were discussed at *kuriltais* held in 1227 and 1229, but in fact all that was undertaken were two probing intrusions – more in the nature of reconnaissances than invasions – into territories east of the Volga. In 1229 two generals, Subetey and Koketey, were despatched to the steppes north of the Caspian where they defeated the 'people of Saksin'[72] and the Polovtsians, who 'fled to the Bulgars'; at the same time Bulgar outposts were also beaten near the river Yaik[73] (the modern Ural, the northernmost river flowing into the Caspian Sea). Subetey and Koketey did not, however, follow up success by invading Bulgar territory, but the Bulgars were sufficiently alarmed by the events to seek a fresh alliance with the Russians in the west (see above, p. 51).

The only other recorded attack on lands neighbouring Russian territory occurred in 1232. This time only the Russian sources provide any information, and thin information at that: 'The Tatars came and took up winter quarters before reaching the Great City of the Bulgars'.[74] Tatishchev gives a little more detail, adding that the Bulgars asked Grand Prince Yury for military assistance, which was not forthcoming, and that the Tatars 'laid waste and conquered much of the lower land of the Bulgars and destroyed their cities'.[75]

During the period of respite which followed the first Tatar invasion of 1223 the Russians cannot have been unaware of the enemy at their gates — they were after all fully informed of the plight of the Bulgars in 1229 and 1232. Yet no steps were taken to strengthen the defences to the east or to the south. Indeed no fortifications or strongholds had been built since the founding of Nizhniy Novgorod in 1221 at the confluence of the Oka and Volga rivers; and that proved of no value when the time of invasion came, for instead of proceeding along the Volga the Tatars attacked far to the south of Nizhniy Novgorod, deep into the principality of Ryazan'.

The decision to invade Eastern Europe was taken at a *kuriltai* in 1234. So great was the scale of the campaign envisaged that Ogedey proposed going himself and was only dissuaded by his nephew Mongke, who impressed upon him that the supreme ruler had no right to take such risks. Eight grandsons of Chinghis Khan were sent west, including two future great khans (Guyuk and Mongke) with the by now experienced general Subetey 'and several others'. An army under Baty, the son of Chinghis Khan's eldest son Juchi, and his three brothers was the first to set off. In February–March 1236 the remainder moved west and met up with Baty near the boundaries of the land of the Bulgars — probably on the river Yaik.[76]

Before embarking on the invasion of Russia, the Tatar armies destroyed all possible centres of resistance to the east and south-east of the Russian principalities. In the territory of the Volga Bulgars the major cities of Bilyar, Bulgar, Kernek, Zhukotin and Suvar were destroyed. The surrounding tribes — the Cheremisy (Mari), the Bashkirs, the Mordvinians and the Burtasy — were subdued, as were the Saksinians from the area of the mouth of the Volga.[77] To the west and south-west of Saksin Mongke's armies neutralized the Ossetians of the northern Caucasian plain and those Polovtsians nomadizing in the Desht-i-Kipchak.[78] By the autumn of 1237 there were no potential enemies left east of the districts of Vladimir-Suzdal', Murom-Ryazan', Chernigov and Southern Pereyaslavl'. The invasion of Eastern Europe could begin.

* * * *

The great Tatar campaigns in the lands of Russia, which lasted for three years (1237–40), can be divided into two separate phases: the first, the invasion of north-east Russia (December 1237 – Spring 1238); the second, the operations in south and south-west Russia (1239–40). As was the case with the invasion of 1223, Russian sources are plentiful, albeit often confusing and contradictory, while eastern historians, Arab and Persian, have little or nothing of value to add, only a few confirmatory details.

Three chronicles contain or reflect the earliest sources of information on the first phase of the invasion: first, the Lavrent'evskiy Chronicle account, which is based on the grand-princely chronicle of Yury Vsevolodovich of Vladimir. As might be expected, the main incidents concern the grand principality of Vladimir — the siege of the capital, the defeat of Yury, the battle of Kolomna and the taking of Moscow. Added to it, somewhat clumsily, are the story of the capture and death of Yury's nephew, Vasil'ko Konstantinovich, a tale which originated in Rostov, and one or two later embellishments, mainly

77

stylistic and of little factual interest. The tone of the basic stories contained in the Lavrent'evskiy Chronicle account is dry and matter-of-fact – a clear pointer to their contemporaneity. Second, the Novgorod First Chronicle account. This represents two quite separate sources – a chronicle of Ryazan' origin which has not survived and the version of Novgorod itself. The most factual – and contemporary – descriptions are those of the taking of Ryazan' in the south-east and the siege of Torzhok in the north-west, both of which were probably written by eye-witnesses. Altogether the version of the Novgorod First Chronicle is strikingly different from that of the Lavrent'evskiy Chronicle factually, ideologically and stylistically: details often differ from or contradict those given in the Lavrent'evskiy; the political slant has nothing in common with that of Yury's chronicler, criticizing as it does the grand prince for not sending military help to embattled Ryazan'; in those parts originating in Ryazan' the attitude to the invaders is strictly neutral – they are neither 'evil', nor 'godless', nor 'drinkers of human blood', nor 'anti-Christians', and the disaster of Ryazan' is attributed not only to the 'sins' of the Russians but also to inter-princely strife ('the hatred of brothers for brothers'), whereas the purely Novgorodian episodes show a considerable anti-Tatar flavour found neither in the Ryazan' section nor in the Vladimir-Rostov version (the Tatars are called 'shedders of Christian blood', 'lawless sons of Ishmael', 'godless and pagan', 'accursed' etc.). Novgorod, never occupied by the invaders, could afford to take a more aggressive attitude towards the conquerors than the survivors of Ryazan', say, or Vladimir.

The third chronicle to record the first phase of Baty's campaign is the Ipat'evskiy, which reflects a strictly south-Russian source. It lacks factual details, is in places vague, inaccurate or confused, and has only a few pieces of additional information which probably derived from oral legends current in post-invasion southern Russia. From an ideological point of view it is of interest only in so far as it clearly attempts to discredit the princes of Suzdalia, for whom the author, as a southerner, had little reason to feel either affection or respect.

As for the accounts found in later chronicles (fifteenth- and sixteenth-century), they provide virtually no new facts; indeed all they do is tidy up and join together the earlier versions, iron out inconsistencies, and by means of padding increase the impression of shock, horror and universal destruction.[79] Only a few small details are added to the basic account of the Novgorod First Chronicle by the author of the composite *Tale of the Destruction of Ryazan' by Baty*, but the main story here is much the same as that of the Novgorod chronicle version and stems from a non-extant Ryazan' chronicle.[80]

* * * *

In the early winter of 1237 the Tatars appeared in the south of the principality of Ryazan', over 200 kilometres from the capital. After setting up temporary headquarters somewhere in the neighbourhood of present-day Tambov, they sent an embassy to Ryazan' requesting, so the chronicler says, a tithe in all things, in 'men, princes, horses . . .', but in all probability demanding immediate surrender. What the Ryazanites' reaction was is hard to say. They had had no previous experience of tackling the Tatars – they were not involved in the Russians' attempt to resist the Tatars in 1223 – and probably the chronicler was right when he said that the princes of Ryazan' and Murom sent an embassy to their ally and virtual suzerain, Yury of Vladimir, requesting military aid. Clearly resistance was unthinkable, especially in view of the fact that no help from Suzdalia was immediately forthcoming.[81] First the southern half of the principality was neutralized: Belgorod and Pronsk to the south-west of Ryazan' were taken.[82] Then the Tatars moved on the capital.

The siege of Ryazan' began on 16 December. By 21 December it was all over. What the casualties were and how great was the damage to the town cannot be gauged. The *Tale of the Destruction of Ryazan'* talks of wholesale death by the sword and drowning, burning and pillage; the chronicle talks of the slaughter of 'the prince [Yury Ingvarevich], the princess, men, women, children, monks, nuns and priests' and the rape of 'nuns, priests' wives, good women and maidens before their mothers and sisters'.[83] But in both cases these expressions of universal disaster are little more than commonplaces used, in the case of the chronicle, to describe the catastrophes that from time to time befell cities at the hands of invaders and, in the case of the *Tale*, to emphasize the feeling of inevitability which permeates the work. All we can say is that the fall of the capital spelt the end of effective resistance to the Tatars in the district of Ryazan'. There was still, however, a detachment under Yury Ingvarevich's brother Roman which met up with a force sent, somewhat belatedly, by Grand Prince Yury of Vladimir to the northernmost tip of the principality of Ryazan', Kolomna, near the junction of the Oka and Moskva rivers. The joint force was surrounded and defeated there. Roman and Eremey – the *voevoda* sent by Yury – were killed; Yury's son Vsevolod managed to escape and inform his father in Vladimir that the Tatars were now at the borders of Suzdalia.

Vladimir, the capital and largest city of Suzdalia, was the first objective of the Tatars after Ryazan'. Moscow, at the time no more than a small town or a fortified outpost, offered little resistance: the local commander was killed and another son of Yury, Vladimir, was taken prisoner or killed[84]; but it held up the Tatars sufficiently to enable Yury to take what he considered to be the only possible defensive measures against the invaders. He decided to quit the capital Vladimir. Leaving his wife and two sons, Vsevolod and Mstislav, with a garrison commanded by one Petr Oslyadyukovich, he moved with his main army north-west and, having crossed the Volga at Uglich, established his headquarters on the River Sit', some 30 kilometres west of the Volga. With him were his three nephews, the sons of Konstantin – Vasil'ko, Vsevolod and Vladimir. Summoning his two brothers Yaroslav and Svyatoslav, he clearly planned to take up a defensive position with all available Suzdalian troops, with the Volga and Mologa rivers as natural defences to the east and the north.[85]

Meanwhile the Tatars marched on Vladimir. They arrived at its walls on 3 February 1238. The details of the siege and capture of the city are given with remarkable vividness and accuracy in the Lavrent'evskiy Chronicle. Having reconnoitred the surrounds, Baty established his headquarters to the west of the Golden Gates and proceeded to erect a palisade around the town, to bring up escalading devices and to station siege guns before the walls. The assault took place on the morning of 7 February. The defences were broken in four places in the western half of the town (*Novyy gorod*). By midday the fighting was over, and as many as could crowded into the Cathedral of the Assumption, including the female members of Yury's family, who had been left behind, Bishop Mitrofan and all the clergy. There they were burned to death or put to the sword by the Tatars. The two princes and the garrison troops fled to the centre of the city (*Sredniy/Pecherskiy gorod*) where they were later killed or taken prisoner.[86]

What happened next is difficult to establish. One source (the Lavrent'evskiy Chronicle) states that in February 1238 six major towns in Suzdalia were captured before Yury's army was defeated on the River Sit' (4 March 1238); another (the Novgorod First Chronicle) lists eight towns in Suzdalia (only two the same as in the Lavrent'evskiy account), and these were taken *after* the Sit' battle; yet a third (the sixteenth-century Nikon Chronicle) adds two more towns to the list not previously mentioned. No details whatsoever are given for the capture of any of the fourteen places variously mentioned. The description of the taking and the sack of Suzdal', to which is devoted more space than to all the rest, is couched solely in terms borrowed by the chronicler from early passages – e.g. the sack of Kiev by the Polovtsians in 1203 – and little credence can be given to it. Not even the destruction of Rostov, which after all had its own annals later to be merged into the chronicle of Vladimir (i.e. the Lavrent'evskiy Chronicle), is described. It looks as though the chroniclers of Vladimir and Novgorod merely listed the major towns of Suzdalia without having any idea as to which, if any, of them was in fact attacked, sacked or even by-passed by the Tatars.

The battle on the Sit', although the story of it clearly originated in Yury's own chronicle, is described with disappointingly little detail and is decked out with the usual emotional epithets, prayers, lamentations and battle phraseology so typical of the Lavrent'evskiy Chronicle ('they marched against Yury'; 'having heard this Prince Yury and his brother [Svyatoslav] . . . marched against the pagans'; 'both clashed'; 'there was a fierce battle'; 'our men fled'). All we learn is that the battle took place on 4 March 1238, that Yury had with him Svyatoslav and his three nephews from the principality of Rostov-Yaroslavl' – Yaroslav evidently had no time to join the main army – and that Burunday was in command of the Tatar army.[87] There were only two princely casualties: Yury, who was decapitated, and Vasil'ko Konstantinovich, captured and later executed by the Tatars.[88] Svyatoslav and the other two princes of Rostov escaped. There is no indication anywhere of the size of the Russian army, of the composition of the Tatar force,[89] or indeed of the gravity of the defeat. It may well be that after the capture of Vasil'ko the bulk of the army fled, killing perhaps the grand prince who attempted to hold them back: not only does the evidence of Yury's severed head point to his death at the hands of his own men,[90] but also the Novgorod chronicler, who in his account of the events of

1237–38 treats Yury with scant respect, casts further doubts on the circumstances of his death: 'He ended his life [on the River Sit']. But God knows how he died, for there are many different opinions about him.' Such speculation as to the outcome of the Sit' battle is hard to avoid, when Yury's own chronicler is so startlingly sparing with details: one may well suspect that he was attempting to cover up the perhaps unsavoury details of what really happened.

The chronicler of Vladimir – Yury's chronicle was replaced after his death by that of his successor Yaroslav – evidently lost interest in what happened outside the territory of Vladimir-Suzdal' during the rest of 1238. After reporting Yaroslav's succession to the throne of Vladimir and his allocation of Suzdal' and Starodub to his brothers Svyatoslav and Ivan respectively, he signs off for that year with the characteristically laconic entry: 'In that same year [i.e. March 1238 to end February 1239] there was peace.' For all the previously reported 'ravages' of the Tatars in north-east Russia, the local chronicler would have us believe that things returned to normal with remarkable rapidity.

But the Tatar armies had by no means finished their campaigns in Russia. While Burunday was confronting Yury on the Sit', another Tatar army was besieging the southeasternmost town in Novgorod territory – Torzhok. The siege lasted longer than that of either Vladimir or Ryazan'. For two weeks the walls were battered by siege-guns. No help from Novgorod was forthcoming, and the inhabitants, 'in fear and perplexity', surrendered on 5 March,[91] the day after the battle on the Sit'. Why the Tatars did not exploit success and follow up the capture of Torzhok by marching on Novgorod is hard to say. The city was only some 300 kilometres distant, a march of fifteen to twenty days; and in early March the thaw would not yet have set in and made the route impassable for the Tatar cavalry.[92] They continued to move west, but when they reached a point, 'the cross of Ignatius, 100 versts [108 kilometres] from Novgorod', they turned south. Novgorod was spared.[93]

Only one more town offered any resistance to the Tatars in the first phase of their Russian campaign,[94] and that was Kozel'sk on the Zhizdra in the north of the principality of Chernigov. Baty surrounded it, but for seven weeks was unable to capture it. Only when reinforcements arrived was the wall battered down and the town taken.[95]

By the summer of 1238 the Tatars had left the lands of Russia. They needed time to rest, regroup and prepare for further conquests in the west. Moreover, trouble threatened the Tatars on the eastern and southern borders of Russia. From the available sources – mainly from Rashid ad-Din's *History* – it would appear that the summer and autumn of 1238 and the winter of 1238–39 were a far from peaceful time for the Tatars. From their encampments on the Kipchak steppes they undertook punitive campaigns against the Circassians and the Ossetians in the north-Caucasian plain, they invaded the Crimea and they clashed with the Polovtsians, killing three of their khans.[96] Nor was all calm on the eastern borders of Ryazan' and Suzdalia: the Russian chronicles mention expeditions against the Mordvinians, the town of Murom and the eastern reaches of the Klyaz'ma river.[97]

The second phase of the invasion of Russia, this time of south and south-west Russia, began in the spring of 1239 when the Tatars took the most southeasterly province, Southern Pereyaslavl'. Few details are known of this the initial venture of their campaign: the chronicles merely state that on 3 March 1239 the town of Pereyaslavl' was taken 'by the lance' and burned and that its inhabitants, including the bishop, were massacred. No mention is made of any prince present in the city or of any resistance by the inhabitants.[98]

Before an attack on Kiev itself could be launched, the principality of Chernigov had first to be neutralized. So far the only Chernigovan town to have been taken was Kozel'sk in 1238. In the summer or early autumn of 1239 a Tatar army under Mongke was sent west across the southern half of Chernigov territory. The number of towns that were captured or bypassed is not known, though Glukhov to the north of Putivl' was in Tatar hands before Chernigov was taken, and Sosnitsa, Khorobor and Snovsk (all east of Chernigov and north of the Seym river) appear to have been captured on the Tatars' march towards the capital.[99] Presumably all the towns in the basin of the Seym river (Kursk, Ryl'sk and Putivl') and perhaps the lower reaches of the Desna as well, were secured before Chernigov itself was approached.

Chernigov was surrounded. The Tatars used a giant catapult (*taran*) capable of 'hurling stones the distance of a bowshot, and the stones could only be lifted by four men'. Mstislav Glebovich, the senior prince of the Ol'govichi after his cousin Mikhail Vsevolodovich, who at the time was still prince of Kiev, made some attempt to defend the town: he led out all his available troops to meet the Tatars in a pitched battle. But he was defeated, and the town fell on 18 October 1239. Bishop Porfiry was spared, led off by the Tatars to Glukhov, and then released.[100]

After the fall of Chernigov the main Tatar army withdrew once again to their encampments in the Kipchak steppes, while a reconnaissance party under Mongke moved south-west to the neighbourhood of Kiev.[101] The Ipat'evskiy Chronicle, which contains the earliest version of this episode, describes how Mongke viewed the city 'from the other bank of the Dnepr', 'was amazed at its beauty and majesty', and sent his envoys to 'Mikhail and the citizens, intending to deceive them'. Having stated that the townsfolk refused to listen to the Tatars' blandishments, the chronicler, who clearly had little love or respect for Mikhail, describes how he 'fled, following his son . . . to the Hungarians' and was replaced first by Rostislav of Smolensk and then by Daniil of West Russia, who left Kiev in the hands of a *voevoda* named Dmitr. Later versions of the same story, doubtless in order to discredit Mikhail, add that he put the Tatar envoys to death.[102]

The rapid change of rulers in Kiev over the last five years can hardly have inspired the inhabitants of the capital with confidence. Forewarned by Mongke's reconnaissance and further alarmed by the departure of two princes in quick succession, the populace must have spent an uncomfortable time awaiting the inevitable assault. The pattern was all too familiar by now: reconnaissance, withdrawal, attack. In the second half of 1240 the Tatars were again in Russian territory. This time they came from the south. Rashid ad-Din describes how Baty and his armies took the field 'against Rus' and the people of the Blackcaps',[103] in other words against the Turkic Karakalpaks, who with the Berendei, the Torki and the Koui had settled permanently in the Ros' river area south of Kiev and who helped the Russians defend the southern borders against nomadic invaders and provided garrisons for such outposts as Torchesk. How long the fortresses on the Ros' held out against the Tatars is not recorded anywhere: the contemporary Russian chronicler had eyes only for the Tatars' ultimate goal.

The story of the siege and capture of Kiev is soberly related in the Ipat'evskiy Chronicle with considerable detail and a refreshing scarcity of cliché and literary embellishment – probably the work of an eye-witness close to the military commander Dmitr, who occupies a prominent role in the narrative.[104] The Tatar army was commanded by Baty and, so the Kievans were told by a suspiciously well-informed prisoner taken early in the proceedings, by nine other Tatar generals, including Baty's brother Orda and two future great khans, Guyuk and Mongke. If the army was as vast as the prisoner said it was, it can have had little difficulty in totally encircling the city and quickly forcing its garrison to surrender. Siege guns were sited near the most south-easterly of the four gates (the 'Polish Gates', *Lyadskie vorota*), as the wooded slope there afforded good cover. The siege guns did their work and the walls fell. There was fierce fighting for a day and a night on the rubble of the fallen walls, but the Tatars soon penetrated the city. The garrison attempted to set up a last-stand stronghold in or around the Church of the Tithe (*Desyatinnaya tserkov'*) in the heart of Kiev, but when the walls of the church collapsed under the weight of the citizens who had fled with their goods and chattels to the vaults, the strongpoint fell. It was the day of the feast of St Nicholas, 6 December 1240.[105] The siege was over. Dmitr, who had been wounded, was spared 'because of his bravery'.

The rest of Baty's Russian campaign seems to have cost him little effort and few casualties. After Kiev there remained only the territories of Volynia and Galicia to be conquered before the assault on Hungary and Poland could begin. The mopping up of resistance took remarkably little time: on the borders of Volynia and Kiev only Kolodyazhin, a town on the river Sluch' endowed with strong natural fortifications, and nearby Kamenets offered any resistance. Kremenets, south-east of Vladimir-in-Volynia, was by-passed. Both Vladimir and Galich fell after short sieges.[106]

The remainder of the story of the great invasion of Europe is well known and need not be related in detail here.[107] Suffice it to say that within four months of the fall of Kiev the Poles, the Czechs and the Teutonic Knights had been shattered at the battle of Liegnitz near Breslau (9 April 1241) and, in the south, the Hungarians routed at the battle of Mohi near the confluence of the Tisa and Sajo rivers. There was panic in Europe.[108] Yet despite the appeals of the king of Hungary to the rulers of the West, no help was forthcoming from any quarter. By January 1242 Croatia had been invaded; most of the Dalmatian coast was overrun. It seemed that little could save Western Europe from sub-jugation. But on 11 December 1241 Great Khan Ogedey died – in all prob-ability of alcoholic poisoning. When Baty heard the news in the spring of 1242 he ordered an immediate withdrawal. Whether this was because he wished to influence the election of the new great khan and 'jockeying for a strong position in Mongol politics seemed more important . . . than continuing the conquest of Europe',[109] or whether it was because he lacked the strength to maintain control over the lands he had conquered, we cannot tell: probably both factors were behind the decision. At any rate Europe was saved.

Baty returned to the Kipchak steppes and set up his headquarters in Saray near the mouth of the Volga, some 100 kilometres north of Astrakhan'. The so-called Tatar Yoke had begun. From Saray, for the next 138 years, the khans of the Golden Horde, as Baty's empire came to be known as, were to exercise political control over all the Russian principalities, and, for a further 100 years, from 1380 to 1480, were to continue to demand, though not always to get, tribute from their Russian 'vassals'.

How did the Tatars manage to overrun Russia with such ease and speed? First, of course, one must look to the size and extraordinary efficiency of the Tatar army. Numerical superiority over their enemies they certainly enjoyed. But how great this superiority was it is impossible to say; indeed it is extremely difficult to arrive at even the roughest estimate of the size of the armies which invaded Russia and Europe. At one end of the scale we have the vague 'countless multitudes' of the Russian chronicles and the vast numbers quoted by western sources; at the other, Rashid ad-Din's estimate of 129,000 as the number of available Mongol troops at the death of Chinghis Khan.[110] Probably the approx-imate figures of 120,000–140,000 troops at Baty's disposal at the beginning of his invasion of Russia arrived at by the Soviet historian Kargalov is reasonably close to the mark, especially if we consider that Tatar khans normally had corps of 10,000 men (*tumen*, or *t'ma* in Russian) under their command and that there were between twelve and fourteen of them serving with Baty.[111]

Many sources, Western and Eastern – Matthew Paris, John of Plano Carpini, the Hungarian Dominican Julian, the Persian historian Juvaini, Rashid ad-Din – talk of their strategy and military tactics and of their skill: of their carefully planned reconnaissance, the attention paid to psychological warfare, the pre-liminary despatch of envoys whose task it often was to sow dissension among the enemy, the swiftness and surprise of their attacks, their skill in manoeuvr-ing, their use of foot-soldiers, conscripted local inhabitants and prisoners of war to bear the brunt of the initial assault, the excellence and accuracy of their bowmen, the speed and endurance of their cavalry, the advanced technique of their siege-drill – rams, catapults, Greek fire –, the minute attention to detail, the strict discipline, the efficiency of their intelligence system, and above all their ability to dispense with extended lines of supply, thanks to the mobility and sturdiness of horses and men and the use of dried meat and cheese for basic rations. The picture given is one of military invincibility, a picture not always supported by facts (Rashid ad-Din, for example, talks of the uprising of two 'emirs', Bayan' and Chiqu, in the Volga Bulgar district and of successful harassment by partisans headed by a Polovtsian robber-chief named Bakhman[112]), but nevertheless suggestive of ruthless efficiency with which the armies of Eastern Europe could not hope to compete.

The reasons for the Russians' inability to cope with the Tatar invasion are not hard to find. Numerically their armies were undoubtedly inferior, but again it is impossible to arrive at any reliable figure. The chronicles make no mention of the size of any of the armies, garrisons or detachments which confronted Baty (with the exception of a 3,000-strong reconnaissance patrol sent south by Yury between the fall of Vladimir and the battle on the Sit').[113] Nor do we know the population of towns in thirteenth-century Russia or the number of troops they could provide. M. N. Tikhomirov hazards a few rough guesses – and very rough they are: 20,000–30,000 for Novgorod; slightly less for Chernigov, the two Vladimirs, Galich, Polotsk, Smolensk, Rostov, Suzdal', Ryazan', Vitebsk and Southern Pereyaslavl'; more for Kiev.[114] If we assume that each of the larger cities could field, say, between 3,000 and 5,000 men, we can arrive at a total of about 60,000 fighting troops. If we add to this another 40,000 from the smaller towns and from the Polovtsians and the various Turkic allies in the principality of Kiev, then the total coincides with the 100,000 estimated by S. M. Solov'ev in his *History of Russia*.[115] But then this is only a rough estimate of the total *potential* number. We have no idea how many towns and districts actually provided troops – it seems unlikely, for instance, that Novgorod sent any at all: certainly none came to the help of their outpost at Torzhok. Perhaps then a half or a quarter – or even a smaller fraction – of the Tatar total was the most the Russians could muster. Then again there is no evidence that more than a handful of princes ever faced the Tatars at any one time: at the battle of Kolomna, for example, the remnants of the Ryazan' force were joined only by an 'advance guard' from Suzdalia, whilst on the River Sit' Grand Prince Yury had with him only his three nephews from the Rostov-Yaroslavl' district and his brother Svyatoslav from Yur'ev.

The Russians had no central command, no central army headquarters, and there was remarkably little liaison between towns and districts. Most damaging of all, there was virtually no intelligence system. At best all the Russian rulers and commanders could hope for was information from stragglers or survivors to tell the tale of earlier defeats and perhaps give an indication of the main line of advance of the Tatar armies. Only on one occasion do we hear of intelligence from the interrogation of a Tatar prisoner – at the beginning of the siege of Kiev – and that sounds suspiciously like planted information. When the attacks occurred, the Russians, it appears, were totally unprepared for them. They knew nothing of the Tatars' techniques in besieging and storming towns, for indeed in the previous invasion of 1223 no towns of any size had been besieged by the Tatars. Yury, as has been mentioned above, took no notice of intelligence concerning Tatar tactics and strength which reached him earlier from his eastern neighbours on the Volga, or if he did, he took no steps to prepare even his own territory of Suzdalia for the invasion which he knew was imminent.[116] Nor were any measures taken to anticipate the invasion of southern Russia: the inhabitants of Southern Pereyaslavl', Chernigov and Kiev, as well as Galicia and Volynia, had nearly a year's respite between the invasion of north-east Russia and the attack on Pereyaslavl'. They must have known what was coming. And yet they did nothing.

But it was not so much military unpreparedness and inefficiency that enfeebled the Russians as lack of unity between the territories in the north, the south and the south-west. There was no suzerain prince who had effective control over *all* Russian lands. The grand prince of Vladimir may have been the most powerful of the princes, but his influence extended only over those districts in the mesopotamian area between the Volga and the Oka where his immediate relatives lived and ruled – and it may well be that his eldest brother, Yaroslav of Northern Pereyaslavl', was not always prepared to obey his commands: it will be remembered that he was not present at the Sit' battle and that earlier, in 1229, he had attempted some sort of coup directed against Yury (see above, p. 70). In the south-east Ryazan', as it turned out, was isolated. For all its close links with Suzdalia during Yury's reign as grand prince, no help was forthcoming when the assault began. Nor did Chernigov, whose princes were closest by birth to those of Ryazan', send help. As for the southern principalities, it has been shown above that the bitter civil war which started in 1235 completely disunited them. Kiev was shuttled between the Rostislavichi, the Ol'govichi, Yaroslav of Northern Pereyaslavl' and Daniil Romanovich. There was no ruler strong enough to guarantee the strength of the district. No mention is made in the sources of any prince in Southern Pereyaslavl' since the 1220s – it might not have existed as far as the chroniclers of Vladimir, Novgorod and south-west Russia were concerned. The rulers of Smolensk and Chernigov were isolated from their neighbours and their forces were exhausted by internecine war; Daniil Romanovich and his brother Vasil'ko were fully occupied in consolidating their authority in Galicia and Volynia, and Daniil, when the time came and he at last took over Kiev in 1240, could do no more than leave a *voevoda* in command, while he himself retired to defend Galich. Is it surprising that the Tatars met with no serious military opposition in Russia?

* * * *

What were the immediate results of the Tatar invasion? As is often the case in early Russian history, there is remarkably little evidence in the written sources to enable us to reach any sort of valid conclusion as to the real damage, political, cultural or economic, inflicted by the Tatars. There is no indication of the number of casualties either military or civil. We do not know how many prisoners of war were taken. The chroniclers, travellers and contemporary historians stubbornly refuse to give even an exaggerated figure: either they are silent, as in the case of Kiev, or they fob off their readers with unhelpful hyperbole ('They slaughtered the old monks and nuns, and priests, and the blind and the halt and the lame and the sick, and all the people'[117]; 'They killed the prince and the princess, and the men, women and children, monks, nuns, priests, some by fire, others by the sword . . .'[118]). Later travellers, the pope's envoy John of Plano Carpini and the Franciscan friar William of Rubruquis, it is true, talk of prisoners of war led off to be herdsmen or slaves, and eastern historians (Rashid ad-Din, Ibn el-Athir), as well as John of Plano Carpini, talk of the systematic conscription by the Tatars of skilled craftsmen and artisans from the conquered cities. But the archaeological evidence of physical destruction and cultural impoverishment is too slender to give us any real picture of the state of Russian towns and countryside after the invasion. The Soviet historian B. A. Rybakov in his *magnum opus, The Crafts of Ancient Russia*, talks of the Russian lands being 'bled dry by the Tatars, the decline and even the total oblivion of complex workmanship, the coarsening and simplification of handicrafts' in the second half of the thirteenth century. But his conclusions seem to be based mainly on the absence of such objects as decorated spindle-whorls (*pryaslitsa*), beads, amulets and bracelets in the burial mounds of the thirteenth and fourteenth centuries and on the disappearance of pottery, ceramics and enamel-ware characteristic of twelfth- and early thirteenth-century archaeological strata.[119]

Certainly it would appear that in north-east Russia the building of cathedrals, churches and monasteries slowed down in the post-invasion period and was nothing like as vigorous as it had been in the twelfth and early thirteenth centuries. But building never came to a halt: there were architects and masons active in the major cities, and there is evidence of considerable building activity in Vladimir and Rostov in the second half of the thirteenth century. Furthermore, new schools of architecture were soon to appear in Tver' and Moscow, where building flourished in the fourteenth century.[120]

Internal commerce, we are told, suffered a serious setback owing to the destruction of city crafts and the inability of the towns to satisfy the demands of the villages;[121] but again this would appear to be based mainly on the reports of Plano Carpini, Rashid ad-Din and Ibn el-Athir, according to which craftsmen and artisans were led off in captivity from conquered towns – reports backed up only by the slimmest of archaeological evidence. As for agriculture, there is little to suggest that it suffered in any way. Indeed, as Rybakov points out, the Tatars deliberately left the peasants alone so that they might, in the words of the Ipat'evskiy chronicler, 'till [the land] for them [and grow] wheat and millet'.[122]

What of the physical destruction? As can be seen from the description of Baty's campaign in Russia, the only towns that we can assume were captured by the Tatars, and presumably suffered in the process, were Ryazan', Vladimir, Torzhok in the north-east; Kozel'sk, Southern Pereyaslavl', Chernigov, Kiev, Kolodyazhin and Kamenets in the south; and Galich and Vladimir-in-Volynia in the south-west. As for the remaining eleven towns mentioned as taken by the Tatars or lying in their path, there is little or no evidence to show that they suffered any damage – indeed, many of them may have been bypassed by the invaders.[123] Even concerning some of those which we can assume *were* captured there is not a great deal of evidence of wholesale destruction. True, John of Plano Carpini, travelling through the district of Kiev five years after the fall of the city, talks of Kiev as 'reduced almost to nothing, for there are at the present time [1245] scarce 200 houses there and the inhabitants are kept in complete slavery', but then in the same breath he talks of the Tatars 'destroying the whole of Russia'.[124] The chronicle which contains so vivid a description of the taking of Kiev (the Ipat'evskiy) makes no mention of the destruction of any buildings or even of any massacre of the inhabitants; only the breaching of the walls and the collapse – through overcrowding in the vaults – of the Tithe Church are mentioned. As for the northern chronicles, the Lavrent'evskiy dismisses the fall of the mother of the Russian cities in two brief sentences, while the Novgorod First completely ignores it. The same chronicles make no mention whatsoever of post-invasion Chernigov or Southern Pereyaslavl'. It was as though the northern chroniclers became even more par-ochially-minded than before the invasion and considered that both towns – as well as Kiev and Smolensk – lay from now on outside their sphere of interest. Indeed, for the second half of the thirteenth century we have practically no information either on any of the south-Russian districts or on which princes, if any, ruled there: probably most of the southern lands came directly under Tatar control.[125]

Ryazan' appears to have suffered some physical damage: the composite *Tale of the Destruction of Ryazan'* mentions the 'great church' (the Cathedral of the Assumption) 'burned and blackened',[126] although the only chronicle to talk in any detail of the taking of Ryazan', the Novgorod First Chronicle, mentions merely the slaughter of the inhabitants, and that in purely conventional terms. As for Vladimir itself, there is little evidence of material destruction. Although the great cathedral of the Assumption (*Uspenskiy sobor*) was allegedly burned in 1238, it was still standing and functioning later in the following year when Grand Prince Yury was buried there.[127] Nor is there anything to show that the other major churches in the city suffered: Aleksandr Nevskiy was buried in the church of the Monastery of the Nativity of the Virgin in 1263,[128] and there is no mention anywhere of damage to Vsevolod III's palace cathedral of St Dmitry, built in the 1190s.

There can be little doubt that there *was* disruption of life throughout north-east and south Russia as a result of Baty's invasions. But it is hard to say how long it lasted. Clearly things returned to normal, or to near-normal, in a remarkably short time. In Ryazan', for example, the senior surviving prince, Ingvar' Ingvarevich, who luckily for him had been in Chernigov at the time of Baty's attack, was quick to begin work on the restoration of his principality. The coda of the *Tale of the Destruction of Ryazan'* describes the aftermath of the invasion in the following terms:

The pious Grand Prince Ingvar' Ingvarevich . . . sat upon his father's throne. . . . And he renewed the land of Ryazan' and built churches and monasteries, he consoled newcomers and gathered together the people. And there was joy amongst the Christians whom God saved . . . from the godless impious khan Baty.[129]

And Mongayt, the Soviet archaeologist and historian of Ryazan', confirms that the city of Ryazan' was quickly restored and that although some crafts were destroyed and trade links declined the district soon returned to normal.[130] The chroniclers of north-east Russia paint a similar picture of restoration and recovery under the new grand prince of Vladimir, Yaroslav Vsevolodovich, and stress the period of calm in Suzdalia which followed the events of 1238. More interest, indeed, is shown by the chroniclers of both Novgorod and Vladimir in the activities of Yaroslav and his son Aleksandr in the west than in the results of the invasion in the rest of Russia. All in all, the picture is hardly one of stagnation or painfully slow recovery after a holocaust, and the 'great consecration' of the palace church of Saints Boris and Gleb in Kideksha near Suzdal' in 1239,[131] Aleksandr Nevskiy's successful activities in the north-west (the victories over the Swedes and the German Knights in 1240 and 1242 respectively) and Yaroslav's defeat of the Lithuanians who invaded Smolensk in 1239, all either illustrate the resilience of the Russians in the north or point to the fact that Suzdalia was not brought to its knees by the invasion of the Tatars.

As for Russia's links with the outside world, again there is little evidence to enable us to pronounce any valid judgements on the effects of the invasion. It might have been expected that commercial connections with the West would have suffered, not so much because of the 'ravages' of the Tatars in the 1230s, as because of increased aggression of Russia's immediate western neighbours – the Swedes, the Germans and the Lithuanians – in the decades following the invasion and the resulting obstruction of trade routes to the sea. Yet trade with the West, either from or via Novgorod and Smolensk, both of which suffered no damage from the Tatars, seems to have been relatively unaffected, especially trade with the Baltic – Riga, Gotland and Lübeck – as is evidenced by the various economic treaties in the second half of the thirteenth century. To what extent eastern trade suffered or increased as a result of the invasion it is even harder to gauge. Some historians consider that the destruction of the Bulgar state on the Volga put a temporary halt to the movement of goods along the Volga[132] – the standard trade route with the east – but there is little to show that imports and exports ceased flowing along the Volga-Caspian route to and from Novgorod, Pskov, Smolensk, Polotsk and Vitebsk in the west and Vladimir and Suzdal' in the north-east.[133]

So we are left with the picture of a Russia struck by yet another steppe invader, more formidable, more efficient both in war and peace and more enduring than the Pechenegs or the Polovtsians. But it was a Russia by no means as shattered, overwhelmed and dispirited as many modern historians would have us believe. True, in the second half of the thirteenth century little is heard of the southern areas – Kiev, Chernigov and Pereyaslavl' – but this is not necessarily evidence of physical destruction or economic stagnation, but rather of a stoppage in the flow of information, the cessation or disappearance of Kievan chronicle-writing and the breach of political and cultural links between Suzdalia and the south. Nor is there anything to show that a mass migration of peoples from the vulnerable south to the relative safety of the north took place as an immediate result of Baty's invasion. If there *was* such a shift in the population of Russia, then it probably occurred nearer the end of the century, when the effect of repeated Tatar punitive raids was beginning to tell.

In the north-east and in the territories of Novgorod and the vast stretches of land north of the Volga, where new centres of interest were to emerge and where the political and cultural life of Muscovy was eventually to develop, the pattern of life seems to have changed remarkably little. Indeed the socio-political structure of post-invasion Suzdalia and Novgorod was much the same as it was before, at any rate in the first years after the invasion. But, as will be seen in the following chapters, which are concerned mainly with north-east and north-west Russia, the presence of the Tatars of the Golden Horde was soon to make itself felt.

REFERENCES AND NOTES

1. The Mongols were originally one of the tribes inhabiting present-day Mongolia. In the twelfth century, however, they were defeated by their neighbours the Tatars. The names 'Mongol' and 'Mongolia' survived thanks to the fact that Chinghis Khan was himself of Mongol stock. The term 'Tatar' was invariably used in contemporary Russian sources, and is used in this book to denote the Mongols in Russia. See Vernadsky, *The Mongols and Russia*, pp. 11–12. Cf. Spuler, *Die Goldene Horde*, p. 11, n. 1.

2. Tizengauzen, *Sbornik*, vol. 1, pp. 25–6. This information is repeated by the Persian historian Rashid ad-Din. See Rashid ad-Din, *Sbornik letopisey*, vol. 1, book 2, p. 229.

3. See Pletneva, 'Polovetskaya zemlya', p. 299. Ibn al-Athir says that after their defeat in the northern Caucasus the 'Kipchaks' fled to the 'Rus'' (Tizengauzen, *Sbornik*, vol. 1, p. 26). It is not known when Mstislav married Kotyan's daughter.

4. Eastern sources (Ibn al-Athir and Rashid ad-Din) have little information of any value.

5. The humiliating nature of the defeat of one Yarun's Polovtsian vanguard before the main battle is stressed, as is the Polovtsians' slaughter of the decimated fleeing Russians after the battle 'some for their horses, others for their clothes'.

6. Up to 1200 *Ipat* is concerned with Kievan affairs. From 1200 to its conclusion it deals almost exclusively with the descendants of Roman Mstislavich of Galicia and Volynia, particularly with his eldest son Daniil.

7. For a detailed investigation of the sources, see Fennell, 'The Tatar Invasion of 1223'. On the dating, see Berezhkov, *Khronologiya*, pp. 317–18. The main chronicle accounts are found in *PSRL*, vol. 1, cols 445–7; *NPL*, pp. 61–3, 264–7; *PSRL*, vol. 2, cols 740–5; vol. 5, pp. 202–7. For a literary appreciation of the *Tale of the Battle on the Kalka* (i.e. the story of the Tatar invasion of 1223), see Fennell and Stokes, *Early Russian Literature*, pp. 81–8.

8. *NPL*, pp. 62, 265. The sixteenth-century compiler of the Nikon Chronicle spares his reader's modesty by changing 'and girls' to 'and so forth'. *PSRL*, vol. 10, p. 89.

9. *PSRL*, vol. 2, col. 741.

10. On Zarub, see Tolochko, *Kiev*, pp. 143–6.

11. *NPL*, pp. 62, 265.

12. *NPL*, pp. 62, 266.

13. Twelve-day, according to Ibn al-Athir (Tizengauzen, *Sbornik*, vol. 1, p. 27).
14. The town was built by Svyatopolk Izyaslavich in 1095 on the site of the defunct town-fortress of Vitichev, 20 kilometres south of Trepol'. See Tikhomirov, *Drevnerusskie goroda*, p. 55; Tolochko, 'Kievskaya zemlya', pp. 35–6; idem, *Kiev*, p. 141.
15. *PSRL*, vol. 5, p. 204.
16. *NPL*, pp. 63, 266.
17. *PSRL*, vol. 1, cols 446–7 60,000 (!) according to *Nik* (*PSRL* vol. 10, p. 92).
18. *NPL*, pp. 63, 267.
19. *PSRL*, vol. 2, col. 741.
20. *PSRL*, vol. 1, cols 446–7.
21. *PSRL*, vol. 2, col. 743.
22. The Brodniki were from the extreme north-eastern area of the Polovtsian steppes (see Pletneva, 'Polovetskaya zemlya', pp. 290–9). They evidently joined forces with the Tatars at some stage in the battle and, in spite of their commander's oath to save Mstislav Romanovich and his two fellow-princes who were holding a hill above the Kalka, enabled the Tatars to capture their redoubt, slaughter all their troops and dine on boards placed over the writhing bodies of the three princes until they died. *NPL*, pp. 63, 266–7.
23. Just before the battle a Polovtsian advance guard fled in disarray, 'trampling in their flight the camps of the Russian princes' (*NPL*, pp. 63, 266).
24. A minor principality situated on the southernmost border of the district of Kiev.
25. See Rapov *Knyazheskie vladeniya*, p. 196.
26. Ibid., p. 196.
27. Ibid., pp. 92, 93.
28. Altogether nine appear to have survived: three Rostislavichi, four Ol'govichi, one West-Russian (Mstislav Yaroslavich of Lutsk) and Daniil of Volynia
29. *PSRL*, vol. 2, cols 746, 753.
30. Pletneva, 'Polovetskaya zemlya', pp. 299–300; Fedorov-Davydov, *Obshchestvennyy stroy*, pp. 27–8, 41–2.
31. *PSRL*, vol. 1, col. 446; *NPL*, pp. 61, 264. Cf. the description of their origins given by Matthew of Paris (Matuzova, *Angliyskie . . . istochniki*, pp. 113, 138).
32. *PSRL*, vol. 1, cols 234, 235–6.
33. *NPL*, pp. 63, 267.
34. In 1226, 1228 and 1232. In 1239 the Mordvinians raided Nizhniy Novgorod. See *PSRL*, vol. 1, cols 448–9, 450–1, 459. For Russo-Mordvinian relations in the 1220s–1230s, see Kuchkin, 'O marshrutakh', pp. 44–5.
35. (a) 1224. Vsevolod sent by Yury, unspecified destination (*PSRL*, vol. 1, col. 447); (b) 1224: Vasil'ko with Yury at Torzhok (*NPL*, pp. 64, 268); (c) 1226: Vasil'ko and Vsevolod with Yury against Oleg of Kursk (*PSRL*, vol. 1, col. 448); (d) 1228: Vasil'ko sent by Yury against the Mordvinians (ibid., col. 450); (e) 1232: all three with Yaroslav against Serensk (ibid., col. 459).
36. (a) 1227: Vasil'ko married to daughter of Mikhail of Chernigov (*PSRL*, vol. 1, col. 450); (b) 1228: Vsevolod married to daughter of Oleg Svyatoslavich (of Kursk?) in Southern Pereyaslavl' (*PSRL*, vol. 25, p. 122).
37. 1227: Vsevolod sent to rule Southern Pereyaslavl' (*PSRL* vol. 1, col 450).
38. Ibid., cols 448–9.
39. Ibid., col. 451. He was back in Yur'ev in 1230, and still in Yur'ev in 1234 (ibid., cols 455, 460).
40. Ibid., cols 451–2.

41. *NPL*, pp. 61, 63–4, 263, 267.
42. Yury married Mikhail's sister Agafia in 1211. *PSRL*, vol. 1, col. 435.
43. *NPL*, pp. 64, 268.
44. 1216: Yury's brother Vladimir married the daughter of Gleb of Chernigov (*PSRL*, vol. 1, col. 438); 1227: Yury's nephew Vasil'ko Konstantinovich married Mikhail of Chernigov's daughter (ibid., col. 450); 1228: Yury's nephew Vsevolod Konstantinovich married the daughter of Oleg Svyatoslavich of Kursk and Novgorod Severskiy, the senior member of the cadet branch of the Ol'govichi (ibid., vol. 25, p. 122). For Oleg of Kursk, see Dimnik, 'Russian Princes and their Identities', pp. 158–65.
45. In 1226 Yury and his nephews Vasil'ko and Vsevolod Konstantinovichi 'marched against Oleg of Kursk to aid Mikhail Vsevolodovich'. Yury managed to solve peacefully what was evidently a family feud amongst the Ol'govichi (*PSRL*, vol. 1, col. 448).
46. The account of the 1232 campaign against Serensk in Chernigov territory (see above, n. 35 (e)) gives no indication that Mikhail was involved in the fighting (*PSRL*, vol. 1, col. 459). Cf., however, *N1 s.a.* 6739 (1231), where Yaroslav is reported as fighting against Mikhail in the area of Serensk and Mosal'sk (*NPL*, pp. 71, 280).
47. Perhaps Vladimir Mstislavich of Pskov (the only surviving first cousin of Mstislav Davidovich apart from Vladimir Ryurikovich of Kiev) succeeded to the throne, or, more likely, Mstislav Davidovich's son Rostislav, who was present, probably as prince of Smolensk, at the Council of Kiev in 1231 (see above, p. 71).
48. *PSRL*, vol. 1, col. 450.
49. Ibid., cols 453–4.
50. In 1225 or 1226 three Rostislavichi (Vladimir Mstislavich of Pskov, his son Yaroslav and his brother David of Toropets) helped Yaroslav combat a major Lithuanian incursion against Torzhok, Toropets, Smolensk and Polotsk. *NPL*, pp. 64, 269; *PSRL*, vol. 1, cols 447–8.
51. *PSRL*, vol. 1, cols 455–6.
52. *PSRL*, vol. 2, col. 753.
53. Ibid., col. 766. In gratitude Vladimir gave Daniil the town of Torchesk.
54. *PSRL*, vol. 1, col. 457.
55. *NPL*, pp. 70, 278.
56. Ibid., pp. 68, 274–5.
57. Ibid., pp. 71, 280.
58. The office of *tysyatskiy* had been transferred to Boris Negochevich in the disturbance preceding Mikhail's recall (*NPL*, pp. 67, 273).
59. In 1225 he left Novgorod shortly after arriving (*NPL*, pp. 64, 268–9). In 1229 he left, again shortly after arrival, but returned in 1230, only to depart once again to Chernigov (ibid., pp. 68, 69, 275, 276).
60. *NPL*, pp. 70, 278.
61. Ibid., pp. 71–2, 280–2.
62. Ibid., pp. 73, 284.
63. The description of the fighting around Chernigov in 1235 (given *s.a.* 1234) and the subsequent truce clearly refers to the Tatar capture of Chernigov in 1239, as described in *Ipat* (*s.a.* 1237), *N4* (*s.a.* 1239) and *S1* (*s.a.* 1239) (*PSRL*, vol. 2, cols 772, 782; vol. 4, pp. 222–3; vol. 5, pp. 218–19). See Dimnik, 'The Siege of Chernigov in 1235'.
64. 'Izyaslav' in *N1* (*NPL*, pp. 74, 284) and *Ipat* (*PSRL*, vol. 2, cols 772–4 with

no patronymic; 'Izyaslav Mstislavich' in *N4* and *S1* (ibid., vol. 4, p. 214; vol. 5, p. 210); 'Izyaslav Mstislavich, grandson of Roman' in *M* (ibid., vol. 25, p. 126); 'Izyaslav Mstislavich of Smolensk' in *Nik* (ibid., vol. 10, p. 104). There can, however, be little doubt that this Izyaslav was a member of the cadet branch of the Ol'govichi, and in fact the grandson of Igor' Svyatoslavich of Novgorod Severskiy and Chernigov. The error of the hypothetical *svod* of 1448 as reflected in *N4* and *S1* was clearly perpetuated in the subsequent *svody*. See Dimnik, 'Russian Princes and their Identities', pp. 107–7, and idem, 'The Struggle for Control over Kiev'.

65. Dimnik ('The Struggle for Control over Kiev', p. 35), however, considers that Mikhail placed not his cousin Izyaslav Vladimirovich on the throne, but Izyaslav *Mstislavich*, Vladimir's nephew.

66. *PSRL*, vol. 2, cols 772–4; *NPL*, pp. 73–4, 284–5.

67. *NPL*, pp. 74, 285. According to *Ipat s.a.* 1235 (*PSRL*, vol. 2, col. 777), he took Kiev from *Vladimir* – not mentioned in *N1*. See, however, Dimnik ('The Struggle for Control over Kiev', p. 37) who suggests that Yaroslav took over Kiev as the result of an agreement between Daniil and Grand Prince Yury, who 'forced Vladimir to vacate Kiev'.

68. *PSRL*, vol. 2, col. 777.

69. Ibid., cols 777–8 (*s.a. 1235*).

70. Saksin was the old Khazar city of Itil'. See Cherepnin, 'Mongolo-Tatary', p. 190; Noonan, 'Suzdalia's Eastern Trade', pp. 372–3; Fedorov-Davydov, *Kochevniki*, pp. 149–50.

71. Tizengauzen, *Sbornik*, pp. 27–8.

72. Khazars perhaps? See Cherepnin, ibid.

73. *PSRL*, vol. 1, col. 453. The expedition is also mentioned by the Persian historian Juvaini (*The History of the World-Conqueror*, vol. 1, p. 190) and by the Arab Ibn Wasil (Tizengauzen, *Sbornik*, p. 73). See also Allsen, 'Prelude to the Western Campaigns'.

74. *PSRL*, vol. 1, col. 459; vol. 25, p. 125.

75. Tatishchev, *Istoriya*, vol. 4, p. 370; vol. 3, p. 227.

76. 'Jaman', according to Rashid ad-Din, perhaps a corruption of Yaik? See Rashid ad-Din, *The Successors of Genghis Khan*, pp. 57–9.

77. Cherepnin, 'Mongolo-Tatary', p. 191. See also the evidence of the Hungarian friar Julian (*Epistola Fr.Iuliani de Bello Mongolorum* in Anninsky, 'Izvestiya vengerskikh missionerov', pp. 83 *et* seq.), who lists under the 'pagan kingdoms' overcome: 'Sasciam (Saksinia), Fulgariam (Bulgars), . . . Merowiam (Mari), Mordanorum regnum (Mordvinians)'; Rashid ad-Din: conquest of the 'Boqshi and Burtas' (Mordvinians) (*The Successors of Genghis Khan*, p. 59); Juvaini, *The History of the World-Conqueror*, p. 249.

78. Rashid ad-Din, *The Successors of Genghis Khan*, pp. 58–9.

79. For a detailed investigation of the Russian sources, see Fennell, 'The Tale of Baty's Invasion'.

80. The earliest MS dates from the sixteenth century, but the *Tale* clearly reflects elements written as early as the thirteenth century. See *Voinskie povesti*, pp. 9–19; Fennell and Stokes, *Early Russian Literature*, pp. 88–97; *Istoriya russkoy literatury X-XVII vekov*, pp. 161–7.

81. 'Yury himself did not march, nor did he hearken to the request of the princes of Ryazan', but he intended to fight by himself.' *NPL*, pp. 74–5, 286. The same chronicle, however, also states that Yury sent one Eremey 'with an advance

guard' (*v storozhikh*), who joined forces with Prince Roman Ingvarevich of Ryazan'
near Kolomna and was beaten by the Tatars (ibid., pp. 75, 287). *L* says that
Yury's son Vsevolod was with Eremey (*PSRL*, vol. 1, col. 460).

82.   *Voinskie povesti*, p. 12. The *Tale* also mentions 'Izheslavets', perhaps Izheslavl'
between Belgorod and Pronsk on the river Pronya. Note that the *Tale* and the
sixteenth-century Nikon Chronicle both say that a battle was fought between the
Ryazanites and the Tatars *before* the siege of Ryazan'. See ibid., pp. 11–12;
PSRL, vol. 10, pp. 105–6.

83.   *NPL*, pp. 75, 287.

84.   Taken prisoner according to *L*, killed according to Rashid ad-Din (*The Successors
of Genghis Khan*, p. 59). For a much later version of the capture of Moscow, see
Gorsky, 'K voprosu'.

85.   According to *N1*, however, Yury went first to Yaroslavl'. From there he sent
out a reconnaissance patrol of 3,000 men. It was surrounded by the enemy. Yury
then took up battle positions (presumably near Yaroslavl'), but fled to the Sit'
river when the Tatars approached.

86.   To this factual account in *L* is added a passage describing the Tatars' attempt
to cow the Vladimirites into submission by parading their prize prisoner, Prince
Vladimir Yur'evich, before the walls of the city. The incident, however, is
dubious – Rashid ad-Din says that Vladimir was killed at Moscow (see above,
n. 84) – and was probably added at a later date to the original chronicle version,
as were many of the hyperbolical embellishments. See Fennell, 'The Tale of Baty's
Invasion', pp. 46–8.

87.   Only in *Ipat. PSRL*, vol. 2, col. 779.

88.   For a detailed textological study of the story of Vasil'ko's capture and execution,
see Fennell, 'The Tale of the Death'.

89.   According to *Ipat*, the Tatars were commanded by Burunday, whose army surrounded Yury's troops. *Ipat* also hints at carelessness on Yury's part or the fact
that he was taken by surprise ('he had no outposts'). *PSRL*, vol. 2, col. 779.

90.   In the *Tale of the Death of Vasil'ko*, attached somewhat clumsily to the account
of the Sit' battle in *L*, Vasil'ko is eventually entombed side by side with the
decapitated body of Yury. M. D. Priselkov was of the opinion that as heads were
rarely cut off by the enemy in early Russian warfare, Yury was betrayed and
killed by his own men. See Fennell, 'The Tale of the Death', p. 36, n. 8.

91.   For the date, see Berezhkov, *Khronologiya*, pp. 270–1.

92.   Cf. Kargalov, *VFR*, pp. 108–9.

93.   *NPL*, pp. 76, 288–9. Kargalov considers that only a reconnaissance squadron
moved west of Torzhok to 'Ignach-krest'. *VFR*, p. 107.

94.   The *Tale of Merkury of Smolensk*, written not before the end of the fifteenth century
and based largely on local legends, tells of how a youth named Merkury saved
Smolensk from a Tatar detachment. There is, however, no evidence whatsoever
in the sources to show that the Tatars went anywhere near Smolensk. See *Russkie
povesti XV–XVI vekov*, pp. 106–7; *Istoriya russkoy literatury X-XVII vekov*,
pp. 169–70.

95.   Reported in *Ipat* (*PSRL*, vol. 2, cols 780–1) and by Rashid ad-Din (*The Successors
of Genghis Khan*, p. 60). The version of *Ipat* contrasts the heroic conduct of the
inhabitants of Kozel'sk under one 'Prince Vasily' with the somewhat cowardly
behaviour of Vsevolod in Vladimir ('Vsevolod was afraid, because he was young') –
another attempt on the part of the southern chronicle to discredit the northern
princes.

96. Rashid ad-Din, *The Successors of Genghis Khan*, p. 60. Kargalov considers that the Tatars invaded the Crimea in the winter of 1239–40. See *VFR*, p. 114.

97. Reported *after* the capture of Pereyaslavl' and Chernigov in 1239 (*PSRL*, vol. 1, cols 469–70). Murom was burned, as was the town of Gorokhovets just east of the influx of the Klyaz'ma into the Oka. The late Tver' chronicle (*Tverskoy sbornik*: *PSRL*, vol. 15, col. 374) says that Gorodets Radilov on the Volga was taken at the same time, but this is probably in error for Gorokhovets.

98. *PSRL*, vol. 1, col. 469; vol. 2, cols 781–2. The date is given in the Pskov First and Second Chronicles (vol. 1, p. 11; vol. 2, p. 79) and *PSRL*, vol. 16, col. 56.

99. They are in fact mentioned in *Ipat* as captured in 1234, but elements of the confused entry of 6742 clearly refer to the Tatar campaign of 1239. See Dimnik, 'The Siege of Chernigov in 1235'; (see above, n. 63).

100. The fullest account of the Chernigov campaign is given in *N4* and *S1*, both of which derive from the fragmentary accounts found in *Ipat* (*s.a.* 1234 and 1237) (*PSRL*, vols 4, pp. 222–3; 5, pp. 218–19; 2, cols 772, 782). *L* briefly mentions the capture of Chernigov and adds 'their princes fled to the Hungarians' — presumably a misplaced reference to the flight of Mikhail Vsevolodovich and his son Rostislav from Kiev (in early 1240, but reported in *Ipat s.a.* 1238). For the date of the fall of Chernigov, see *PSRL*, vol. 16, col. 51; *P1L*, p. 12.

101. *PSRL*, vol. 1, col. 469. Note that according to *N4* and *S1* (*PSRL*, vols 4, p. 223; 5, p. 219) the Tatars 'came to Kiev with [offers of] peace and they made peace with Mstislav and Vladimir and Daniil. This coda, which is also found at the end of *Ipat's* description of the siege of Chernigov in 1235, seems to me to be misplaced here: it would be hard to see what the princes of Chernigov, Smolensk and Galich were doing in Kiev at the end of 1239. See, however, Dimnik, 'The Siege of Chernigov in 1235', pp. 401–3.

102. *PSRL*, vol. 2, col. 782; cf. vol. 25, p. 131; vol. 20, p. 158; vol. 23, p. 77; vol. 10, p. 116 — i.e. the version of the 'svod' of 1472–9'.

103. Rashid ad-Din, *The Successors of Genghis Khan*, p. 69

104. See Pashuto, *Ocherki*, pp. 85–6. The account of *Ipat* is repeated, with slight variations, in *N4*, *S1*, *M*, *E*, *L'v* and *Nik*. *N1* makes no mention of the taking of Kiev, and *L* restricts its entry to a few words.

105. The siege lasted nine days according to Rashid ad-Din (*The Successors of Genghis Khan*, p. 69). According to later Russian sources it lasted '10 weeks and 4 days', from 5 September to 19 November. See *PSRL*, vol. 16, col. 51; *P1L*, p. 12; *P2L*, p. 81.

106. *PSRL*, vol. 2, col. 786. Repeated in *N4*, *S1*, *M*, *E*, *L'v*, Rashid ad-Din (ibid., p. 69).

107. For an account of Baty's campaign in the West, see Vernadsky, *The Mongols and Russia*, pp. 52–8; Pashuto, 'Mongol'skiy pokhod'; Spuler, *Die Goldene Horde*, pp. 20 et seq.; Grousset, *L'Empire des Steppes*, pp. 330–3.

108. See Matthew Paris (in Matuzova, *Angliyskie . . . istochniki*, pp. 110 et seq.). According to him there was a glut of herrings in Yarmouth in 1238: overseas buyers were too scared by the Mongol threat to travel to England (ibid., pp. 111, 136).

109. Vernadsky, *The Mongols and Russia*, p. 58.

110. Rashid ad-Din, *Sbornik letopisey*, vol. 1, book 2, p. 266.

111. Kargalov, *VFR*, pp. 74–5. The total numbers are especially hard to arrive at as the Mongols added detachments from the people they conquered to their own forces. See the letter of the Hungarian monk Julian to the bishop of Perugia

(Anninsky, 'Izvestiya', pp. 83–90); Matthew Paris (Matuzova, *Angliyskie* . . . *istochniki*, pp. 112, 137).

112. Rashid ad-Din, *The Successors of Genghis Khan*, pp. 57, 58. Allsen, 'Prelude to the Western Campaigns'.

113. *NPL*, pp. 76, 288.

114. Tikhomirov, *Drevnerusskie goroda*, pp. 139–41.

115. Solov'ev, *Istoriya Rossii*, vol. 3, pp. 23–4.

116. According to the Hungarian Dominican Julian, who travelled to the district of the Volga Bulgars in 1237–38, Yury learned from the Tatar ambassadors to Hungary, whom he intercepted, that the Tatars planned to attack Hungary, overcome Rome and march still further west. See Anninsky, 'Izvestiya', pp. 88, 106.

117. In Suzdal'. *PSRL*, vol. 1, col. 462.

118. In Ryazan'. *NPL*, pp. 75, 287.

119. Rybakov, *Remeslo drevney Rusi*, pp. 525–38.

120. Voronin, *Zodchestvo*, vol. 2, pp. 131–8.

121. Vernadsky, *The Mongols and Russia*, p. 343; Rybakov, *Remeslo drevney Rusi*, p. 534.

122. Rybakov, ibid., p. 525. *PSRL*, vol. 2, col. 792.

123. Voronin is of the opinion that Yaroslavl', Rostov, Uglich, Kostroma, Northern Pereyaslavl', Tver' 'and other towns' surrendered without a fight and were spared. *Zodchestvo*, vol. 2, p. 130.

124. *The Mongol Mission*, p. 30.

125. Grushevsky, *Ocherk*, pp. 447 *et seq*.

126. *Voinskie povesti*, p. 15.

127. *PSRL*, vol. 1, cols 467–8.

128. *NPL*, pp. 84, 312.

129. *Voinskie povesti*, pp. 18–19.

130. *Ryazanskaya zemlya*, pp. 355–9. The capital was transferred to Pereyaslavl' Ryazanskiy in the fourteenth century mainly as a result of the vulnerability of Old Ryazan' and frequent attacks by the Tatars. Pereyaslavl' enjoyed good protection from the surrounding forests. See Mongayt, *Staraya Ryazan'*, p. 28.

131. The church was built in 1152 and reconsecrated (presumably after building alterations) by Bishop Kirill of Rostov. *PSRL*, vol. 1, col. 469.

132. For example Kargalov, *VFR*, pp. 210–11.

133. See Limonov, 'Iz istorii'.

CHAPTER FIVE

The Aftermath 1238–1263

THE STRUGGLE FOR POWER 1238–1252

For the first thirteen years after the battle on the river Sit' the Tatars left northern Russia in peace. They committed no acts of military aggression against any of the descendants of Vsevolod III or their subjects, or if they did, they were not recorded. It meant that the princes were able to squabble amongst themselves, to manage their own business, to defend themselves against enemies in the west, and even occasionally to interfere in the affairs of their old neighbours in the south. Of course for the first four years, 1238–1242, the Tatars were elsewhere engaged – in south and south-west Russia and in eastern Europe – and had neither the opportunity nor the time to control the affairs of the conquered Russians. But in the ten years after establishing their capital and headquarters in Saray on the Volga, although Khan Baty and his son Sartak kept a sharp watch on their new subject princes and nominally at least made them ratify their right to rule by presenting their credentials at the court of the khan, they showed no inclination to step in and control affairs in Vladimir, Suzdal', Rostov or Novgorod. They sent no punitive expeditions. There is no record even of Tatar officials or Tatar troops being stationed in the major towns of the north. This may have been due to the Russians' submissiveness, their unwillingness to tread on the Tatars' toes in the early years, a tentative policy of wait and see; or again it may be merely symptomatic of the Tatars' unreadiness at this stage to exercise firm military and economic control over the Russians. But at any rate this was a period of inactivity as far as the Tatars' policy in Russia was concerned, and it looks as though the Russians were free to run their own lives.

As has been mentioned above, life in north-east and north-west Russia went on much as before the invasion. Of course there was rebuilding to be done in a few of the towns, as well as a certain amount of resettlement and repopulation. But the same princes ruled the same districts; the same chronicles were kept in the same centres – Vladimir, Rostov and Novgorod; and the same enemies harassed the same segments of the western frontiers. As for relations with the southern and south-western districts of Russia we hear far less than before, perhaps owing to the fragmentary and sporadic nature of the southern sources: Kievan chronicle-writing, if it existed at all in the post-1240 years, is only dimly reflected in later compilations, and the great Volynian-Galician (Ipat'evskiy) Chronicle records only what concerned Daniil of west Russia, his family and his – usually stormy – relations with the countries of eastern Europe.

It was also, however, a period of momentous decision and change. Once again the descendants of Vsevolod III were split into two factions with radically opposed policies. But this time it was not just a question of who should rule Suzdalia or where the centre of power should be, Vladimir or Rostov. The question now was twofold: what was to be the attitude of the Vsevolodovichi to the Tatars: resist or submit? And what was to be their policy vis-à-vis western Europe? On the answer to these questions hung the future of Russia. Furthermore, what appears to have been the virtual divorce between the north and the south of Russia, the near-severance of political and cultural relations between Vladimir and the principalities of the south, as well as Daniil of Galicia's absorption in local and east-European affairs to the exclusion of his previous concern with Kiev – all this marked the beginning of the isolation of most of what had once been the Kievan empire.

*   *   *   *

In order to understand the division of land and the transference of authority from prince to prince in the north-east it is necessary to bear in mind which of the descendants of Vsevolod III survived the events of 1237–38 and what their positions were in 1238. After the death of Yury and his three sons, his eldest surviving brother Yaroslav became grand prince of Vladimir. Aged 48, he was easily the most experienced and politically the toughest of all the Vsevolodovichi. Most of his early career had been spent in his patrimony of Northern Pereyaslavl', which at the time included the town of Tver' in the west and which bordered on Novgorod territory. In the 1220s and 1230s he had gained enormous experience in controlling Novgorod, with or without the assistance of his sons Fedor and Aleksandr, in dealing with its recalcitrant citizens and in combating the schemes of his adventurous and ambitious enemy, Mikhail of Chernigov. Not surprisingly, no one disputed his accession to the throne of Vladimir. His two brothers, Svyatoslav and Ivan, caused him no worry. Svyatoslav, who had already been granted Yur'ev Pol'skiy as his patrimony in 1213 (see above, p. 47) and who had remained there quietly for a quarter of a century, was given the town and district of Suzdal' in 1238 as a mark of his seniority – he was next in line for the throne of Vladimir. Ivan, who for forty years had had no patrimony at all, was given the minor district of Starodub on the Klyaz'ma, which had previously been held by his brother Vladimir until the latter's death in 1228 (see above, p. 50) and which was now vacant.[1]

As for the next generation, the grandsons of Vsevolod III, only two family groups need concern us here – the descendants of Konstantin of Rostov and those of Grand Prince Yaroslav. Konstantin's eldest son, Vasil'ko, it will be remembered, had been executed by the Tatars after the battle on the river Sit' in 1238. His major share of Konstantin's patrimony, Rostov, fell not to his eldest brother, but, according to the rule of primogeniture which from 1238 onwards seems to have been observed in the main by the descendants of Konstantin during the thirteenth century, to his eldest son Boris, while the northern district of Beloozero fell to his second son Gleb (see below, p. 153). The fate of Konstantin's second son, Vsevolod of Yaroslavl', is not known; probably he died in 1238 or shortly afterwards, as nothing more is heard of him after the brief announcement in the chronicle to the effect that he fought at the battle on the Sit'. His eldest son Vasily evidently became ruler of Yaroslavl'.[2] The third son Vladimir, the only one known to have survived the events of 1238, was prince of Uglich when he died in 1249.[3] Thus the three branches of the descendants of Konstantin ruled in the vast north-western sector of Suzdalia, with the senior branch in Rostov and Beloozero, the second in Yaroslavl', and the third in Uglich.

Very little is known about the activities of Grand Prince Yaroslav's children before 1238. Fedor, the eldest, died aged 14 in 1233. Aleksandr, born in about 1220,[4] spent most of his childhood and youth in Northern Pereyaslavl', but he was also exposed to long sojourns in Novgorod with his father and elder brother. In 1236 Yaroslav left him as sole ruler in Novgorod when he set off south to try his hand in Kiev (see above, p. 75), and there he evidently remained for the next four years, and peacefully too – the Novgorodian chronicler records no disturbances in the town until Aleksandr left after a disagreement with the citizens in 1240 (see below, p. 104). As for the other sons of Yaroslav – Andrey, Konstantin, Yaroslav, Daniil and Mikhail – the chronicles first mention them in 1239 as having survived the Tatar invasion.[5] The same applies to Svyatoslav's son Dmitry. Ivan's son Mikhail is mentioned only by Tatishchev under the years 1276 and 1281 as prince of Starodub,[6] which he must have inherited from his father.

The only outward sign of Tatar occupation, as has been pointed out above, was that all these rulers of the patrimonies of Suzdalia were obliged from time to time to travel to the headquarters of the Golden Horde at Saray to pay allegiance to the khan and to have their appointment as prince of this or that district confirmed. Altogether in the years 1242–52 no less than nineteen visits were paid by Suzdalian princes to Baty or his son Sartak, and on four occasions the princes concerned were made to make the long and arduous journey from Saray to the great khan in Karakorum. Two of the Rostov princes made the journey three times between 1242 and 1250, presumably to regularize changes of ownership which were taking place. Three southern princes are also recorded as having been summoned to the Horde: one to be killed there, a martyrdom which won him canonization (Mikhail of Chernigov in 1246),[7] one to pay an unexpectedly submissive homage to the khan (Daniil of Volynia-Galicia in 1245)[8] and one to be despatched for some unknown reason to Karakorum (Oleg of Ryazan' in 1243).[9] Even the grand prince of Vladimir had to go, and Yaroslav went twice – in 1243 to receive the patent for the throne of Vladimir ('O Yaroslav, may you be the senior of the princes in the Russian land', Baty is reported as saying to him)[10] and in 1245, with his two brothers and two of the princes of Rostov. On this occasion he was sent to Karakorum.

Yaroslav survived the Tatar invasion of Suzdalia by eight years. In this period it was only in 1239 that he showed any signs of the old aggressiveness which had so marked his career before the Tatar invasion. In that year he attacked the town of Kamenets on the Khomora river near the border of Kiev and Volynia. The aim of this extraordinary expedition to a town so remote from Suzdalian Vladimir becomes clear when we realize who was occupying it at the time. It would appear that none other than Mikhail of Chernigov, the current prince of Kiev, was there, having evacuated his wife and her retinue to this westernmost outpost of the territory of Kiev in face of the growing threat to the capital. The town itself was under Mikhail's cousin Izyaslav Vladimirovich, whom four years previously he had temporarily placed on the throne of Kiev (see above, pp. 74–5). Yaroslav's attack succeeded, and not surprisingly, for Mikhail could hardly have anticipated anything so unexpected from his old but by now distant enemy whom he had recently displaced in Kiev itself. Mikhail managed somehow to escape to Kiev. But Kamenets was taken, and Yaroslav led off Mikhail's wife and a number of his boyars in captivity to Vladimir.[11] It was an act of personal revenge and not of political expediency, and it availed Yaroslav little, for neither did he capture his old enemy, nor would it have made much difference if he had: Mikhail's days as a force in the politics of southern Russia were by now numbered.

This was not Yaroslav's only military act in 1239. Towards the end of the year we find him, perhaps while he was on his way back from Kamenets, fighting the Lithuanians, who had invaded Smolensk territory. There are no details of the encounter except the bald statement that Yaroslav defeated them and 'captured their prince', whoever he was; but the chronicle entry adds that he 'arranged the affairs of the people of Smolensk' (*Smol'nyany uryadiv*) and 'placed Prince Vsevolod [Mstislavich] on the throne'.[12] This act of interference in the affairs of Smolensk – evidently Yaroslav settled some dynastic problem there, perhaps replacing Svyatoslav Mstislavich, the last known ruler of Smolensk, with his brother – shows not only the decline of the power of the Rostislavichi, no longer a force to be reckoned with, but also the recognition by them of the authority of the grand prince of Vladimir.

However, it was virtually the last of his actions to be recorded – and indeed the last time a prince of Suzdalia was to influence the affairs of Smolensk. Apart from his visits to the Horde in 1243 and 1245, the chronicles mention no other activity on his part. What the results of the first of these visits in 1243 were, apart from his confirmation as senior prince, is hard to say. Perhaps he was given control not only over the districts of Suzdalia, but also over Kiev, as it appears that a governor of his, one Dmitr Eykovich, resided there in 1245.[13] But nothing more is heard of this his Kievan connection.

As for his second trip to the Golden Horde in 1245, the events connected with it are reported with such extreme brevity by the only two sources to mention it, the chronicle of Vladimir and the account of Friar John of Plano Carpini, Pope Innocent IV's envoy to Mongolia, that any explanation of them can only be hypothetical. All we know is that he was summoned by Baty, that he set off with two brothers and three nephews, that he was diverted to the capital of the empire, Karakorum in Mongolia, with a large retinue, most of whom perished on the way, and that he either died on the return journey (Russian chronicle version) or was poisoned in Karakorum (30 September 1246) by Great Khan Ogedey's widow (John of Plano Carpini's version).[14] Various explanations have been put forward by scholars: the Soviet historian Pashuto, for example, thinks that the fact that Yaroslav seemingly had agreed to talks with the Curia may well have been a reason for the poisoning, if such it was, as was also the desire of the great khan (Guyuk) and his mother to have their own creature on the throne of Vladimir;[15] the American historian Vernadsky, on the other hand, points to the 'tenseness of relations' between the new Great Khan Guyuk (Ogedey's son) and Baty and the possibility that the former considered Yaroslav the tool of the latter and therefore 'found it necessary to get rid of him quietly';[16] a further possibility is that Yaroslav in fact merely died from natural causes, from the exertions of the return journey, as did many of his retinue on the outward journey. On the whole the poisoning version of Innocent IV's envoy to Mongolia seems to be the most likely: after all John of Plano Carpini was there at the time and he would have had no trouble in obtaining the information from the surviving members of Yaroslav's suite; while the laconic statement of the vestigial remains of Yaroslav's own grand-princely chronicle to the effect that he 'died amongst foreigners while travelling from the great khans [i.e. from Karakorum]' represents in all probability the efforts of the contemporary chronicler – or, more likely, later editors – to avoid any mention of Tatar participation in his death, a typical show of unwillingness to offend the Tatars or to include in the record any information which might be construed by them as invidious.

If the last six years of Yaroslav's reign were marked by an untypical inactivity, almost, one might say, passivity, on his part, the same years saw the beginning of the career of his son Aleksandr. They were years of vigorous activity in the west and the north-west. Yaroslav had clearly entrusted his son with the defence of the frontiers of Novgorod and Pskov.

Already before the Tatar invasion pressure had been building up in these areas. During the first three decades of the thirteenth century the German Knights of the Catholic Order of Livonian Swordbearers, as they were known – later to be joined by the Teutonic Order (1237) – had gradually been pushing eastwards, north of the Western Dvina river, into what is now Estonia[17] (then called Chud') and Livonia (in the area of modern Latvia). But no raids into Russian territory are recorded from the beginning of the thirteenth century to the Tatar invasion: most of their military activities were directed either against the local Baltic tribes or against the ever-strengthening state of Lithuania. On their side the Lithuanians showed more and more aggressiveness, and frequent raids into the territories of Novgorod, Polotsk and Smolensk are recorded in the Russian chronicles during the 1220s and the 1230s. They were not, however, coordinated attacks, nor did they have as their goal the annexation of any Russian lands. Rather they were in the nature of razzias and their aim was to capture prisoners and to loot the countryside.

The true expansion of Lithuania can be said to have begun in 1238 with the accession of Mindovg (Mindaugas) as ruler. His policy was one of gradual penetration into the neighbouring territories, and although he achieved no success in gaining a foothold in the lands of Novgorod and Pskov, nevertheless he presented Aleksandr with more of a threat than did the Germans in the north. For the truly vulnerable districts of Russia were not Novgorod and Pskov or even the northern part of Smolensk at this time, but the crumbling principality of Polotsk, through which innumerable Lithuanian raiding parties had passed during the pre-Tatar period, and the old lands of Turov and Pinsk on the north-eastern borders of Volynia. The importance of the principality of Polotsk, sand-wiched between Smolensk, where Yaroslav in 1239 had shown signs of establishing his authority (see above, p. 100), and Lithuania, was recognized by Aleksandr, for in 1239 he married Aleksandra, the daughter of the senior prince of Polotsk, Bryacheslav. The marriage took place not in Polotsk itself, but, significantly, in the northernmost city of Smolensk, Toropets, one of the key towns in the defence of Novgorod and Smolensk territories against the inroads of Lithuanian raiders.[18] And Aleksandr maintained links with his wife's family in Polotsk – we know that his first-born son was in the easternmost town of Polotsk, Vitebsk, in 1245, when Aleksandr moved him to the safety of Novgorod in the face of a large-scale Lithuanian invasion.[19]

But there was nothing Aleksandr or Yaroslav could do to save Polotsk from the Lithuanians. Mindovg's centralizing policy and his conversion of the districts of some of the large landowners into service fiefs led to civil war between himself and his nephews, the princes of Zhemaytiya (Žemaitija) in north-western Lithuania. The vicissitudes of this internal war, in which the Teutonic Knights and Daniil of Galicia-Volynia were involved and which led to Mindovg's temporary conversion to Christianity and his acceptance of a crown from the archbishop of Riga, need not concern us here. All we need to note is that eventually it ended in the early 1250s with a truce being concluded by Mindovg's son Voyshelk (Vaišvilkas) according to the terms of which Black Russia – the westernmost district of Polotsk in the basin of the upper Neman and its tributaries – was recognized as part of Lithuania.[20] It was the beginning of Lithuania's vast expansion at the expense of the old lands of Kievan Russia: later in the thirteenth century and early in the fourteenth the remainder of the principality of Polotsk, the western portion of what had once been the principality of Turov-Pinsk on the upper reaches of the Pripyat' and the northern triangle of Volynia with Berest'e (Brest) on the middle Bug, were all annexed by Lithuania.

If Aleksandr was able to do so little to prevent the gradual lapse of Polotsk into Lithuanian dependency, he was at least successful in stopping any permanent breach of the frontiers of Novgorod and Pskov by Lithuanian raiders. After two attacks in 1239, on Kamno (Belyy kamen')[21] and Smolensk (see above, p. 100), he erected a number of fortifications along the Shelon' river,[22] south-west of Novgorod, to protect the city from invasions from the south. By far the greatest and most determined invasion of Russian territory took place in 1245. What started off as a raid on Bezhichi in the east and Torzhok developed into a full-scale pursuit over the eastern and southern areas of the land of Novgorod. As well as an army from Novgorod under Aleksandr, troops from Pskov, Tver' and Dmitrov took part. Two major battles took place, at Zhizhets (modern Zhizhitsa) and Usvyat (modern Usvyaty) in the north of Smolensk and the east of Polotsk respectively. More than eight Lithuanian 'princelings' were killed and any booty taken by them in the early stages was recaptured.[23] Only one more Lithuanian raid is recorded before Aleksandr's accession to the throne of Vladimir in 1252 and that was in 1248 when his brother Mikhail was killed and the 'princes of Suzdal'' defeated the Lithuanians at Zubtsov near the Smolensk border.[24]

Perhaps the best indication of what contemporaries thought about Aleksandr's dealings with this heathen enemy is to be found in his *Life*. Describing what was probably a fictitious invasion immediately after the battle on Lake Peypus in 1242 (see below, p. 105), the author writes:

At that time the [attacks of the] people of Lithuania were multiplied, and they began to lay waste the lands of Aleksandr. But he went out and slaughtered them. On one occasion he sallied forth and defeated seven armies in one sortie, and he killed a multitude of their princes and others he captured by hand. His service men (*slugy*), mocking them, bound them to the tails of their horses. And from then on they began to hold his name in awe.[25]

The author of Aleksandr's *Life* was even more expansive on his successes against the Swedes and the Germans. The two relatively minor victories over the Swedes on the river Neva (1240) (hence the sobriquet *Nevskiy* given him by a fifteenth-century chronicler) and over the German Knights on the ice of Lake Peypus (or the Chud' Lake – *Chudskoe ozero*) are blown up to epic proportions in the *Life*. They are given the full hagiographical treatment with prayers, visions of Saints Boris and Gleb, angelic aerial assistance, clichés and hyperbole. But the *Life* was written in all probability some forty years after the events themselves and it was written or commissioned by a man who had every reason to be antagonistic to the West, particularly to the Catholic West – Metropolitan Kirill. Kirill, whose career started as Daniil of Volynia-Galicia's chancellor, was sent in 1246 by his sponsor Daniil to be consecrated as metropolitan of Kiev to the oecumenical patriarch. He spent three to five years in Nicaea – Constantinople was still occupied by the Latins – and eventually returned not to south-west Russia but to the north where he remained for the last thirty years of his life as the firm supporter of Aleksandr in all his ventures. It is hardly surprising that after his sojourn in what was probably the most anti-Catholic centre in the world and with the knowledge that his former master Daniil had not only begun flirting with the Curia in 1246 but had eventually accepted a crown from the pope, he should in his attempt to pave the way for Aleksandr's canonization glorify in his hero the mighty champion of the Orthodox faith, the great fighter against Catholic aggression.[26]

The ascertainable facts about Aleksandr's dealings with the West are somewhat different from those given in his *Life*. In the first half of July 1240 a Swedish force consisting of Swedes, '*Murmane*' (Norwegians?: perhaps a few Norwegian knights) and Finns and headed by 'a prince and bishops' landed on the banks of the Neva river. Why the Swedes chose to invade at this particular juncture is hard to say. The Soviet historian Shaskol'sky, who specializes in Russo-Scandinavian relations in the early period and who is ever anxious to stress the 'Western menace', considers that it was part of a concerted plan hatched by the Swedes, the Germans and the Danes and master-minded by the pope. Suspecting Russian weakness after the Tatar invasion, they hoped – and here Shaskol'sky draws on the only Russian source apart from the *Life* of Aleksandr, the Novgorod First Chronicle – to gain a foothold on the banks of the Neva and Lake Ladoga and then move south and conquer Novgorod and its territory.[27] However, there is no evidence of any coordination of action between the Swedes, the Germans and the Danes, nor is there anything to show that this was more than a continuation of the Russo-Swedish conflict for mastery over Finland and Karelia.[28]

The battle took place on 15 July and ended in a victory for Aleksandr and the troops he had hurriedly mustered from Novgorod and the district of Ladoga. The chronicle talks of 'a great multitude' of enemy killed, but also mentions the remarkably small number of Novgorodian casualties – twenty. This and the fact that neither the Suzdalian chronicle (the Lavrent'evskiy), nor any of the Swedish sources make any mention whatsoever of the occasion would lead one to believe that the 'great battle' was little more than one of those periodic clashes between Swedish raiders and Novgorodian defenders which took place from time to time in the thirteenth and fourteenth centuries. It is indeed surprising that the 'great force' of the Swedes and the presence of 'prince' and 'bishops' in their army completely escaped the notice of any chronicler except the Novgorodian.[29]

While the Novgorodians welcomed Aleksandr's assistance in dealing with the Swedish intrusion, it is clear that he had his enemies in Novgorod – and in Pskov too – as the subsequent events of 1240–42 show. In the same year as the Neva battle a force of German Knights assisted by local inhabitants from southern Estonia and by the prince-ruler of Pskov himself, Yaroslav Vladimirovich, seized the important fortress of Izborsk south-west of Pskov. The local Pskovites tried to recapture the town, but the Germans defeated them, marched on Pskov and occupied it, when the *posadnik*, evidently in league with Yaroslav Vladimirovich, opened the gates to them.

Yaroslav Vladimirovich and the Germans had their supporters in Novgorod too: no sooner had Aleksandr returned to Novgorod from the Neva than 'great sedition (*kramola velia*) arose' in the city. What the 'sedition' was all about is not stated in any of the sources, but it was enough to make Aleksandr 'fall out' (*rospretisya* is the verb used) with the Novgorodians and leave for Pereyaslavl' in a huff 'with his mother, his wife and all his court [i.e. his army and administration]'.[30] The 'German party', if such it was, had clearly won the day. In the winter of the same year we find the Germans making determined inroads in the north of Novgorod territory. Operating in the area of the Luga river, they took Tesov, 35 kilometers from Novgorod, and built a fortress at Kopor'e east of the mouth of the Luga and some 16 kilometres from the Gulf of Finland. As usual the Novgorodians could do nothing without a prince to lead their troops and to provide his own army. So anxious messengers were sent to the grand prince asking for Aleksandr to be returned to them. Yaroslav offered them his second son Andrey. But the Novgorodians would have none of this and tried again. This time they were successful. But when Aleksandr arrived in 1241 to the joy of the anti-German faction, he took drastic measures. He hanged 'many of the instigators of sedition' in Novgorod and, having captured Kopor'e, executed the local 'traitors' there who had assisted the Germans.[31]

Pskov presented more of a threat than the German presence in the north, and Aleksandr, this time with his brother Andrey, marched on Pskov as soon as he had dealt with Kopor'e. The town was taken with little difficulty and Aleksandr, determined to exploit success, crossed the frontier into Estonian-German territory. A confrontation was inevitable. After a Novgorodian reconnaissance detachment had been soundly beaten, Aleksandr and Andrey drew up their army on what some of the sources say was the ice of Lake Peypus. The German Knights, supported by Estonian conscripts, attacked in wedge formation, penetrated the Russian lines, but were defeated (5 April 1242). The prisoners were led back to Pskov. Later in the year the Germans agreed to relinquish any Russian territory they still occupied and to exchange prisoners of war.[32]

So ended what many historians have called one of the great decisive Russian victories of the thirteenth century, the crushing of the crusade of the Teutonic Knights against Novgorod and Pskov, the rout of the Germans, the heroic defence of the western frontiers against papal aggression, the turning-point in relations between Russia and the West, and so on. Many of the descriptions of the battle itself – in the *Life* and in the later chronicle versions – are decorated with details which are clearly no more than fruits of the writers' imaginations. Numbers of participants are exaggerated. Comparisons are made with Moses' victory over Amalek and David's over the Philistines; the Pskovites are upbraided for their stupidity in allowing the Germans to take their city and are told that if they ever forget Aleksandr's great feat they will be 'likened unto the Jews whom the Lord fed in the wilderness with manna and baked quails'.

But was this so great a victory? Was it a turning-point in Russian history? Or was it simply Metropolitan Kirill, or whoever wrote the *Life*, blowing up Aleksandr's victories in the west to compensate for what must have struck many of his contemporaries as his subsequent kowtowing to the Tatars? As usual, the contemporary sources are not particularly helpful. The Novgorod First Chronicle gives the fullest account, while in the Suzdalian chronicle, in which, for this particular entry, no elements of Aleksandr's personal grand-princely annals have survived, the whole affair is played down – so much so that the only hero to emerge is not Aleksandr but his brother Andrey: 'Grand Prince Yaroslav sent his son Andrey to Novgorod the Great to help Aleksandr against the Germans, and they defeated them beyond Pskov on the lake and took many prisoners. And Andrey returned to his father with honour'.[33]

Again, the only indication of the dimensions of the battle comes from the number of casualties quoted, this time only of the enemy: the Novgorod First Chronicle reports '400 Germans killed and 50 taken prisoner' as well as 'innumerable Chud' (Estonians)'. If these 450 were knights, then the number is clearly a gross exaggeration, for at the time of the battle the most the two Orders were able to field was little over one hundred,[34] and probably many, if not most, of these were engaged elsewhere fighting other enemies in Courland under the Landmaster of Livonia, Dietrich von Grüningen.[35] In any case the oldest and most original western source, the Livonian Rhymed Chronicle, written in the last decade of the thirteenth century, says that only twenty knights died and six were taken prisoner – hardly indicative of a major encounter even if we take into consideration epic minimalization of the home side's losses.

Although Aleksandr's claim to be considered the mighty Russian bastion against German, and particularly papal, aggression in the west cannot be taken as seriously as many Soviet historians would like us to take it – especially those writing at the time of and just after the Second World War[36] – nevertheless he showed himself to be competent, shrewd and firm during the last five years of his father's life, ready to quit Novgorod and leave it to its own devices when faced with tough political opposition, yet quick to defend the frontiers when the need arose. Had his father outlived his own two brothers, Svyatoslav and Ivan, Aleksandr might well have succeeded him as grand prince: he would have been next in line according to the law of succession by seniority. But Yaroslav died in Mongolia in 1246 (see above, pp. 100–1), and a period of bitter conflict between uncle and nephew, brother and brother ensued. Once again the inability of the princes – this time the relatively closely knit family nest of the Vsevolodovichi – to live in peace with one another contributed to their ultimate enfeeblement and to political instability in Suzdalia.

The events of the three years following Yaroslav's death are involved and reported, often highly contradictorily, from a number of different angles in a number of different sources.[37] What appears to have happened is as follows: Svyatoslav Vsevolodovich acceded to the grand-princely throne (1247), as was to be expected, when news of Yaroslav's death reached Suzdalia. All we know of his brief reign is that he 'placed his nephews in towns as their father Yaroslav had drawn up a contract for them' – in other words he merely confirmed the settlement of Yaroslav's will concerning his sons' patrimonies. Within a year of his accession he was ousted (1248), not by his younger brother Ivan, whose fate after his trip to the Golden Horde in 1245 is unknown, nor by Yaroslav's eldest son Aleksandr, but by his second eldest Andrey. No reasons are given in any source for this the first breach of the order of lateral succession by seniority since Konstantin Vsevolodovich's accession to the grand-princely throne of Vladimir in 1216 (see above, p. 49). It was presumably a usurpation, a military coup, though where Andrey got his troops from or indeed what patrimony he had been left by his father is not known. In fact nothing is known of Andrey's early life except that he was born some time after 1220 and that he was sent by Yaroslav to fight against the Germans in 1242 (see above, p. 105).

It was not to be expected that Aleksandr would take his younger brother's usurpation of the throne lightly or that Svyatoslav would remain quietly in the background. But neither Aleksandr nor Svyatoslav were able to do anything about it without the support of the Tatars. Nor could Andrey retain his throne without a patent. So all three made their way separately to Saray. Andrey was the first to go, followed closely by Aleksandr. Baty despatched them both to Karakorum in Mongolia. What happened there it is hard to say. Evidently there was heated haggling, the outcome of which was that the regent, Guyuk's widow, decided to give Andrey the patent for the grand-princely throne of Vladimir, while Aleksandr was granted 'Kiev and all the land of Rus'' (i.e. all southern Russia). One can only guess at the reasons for this support of the younger son, and Pashuto's guess is as good as any: the regent, Oghul-Ghaimish, in his opinion, was hostile to Baty and as she considered that Aleksandr had too close links with the Golden Horde, she supported Andrey.[38] As for Svyatoslav, little more is heard of him. In the autumn of 1250, three years after being ousted, he set off to try his luck in Saray. Nothing more is known of him until his death in February 1253.[39]

Andrey and Aleksandr came back to Russia in the winter of 1249. In spite of his appointment to the throne of Kiev, Aleksandr returned with Andrey to Vladimir, and left for Novgorod in the following year.[40] Practically nothing is known of Andrey's five-year rule as grand prince. There are no indications of conflict with any of his brothers, and if indeed he was obliged to struggle for the retention of his throne, as was only too likely, his or later chroniclers saw to it that all traces of discord were removed from the record. All we hear concerning his private life is that Metropolitan Kirill officiated at his marriage to the daughter of Daniil of Volynia-Galicia in the winter of 1250–51.

Irritatingly reticent though the sources may be, it is clear that trouble was brewing in the last three years of Andrey's reign. In 1252 the crisis occurred. In that year Aleksandr went to the Horde; a double Tatar expedition was despatched: under Nevryuy against Andrey, and under Kuremsha against Daniil of Galicia.[41] The latter had little difficulty in resisting the Tatars, but Andrey and his brother Yaroslav were defeated at the battle of Northern Pereyaslavl' (May or July 1252). Andrey, after seeking refuge in vain in Novgorod, fled to Sweden; and Aleksandr returned to Vladimir with 'seniority over all his brothers' to assume the grand-princely throne. Such are the bare details which can be extricated from the numerous sources, many of which contain fragments surviving from divers grand-princely chronicles: those of Andrey, Svyatoslav, Aleksandr and Yaroslav Yaroslavich. The facts are abundantly clear but the motives behind the actions of the two main protagonists, Andrey and Aleksandr, can only be arrived at by deduction.

Most of the sources, doctored, sometimes clumsily, at a later stage to justify Aleksandr's behaviour, portray Andrey merely as the hapless victim of circumstances. Defeated by the Tatars at Pereyaslavl', he is shown as having no alternative but to flee the country; in the Lavrent'evskiy Chronicle account – a curious and jumbled mixture of Aleksandr's chronicle and faint fragments from that of Andrey – he is made, even *before* the appearance of the Tatars, to take council with his advisers and decide to 'flee rather than serve the khans'. Having criticized Andrey for the laxity of his rule, the sixteenth-century compiler of the Nikon Chronicle, with equally little concern for chronology of events, puts a moving little speech into Andrey's mouth, again *before* the battle: 'O Lord!

Why do we squabble amongst ourselves and lead the Tatars against one another [but nobody had done yet!]? It were better for me to flee to a foreign land than to be friends with, and to serve, the Tatars.' But even in these garbled and largely fictitious accounts there are hints of Andrey's true motives: 'it were better not to be friends with and not to serve the Tatars' – this surely must be construed as an expression of Andrey's desire to resist Tatar domination, not to cooperate, not to become a vassal of the khans. He was not alone. All the accounts stress the close cooperation between Andrey and his brother Yaroslav, both of whom were beaten at the battle of Pereyaslavl'.; nor was it by chance that the punitive force sent against Andrey's father-in-law Daniil happened to coincide with that of Nevryuy's expedition. Can we not then assume that resistance to the Golden Horde was envisaged by at least two of the senior princes of Suzdalia with the backing of the rulers of Volynia and Galicia? One distinguished Soviet orientalist has even gone so far as to posit an armed uprising between 1249 and 1252, an uprising which was suppressed by the khan with the connivance of Aleksandr.[42]

What of Aleksandr's exploits in 1252? Not one chronicler of course imputes to him any blame for the defeat of his brothers, just as later in the fourteenth century none of the sycophantic Muscovite chroniclers dared to hint at Ivan I's responsibility for the Tatar destruction of Tver' in 1328.[43] But the coupling of Aleksandr's trip to the Horde with the despatch of Nevryuy's punitive expedition and the sandwiching of the military action between his arrival at Saray and his triumphant departure for Vladimir leave little doubt as to his complicity. Quoting perhaps from an earlier source which escaped the chronicles, the eighteenth-century historian Tatishchev adds considerable plausibility to the whole story by making Aleksandr complain of his brother to Baty's son Sartak for 'deceiving the khan, taking the grand principality from the senior prince [Aleksandr] and not paying in full the taxes and tributes to the khan'.[44]

Aleksandr returned in triumph to Vladimir where he was met 'at the Golden Gates [by] the metropolitan and all the abbots and the citizens'. There he was placed 'upon the throne of his father Yaroslav', and 'there was great joy in the town of Vladimir and in all the land of Suzdalia'.[45] His return marked the end of a period of conflict of interests among the descendants of Vsevolod III and the beginning of a new era of Russia's subjugation to Tatar overlordship. Andrey and his supporters were a finished force. True, he was eventually to return from Sweden and to be given Suzdal' and Nizhniy Novgorod as a patrimony by Aleksandr after some sort of reconciliation had been patched up between them. And true his ally Yaroslav was eventually to become grand prince of Vladimir. But nevertheless this was the end of any form of organized resistance to the Tatars by the rulers of Russia for a long time to come. It was the beginning of Russia's real subservience to the Golden Horde, which was to last for over a century and a quarter. The so-called 'Tatar Yoke' began not so much with Baty's invasion of Russia as with Aleksandr's betrayal of his brothers.

The fourteen years between the Tatar victory over Yury Vsevolodovich on the Sit' and the defeat of his nephews Andrey and Yaroslav at Pereyaslavl' were also marked, as has been pointed out earlier (see above, p. 98), by yet another sweeping change in the structure of all the Russian lands — the virtual end of political relations between north and south. All we know about the links between Vladimir and Kiev during this period is that in 1245 Kiev, according to the not always reliable Ipat'evskiy Chronicle, was ruled by Grand Prince Yaroslav's 'boyar Dmitr Eykovich' (see above, p. 100). In 1248 or 1249, however, Aleksandr was given nominal control over Kiev by Guyuk's widow. But we know that he never went there. He returned instead from Mongolia to Vladimir and Novgorod.[46] From then onwards there are no known political links between Suzdalia and the south,[47] no reports of any missions to the old capital, and only formal connections between the head of the church, who was still 'metropolitan of Kiev and all Rus'', and his see. Kiev and the south had as it were slipped from the hands of the rulers of north-east Russia, and even the princes of Volynia and Galicia showed little interest in their eastern neighbour. In just over a century Lithuania was to absorb most of the old Kievan empire in the south as well as the eastern half of Volynia: from then on the struggle for control over the rich Ukrainian lands was to drag on for centuries, involving Moscow in exhausting wars with the West.

The beginning of Aleksandr Nevskiy's reign was in more ways than one a cataclysmic turning-point in the history of Russia.

THE REIGN OF ALEKSANDR NEVSKIY 1252–1263

The brief reign of Aleksandr Yaroslavich as grand prince of Vladimir followed a predictable pattern. It was marked by precisely the sort of policy of appeasement Aleksandr's previous activity would lead us to expect: strong links with the Tatars of the Golden Horde and obedience to the every wish of the khan; decisive dealings with the West; an uncompromising attitude to the Catholic Church and a firm support of the Orthodox Church; a no-nonsense policy towards oppositional elements in Novgorod; swift suppression of any signs of rebellion or of opposition to his and the Tatars' policy; resolute control exercised over his relatives. It was exactly the sort of reign one could reconstruct with hindsight from the exuberant praise of whoever wrote the *Life* some twenty years after his death. Unfortunately, the less unreliable sources, the chronicles, are remarkably elliptical for this period, as indeed they are for the preceding one — not because this was any more an age of cultural barrenness than any other preceding period of Russian history, but because of the peculiar quirks of the lateral system of succession: the fact that Aleksandr was followed as grand prince by his two brothers, one of whom was undoubtedly hostile to him, then by his two sons, then by the hostile brother's son, meant that the details of his private chronicle were erased or altered, then reconstituted, and then again erased or altered. Small wonder that most information about his reign comes not from the chronicle of Vladimir, but from the somewhat more objective Novgorod chronicle. The *Life*, as might be expected, adds nothing to what is known from the chronicles. Indeed, it severely compresses or simply omits anything which might have been construed as embarrassing or damaging to Aleksandr's image.

Even in spite of Andrey's usurpation of the throne of Vladimir in 1249, Aleksandr was never faced with a succession problem vis-à-vis his cousins, the Rostov branch of the Vsevolodovichi, the descendants of Konstantin. According to the curious law of 'succession by seniority' which we can assume held, or at any rate was observed, throughout much of the thirteenth century for the throne of Vladimir, the right of seniority (i.e. to be grand prince) passed horizontally from brother to brother, and when one generation of princes became defunct the throne passed to the eldest son of the eldest brother. However, the children of those princes who predeceased either their father or their ruling uncles were together with their descendants automatically debarred for ever from the succession. This is precisely what happened to the senior branch of the Vsevolodovichi. The two eldest sons of Konstantin, Vasil'ko of Rostov and Vsevolod of Yaroslavl', had both died in 1238; as a result all their descendants were out of the race. As for the third son, Vladimir of Uglich, he died in 1249, thus predeceasing Svyatoslav, who, although he lost the throne in the preceding year, did not die until 1253. Consequently his children too were seemingly debarred from the succession to the title of grand prince. As Yury's children all died in 1238 leaving no offspring, the field was open for the descendants of Yaroslav, and indeed the title of grand prince of Vladimir, later of Moscow and all Russia, was to remain in his branch of the family until the end of the sixteenth century: no members of the family of Svyatoslav or Ivan were ever to lay claim to the golden throne. They too for some reason were excluded from the succession.

It is hard to say what precisely were the relations between Aleksandr and Konstantin's offspring, the princes of Rostov, Yaroslavl', Uglich and Beloozero. Did they form a completely separate part of the princely family with its own laws, its own ties of fealty? Or were they under some sort of obligation to the grand prince of Vladimir? No records of treaties exist, and one can only hazard a guess as to the nature of this relationship. It would, however, appear that in some way or other the Konstantinovichi were under a form of service contract to the grand prince. There was a precedent for this: in 1227 Grand Prince Yury disposed of his nephew Vsevolod Konstantinovich, sending him off to rule Southern Pereyaslavl' as though he were his son or younger brother. And during Aleksandr's reign we find much the same sort of thing happening: in 1256 he sent the senior prince, Boris of Rostov, to the Golden Horde with the delicate mission of 'asking forgiveness' for Andrey who had returned from Sweden in the previous year.[48] Two years later Boris was in the group of princes who set out to the Horde under Aleksandr's leadership, and in 1259 he went with Aleksandr and Andrey to Novgorod to enforce the Tatar census in the city (see below, p. 117). On all these occasions he appears to have acted as Aleksandr's subordinate.

Aleksandr's two uncles, Svyatoslav and Ivan, gave him no trouble, or no trouble that was recorded. Svyatoslav, after a fruitless visit to the Horde in

1250, presumably to complain of his nephew's usurpation of the throne, died in early 1253 (see above, p. 107). All he had to leave to his only son Dmitry was his original tiny patrimony of Yur'ev Pol'skiy tucked away between Vladimir and Pereyaslavl' – Suzdal' he had either abandoned on accepting the throne of Vladimir or lost when ousted in 1249.[49] As for Ivan, he died some time after 1247, probably even after 1264 (see below, p. 128); so insignificant was he that the chronicles do not even mention his death – a rare occurrence for a prince's demise. His son Mikhail inherited his, the least of all the principalities in Suzdalia – Starodub on the Klyaz'ma, east of Vladimir.

Aleksandr's two brothers, Andrey and Yaroslav, however, played a more significant role. After his defeat at the hands of the Tatars in 1252 Andrey fled to Novgorod, hoping to find support among Aleksandr's opponents there. But he misjudged the mood of the city: there had been no open conflicts with Aleksandr in Novgorod since 1242, and in 1251 a new archbishop, Dalmat, had been consecrated by the metropolitan in the presence of Aleksandr. Perhaps too at the time the office of *posadnik* was in the hands of a representative of the 'greater' boyars, who were later to prove the mainstay of Aleksandr's supporters in the city (see below, p. 115). At any rate the Novgorodians were in no mood to irritate the defender of their frontiers. In Pskov, his next port of call, he was given a more friendly welcome and was allowed to await the arrival of his wife who had managed to leave Vladimir and escape the Tatars. From there he went to Revel' (Tallinn) on the Baltic coast, whence he travelled to a safe refuge in Catholic Sweden.

Andrey's ally, his brother Yaroslav, was less fortunate. After the battle of Pereyaslavl' in 1252 his children were taken prisoner by the Tatars and his wife and the commander of his army were killed by them. Somehow or other he managed to get back to his patrimonial town of Tver' near the Novgorod border. But even there he was not safe. In early 1254 he was on the run. He first fled 'with his boyars' to Ladoga in the north of Novgorod territory, intending perhaps to join his brother Andrey in Sweden from there. But for some reason his plans changed, and from Ladoga he proceeded to Pskov, always a haven for elements hostile to the controlling party in Novgorod or the grand prince of Vladimir. His arrival in Pskov coincided with a radical change of mood amongst the ruling elements in Novgorod – perhaps with the appointment of the new *posadnik*, Anan'ya, an opponent of the pro-Aleksandr party. He was brought from Pskov by the Novgorodians and placed upon the throne of Novgorod evacuated by Aleksandr's son Vasily, whom they drove out as a gesture of defiance directed against the grand prince. It was a moment of crisis and revolt in Novgorod. What happened to Yaroslav it is hard to say. The chronicler merely states that he was reported as having fled earlier in the proceedings. At any rate nothing more is heard of him for some three years. Presumably he returned to Tver' and some sort of reconciliation between him and Aleksandr was patched up.[50]

Aleksandr could not hope peacefully to rule Suzdalia with his two brothers in direct opposition. Andrey and Yaroslav obviously enjoyed considerable support among the population of the Suzdalian principalities as well as in Novgorod and Pskov, and the inhabitants of the larger cities, as was later to become all too evident, were clearly unwilling to go along with Aleksandr's policy of appeasement and his support for Tatar control over their lives and their pockets. Furthermore, a Swedish invasion, or worse a joint German-Swedish invasion, backed by Andrey and with internal support from Yaroslav, was the last thing Aleksandr wished to be faced with at the beginning of his difficult and precarious reign. The only solution was to make his peace with his two brothers, and this he did with all speed.

Andrey was the first to be dealt with. Some sort of inducement was necessary to persuade him to return, and it seems likely that the bait included the town and district of Suzdal', vacated some time earlier by his uncle Svyatoslav. He returned to Russia in 1255 and was warmly welcomed by his brother Aleksandr. According to Tatishchev – the only source to mention his return – Aleksandr was having second thoughts about granting him Suzdal'. It was not because he feared his brother's potential power as prince of Suzdal' – the reconciliation seems to have been complete – but because he had not obtained the khan's approval for his return to favour.[51] The installation of Andrey in Suzdal' had to wait for at least two years: in 1255 Aleksandr was too absorbed with troubles in Novgorod, and it was only in 1256 that he was able to send Boris of Rostov to the Horde with a request for the new Khan Ulaghchi's 'forgiveness' of Andrey and approval.[52] In the meantime Andrey was given the additional towns of Gorodets on the Volga and the new town of Nizhniy Novgorod founded by his uncle Yury on the extreme eastern border of Suzdalia: he was taken there to be installed in 1256.[53] From then on until his death in 1264 we hear little of 'Andrey of Suzdal''.[54] All we know is that he twice accompanied his elder brother on delicate missions – to the Golden Horde in 1258 and to Novgorod in 1259 to enforce acceptance of the Tatar tax-collectors (see below, p. 118). Aleksandr had converted him from a dangerous rival and rebel to a complaint service prince.

Yaroslav's career after the Novgorod débâcle of 1255 seems to have been very similar to that of Andrey after his return from Sweden. In 1258 we find him travelling with Aleksandr to the Golden Horde. In the following year Aleksandr had the good sense not to take him with him on his mission to Novgorod, but in 1262 he accompanied Aleksandr's son Dmitry in the campaign against Yur'ev[55] (see below, p. 114). No more is heard of him until his accession to the throne of Vladimir in 1263.

If Aleksandr had to tread warily with his two brothers, he fostered and enjoyed the warm support of the Orthodox Church throughout his reign. The cooperation of Metropolitan Kirill was unflagging, and Aleksandr could hardly have wished for a truer ally. The metropolitan met him with all the church dignitaries when he arrived in Vladimir from the Horde in 1252, he crowned him grand prince, he even accompanied him on one of his military campaigns,[56] he buried him with full honours, he pronounced a funeral oration over him ('The sun of the land of Suzdal' has set'[57]), he resided for most of the time in his city of Vladimir rather than in the metropolitan see of Kiev. Most important of all, in 1261 he established a bishopric in Saray, the capital of the Golden Horde, thus providing a constant link between khan and Church in Suzdalia as well as a handy diplomatic link with the Byzantine empire.[58] Altogether the Russian Church looked eastwards rather than westwards. Symbolically enough, Aleksandr's *Life* contains a curious incident which indicates only too well the political and ideological trend of the Orthodox Church at the time. 'At one time', the narrative runs, 'envoys from the pope . . . came to him saying, "Our pope speaks thus: 'We have heard that you are a pious and glorious prince and that your land is great. For this reason we have sent you two of the most skilled of the twelve cardinals, Gald and Gemont. May you listen to their teaching concerning the law of God.'"' Aleksandr's answer to this offer of conversion to Catholicism was predictably blunt: 'We know all this full well and we are not accepting any teaching from you.'[59]

The Church's attitude is hardly unexpected. The clergy had everything to lose from exacerbating relations with the Tatars and had little to gain from close relations with the West. For the Church was the one institution that was not subject to the census. Taxation and conscription were spared it from the first. When in 1257 the Tatar census officials 'counted all the Suzdalian land and the land of Ryazan' and Murom' and divided the country into tens, hundreds, thousands and myriads for the purpose of determining the numbers of taxpayers and recruits for the Mongol armies, members of the Church were specifically excluded: 'The only ones they did not count were the abbots, the monks, the priests, the *kriloshane* [servitors, officials, readers, singers or perhaps just minor clergy?], [those] who look towards the holy Mother of God and towards the Lord'.[60] Whether these latter categories included all those living on church or monastic estates, or whether it simply meant any layman employed in a church or a monastery, clearly the chronicle entry implies a vast degree of protection for ecclesiastical personnel and property. Such a privilege, later to be encapsulated in various Tatar immunity charters, meant that the Church enjoyed a freedom and protection unknown to other sections of society in Russia. Under such circumstances the Church could hardly be expected to do anything but afford Aleksandr all possible support in the pursuance of his pro-Tatar policy and to foster in his *Life* the image of him as the great champion of Orthodoxy in the face of papal aggression.

His military encounters with the West, or such few as are reported in the contemporary chronicles, read like a continuation of his early career: there were the same enemies – Lithuanians, Germans, Swedes – and much the same areas of conflict – the principality of Smolensk and the west and north-west districts of Novgorod territory. Nothing seems to have changed in this curiously resultless border skirmishing: as before, the Lithuanians proved to be the most dangerous and destructive. They attacked deep into Novgorod territory (Torzhok, 1258) and into Smolensk (Toropets, 1253; Smolensk, 1258). But nothing came of these forays, and eventually, in 1262, Grand Prince Mindovg's policy towards Suzdalia took a radical turn. In that year he broke off all relations with Rome and the Teutonic Knights and concluded a treaty with Aleksandr,[61] as a result of which a joint Lithuanian-Polotskian army joined in the Russian attack on Yur'ev (Tartu, Dorpat) (see below). Only the murder of Mindovg, of his nephew Tovtivil (Tautvilas) of Polotsk and of two of his sons, and the accession of Voyshelk, Mindovg's son, as grand prince of Lithuania put an end to what might have been a fruitful alliance.[62]

The German Knights were less active. Their only military venture was an unsuccessful attack on Pskov in 1253.[63] Indeed the initiative seems to have been rather on the side of the Russians. Not only did they counter-attack across the Narova river in 1253 after driving the Germans from Pskov, but nine years later they mounted a large and highly successful invasion of German territory. The expedition, nominally under Aleksandr's youthful son Dmitry, consisted of Novgorodian, Tverite, Polotskian and Lithuanian detachments. The combined army succeeded in capturing Yur'ev (Tartu, Dorpat) one of the easternmost German-held towns in southern Estonia, just west of Lake Peypus.[64] It was a major setback for the Teutonic Knights.

As ineffectual as the Germans were the Swedes. Their only approach to Russian territory occurred in 1256 when, perhaps in answer to a call by Pope Alexander IV for a general crusade against the 'heathens' of eastern Europe,[65] they attempted to build a fortress on the Narova river with a party of Finnish auxiliaries (Em' and Sum') and perhaps a detachment of Danes.[66] All the Novgorodians had to do was to send to Suzdalia for an army and to muster their own local forces. It was enough to scare the Swedes, who 'hearing of this fled beyond the sea'. That same winter Aleksandr led a force consisting of Suzdalian and Novgorodian troops first to Kopor'e, then to southern Finland. Although somewhat curiously and ambiguously reported in the Novgorod Chronicle – the metropolitan accompanied him as far as Kopor'e; the Novgorodians 'did not know where the prince was going'; 'their route was bad, as though they knew neither day nor night' – the expeditionary force managed to slaughter and capture a satisfactory number of Finns and 'all returned safely', the cliché normally employed to indicate a not unsuccessful campaign. Even though the expedition did not achieve the success it set out to achieve, it led to the cessation of Swedish inroads for a quarter of a century.

*　　*　　*　　*

Neither Aleksandr's relations with the members of his clan, nor his dealings with the Orthodox Church, nor his military activities give anything like the whole picture of his overall policy, of his fundamental attitude to the great problems of the age, of his answer to the fearful questions: what stance should Russia take within the Mongol empire? What should be the attitude of Suzdalia, Novgorod and Pskov to the khans of the Golden Horde? Should the grand prince of Vladimir, as virtual suzerain of Novgorod and all the territories north of the Oka, strive for independence from Saray and Karakorum and attempt to unite all the Russians within his sphere of influence with the ultimate aim of rejecting the overlordship of the Horde? Or should he submit to the demands of the khans, however humiliating they might be, avoid all possible military confrontation with the Tatars and thus be permitted to exercise a certain amount of limited freedom in the internal management of the grand principality? In order to understand Aleksandr's position – or perhaps predicament – and to attempt to glimpse the goal of his statesmanship, if such it can be called, we must investigate his dealings with Novgorod in the crisis years of 1255, 1257 and 1259/60 and examine his attitude to the great uprising of 1262 in the northern cities of Russia.

Nothing is known of internal conflicts within Novgorod for the decade following the battle on Lake Peypus (1242). The chronicler makes no mention of any 'upheaval' or 'revolt' during these ten years; it looks as though the 'treasonable' activities of certain anti-Aleksandr elements in the city in the early 1240s were effectively silenced for the time being by Aleksandr's uncompromising treatment of them (see above, pp. 104–5). However, there was still considerable opposition to Aleksandr and all he stood for, particularly amongst those sections of the population which favoured strong links with the West. While Aleksandr was nominally in control of Novgorod before he became grand prince, there was little the opposition could or dared do: for much of the time Aleksandr was either in Novgorod itself or in his patrimony of Pereyaslavl', close enough for him to quell any signs of incipient trouble. But when, shortly after his accession to the throne of Vladimir in 1252, he appointed his eldest son Vasily as prince of Novgorod,[67] the hostile elements in the city realized that the time had come to take action. For Vasily could not have been much more than twelve at the time – Aleksandr's marriage to Aleksandra of Polotsk took place in 1239.

An opportunity soon presented itself. As has been mentioned above, in early 1254 Aleksandr's brother Yaroslav, who had allied himself with Andrey in 1252, fled from his patrimony of Tver' and after a brief stay in Ladoga moved to Pskov. From there he was summoned to Novgorod in 1255 by members of the anti-Aleksandr party, who drove out Vasily and put Yaroslav on the throne in his place. Aleksandr's reaction was immediate: he collected an army and marched on the city. The chronicler quite clearly differentiates between the two parties in Novgorod. On the one hand there were the 'greater' boyars, who supported Aleksandr; on the other the 'lesser' boyars headed by the current *posadnik*, Anan'ya Feofilaktovich, and supported by the 'common people' (*chern'*), the 'well-to-do' (*zhit'i*) and the merchants: it was they who had engineered the ousting of Vasily and the invitation of Yaroslav, who by this time had fled the city. Aleksandr immediately made his demands known: the hand over of his 'enemies'. Both sides had armed forces drawn up and both held assemblies (*veche*) in different parts of the town at which their demands and counter-demands were voiced. At first the 'lesser' boyar party was determined to 'stand to a man and to [sacrifice] life or [suffer] death for Novgorod's justice, for the fatherland', while the 'greater' boyars were preparing to 'defeat the lesser boyars' and 'to bring in the prince [Aleksandr] according to their will'. Somehow or other bloodshed was avoided, thanks perhaps to the intervention of the archbishop. In the face of determined opposition by the 'lesser' boyars and the *posadnik*, Aleksandr dropped his demand for the surrender of all his 'enemies' and merely requested that Anan'ya be handed over. If his request was not complied with, he would no longer be 'prince of Novgorod', in other words he would tear up his contract with the city and would march against Novgorod 'in war' (*rat' yu*). After yet further negotiations – the archbishop and the *tysyatskiy* were sent to parley with Aleksandr – his demands were reduced to the relinquishing by Anan'ya of the office of *posadnik*. The compromise was accepted. Mikhalko Stepanovich, the grandson of the pro-Suzdalian Tverdislav (see above, p. 55) and the candidate of the 'greater' boyars, became *posadnik*. Aleksandr entered his city in triumph, was met by 'Archbishop Dalmat and all the priestly hierarchy' and 'sat upon his throne'. When he left Novgorod, however, he did not appoint his son as his representative for a whole year; he could rely on the new *posadnik* to keep the city in order.[68]

The significance of the events in Novgorod in 1255 cannot be overemphasized. This time it was not just a clash between rival factions on the question of who should be prince of Novgorod and who should be invited to defend the frontiers. It was an echo of the crisis of 1252 when the question had been: what is to be the attitude of the Russians to the Tatars, resist or submit? Surprising in this account is the evident strength of the opposition to Aleksandr. For three days between the grand prince's last two demands the city was on the brink of war. Both sides, fully armed, waited for the fighting to begin, and the party of the 'lesser' boyars, which clearly included the majority of the population, were prepared to lay down their lives 'for their rights (*za svoyu pravdu*)'. Significant too is the fact that it was Aleksandr and the 'greater' boyars who were forced to compromise in the end. The revolt of the Novgorodians can only have alerted Aleksandr to the danger within the country and the strength of the opposition to his policy of appeasement. Indeed it may well be that it was only as a result of the events of 1255 that he agreed to allow Andrey to return from Sweden. In fact in the only source to mention Andrey's return, Tatishchev's *History*, it is inserted *after* the description of the events in Novgorod.

Although Aleksandr may have reached an amicable settlement with his two brothers and returned them to the fold, his troubles in Novgorod were by no means at an end. In 1257 an even more serious manifestation of opposition to the grand prince occurred. This time it directly concerned Aleksandr's support of the actions of the Tatars: 1257 was the year of the first recorded Tatar census in Russia. The census began with 'all the land of Suzdal'', in other words all the principalities subordinate to the grand prince of Vladimir, and it included the districts of Murom and Ryazan'. The only chronicle to record this (the Lavrent'evskiy) makes no mention of any resistance; it merely states that the census officials (*chislenniki*) 'counted' the population in order to assess them for taxation and recruitment purposes, appointed overseers responsible for groups of ten, one hundred, one thousand and one hundred thousand (*desyatniki i sotniki, i tysyashchniki, i temniki*) – presumably Russians and not Tatars, as the chronicle makes no mention of their nationality – and absolved the clergy from the census.

The Tatars, needless to say, had no intention of confining the census to Suzdalia, Murom and Ryazan'. Novgorod was also included, and in the summer news reached the city of the census officials' impending visit and their intention of levying a tithe as well as a customs tax (*tamga*), evidently a percentage of the merchants' capital. The announcement led to uproar: 'The people were confused throughout the whole summer', writes the chronicler. To make matters worse the ex-*posadnik* Anan'ya 'died' (murdered?) on 15 August and his successor Mikhalko Stepanovich was put to death in the beginning of the winter, both events doubtless the result of the 'confusion'. Indeed it looks as though Mikhalko was killed to avenge the death of his predecessor: the chronicler, a partisan of Anan'ya and the 'lesser' boyars, adds a sour adaptation of Proverbs 28.10 to Mikhalko's murder: 'If a man does good to another, then it is good [for him]; but he who digs a pit for another man shall himself fall into it'. Aleksandr's son Vasily and his advisers were on the side of the 'lesser' boyars as well. As soon as the Tatar officials, accompanied by the grand prince himself, arrived in the city, Vasily fled to Pskov.

If Aleksandr expected that the census would be plain sailing, he was mistaken. The Tatars 'began to ask for tithe and *tamga*', but were met with a blunt refusal. Instead the Novgorodians loaded the census officials with gifts for the khan and somehow persuaded them to leave. Aleksandr had not enough troops to enforce the census. Instead he remained behind and meted out suitable punishment to his son, his son's advisers and the rebellious Novgorodians. Vasily was arrested in Pskov and sent back to Suzdalia in disgrace. One Aleksandr, presumably the *voevoda* of Vasily's bodyguard, was executed together with his *druzhina*, while those who 'led Vasily into evil' either had their noses cut off or their eyes gouged out. Again the chronicler adds a rider, but this time an ironical one: 'for every bad man shall come to a bad end'. Leaving behind him a savage reminder that insubordination could be punished by execution or mutilation, Aleksandr returned to his capital, one Mikhail Fedorovich, imported from Ladoga, having been given the thankless task as the new *posadnik* of restoring some sort of order to Novgorod.[69]

There can have been no doubt in Aleksandr's mind that he would be called to task by the Tatars for his set-back in Novgorod. The bribes sent to the khan and Aleksandr's vicious punishment of those he deemed guilty of disobeying Tatar commands were hardly enough to satisfy the Golden Horde. In the following year, 1258, he was sent for – not alone this time, but with his two previously refractory brothers Andrey and Yaroslav and with Boris of Rostov, the senior representative of the Konstantinovichi. It would be too much to expect that the strongly expurgated chronicle of Vladimir and Rostov, the only one to mention the visit to the Horde, would add any explanation or say what happened apart from noting that they 'paid honour to [Khan] Ulavgiy [Ulaghchi, Sartak's son and successor] and all the *voevody* and were sent back [not 'with honour', be it noted] to their patrimony'.[70] It would be still more surprising to find the deferential author of Aleksandr's *Life* even mentioning the episode. It is not, however, hard to guess at the reason for the summons or the instructions given to the princes at Saray. The events of the following year point to both only too clearly.

The Novgorodians were given warning of what was about to happen. At the end of 1259 or the beginning of 1260[71] a messenger arrived from Vladimir with the naked threat: accept the census or you will be invaded; 'the armies are already in the Lower Lands [i.e. Suzdalia]'. Novgorod agreed to admit the Tatars. They arrived soon after, together with a large body of officials. They were accompanied by Aleksandr, his brother Andrey and Boris of Rostov[72] – in other words, the same group that had journeyed to the Horde in 1258 less Yaroslav of Tver': in view of his previous connections with the dissident elements in Novgorod Aleksandr deemed it wiser to omit him from the party. The Russian princes with their *druzhiny* and the Tatar troops remained in waiting in Gorodishche, the fortress on the Volkhov just south of the town, while the census officials set about their task. In spite of their formal agreement the Novgorodians rebelled as soon as the Tatars began collecting tribute and conducting the census: 'There was a great upheaval in Novgorod', writes the Novgorod chronicler, 'and the accursed Tatars did much evil while collecting the tax (*tuska*)[73] throughout the districts', an indication that they set about their collecting in the rural areas first.

The population was split into two parties: the 'lesser' boyars, the 'common people' (*chern'*) and the merchants had no wish to submit; the 'greater' boyars were anxious to obey Aleksandr and to oblige their opponents to allow the census to proceed. There was physical opposition too, and the Tatars were harassed by urban guerrillas. 'Give us guards, otherwise they will slaughter us', the Tatars complained to Aleksandr, whose answer was to order 'the *posadnik*'s son and the "boyar children" [i.e. minor service people] to guard them by night'. Again the city was on the brink of civil war, and it was only when Aleksandr and 'the accursed Tatars' rode into Novgorod from Gorodishche that the opposition yielded. 'The accursed ones', so the chronicler wound up his narrative, 'began to ride through the streets, writing down the houses of the Christians; for our sins, God has brought these wild beasts from the desert to eat the flesh of the strong and drink the blood of the boyars.' This time Aleksandr had succeeded in imposing the will of the Tatars on the people of Novgorod. The tax was collected, the census was completed. To what extent this was the beginning of a regular system of taxation in Novgorod and how many soldiers the city provided for the Mongol armies as a result of the census is not known. But the khan of the Golden Horde could only have been gratified by Aleksandr's loyal cooperation. At long last Novgorod had submitted – if only nominally – to the authority of the 'accursed' Tatars.[74]

It is hard to say for certain how far the disaffection of the bulk of the citizens of Novgorod was also reflected in the towns of Suzdalia. Certainly the chroniclers of Vladimir and Rostov, reporting the 'counting' of the population in 1257, make no mention of any resistance to the Tatar officials or to Aleksandr himself. But then it must be remembered that the chronicle in which their reports appeared, the Lavrent'evskiy, reflected Aleksandr's *own* grand-princely chronicle for this period, and even if it was altered by his successor and erstwhile opponent, Yaroslav of Tver', it was probably reconstituted in something like its original form, though somewhat emaciated, by Aleksandr's sons in the last decades of the thirteenth century. So it is no surprise to find the bare statement to the effect that the officials 'counted all the land of Suzdal' and Ryazan' and Murom'. But was there no resistance to these 'wild beasts', these 'accursed' Tatars? The great uprising of 1262 gives the answer to that question.

Tax-collecting and recruitment for the Tatar armies had been going on in north-east Russia ever since the census of 1257, but it was not until 1262 that we have any details of the suffering caused or the reaction of the population to the tax-collectors. The Lavrent'evskiy Chronicle gives the earliest and most vivid picture of the events of that year.[75] It was a purely popular uprising. Assemblies (*vecha*) were summoned in the major towns of Rostov, Vladimir, Suzdal' and Yaroslavl'[76], and, as if by common consent, the people drove out the Tatars. The tax-collectors' practices had become intolerable; apart from such general expressions as 'great destruction', 'violence', 'suffering', 'misfortune', the chronicler implies not only that the Tatars, who are termed indiscriminately both Moslems (*besurmene*) and heathens (*poganye*), obliged those who were unable to raise the money to pay off the interest by work or slavery (*rabotyushche* [*lyudi?*] *rezy*), but that they split up families by sending off members for conscription in the Mongol armies or to the slave markets (*mnogy dushi krest'yanskyya razdno vedosha*). Further light is thrown on their practices by the example of the 'renegade' Zosima. Monk turned Moslem, he worked in Yaroslavl' as the agent of one Kutlu Beg, an envoy[77] of the khan of the Golden Horde. With Kutlu Beg's help he 'caused grave offence to the Christians'; it may well be that he even attempted to extort taxes from the clergy as he is described as 'mocking the cross and the holy churches'. The townsfolk of Yaroslavl', 'having risen against their enemies the Moslems' and 'driven out some and killed others', put him to death and threw his corpse to the dogs and the ravens.

It was clearly a mass uprising preceded by individual outbursts and coordinated to some degree – it is unlikely that the action was entirely spontaneous in *all* the towns of Suzdalia. The Nikon Chronicle, in an attempt to add a little lustre to the reputation of the princes, makes *them* the initiators of the rebellion: 'The Russian princes agreed amongst themselves and drove out the Tatars from their towns';[78] and the sixteenth-century chronicle of Ustyug adds to its brief report on the uprising a purely fictitious and highly folkloric tale of a tax-collector called Bugha whose Russian concubine ('taken to bed in lieu of tax') informed him of instructions from 'Prince Aleksandr to kill the Tatars'.[79] But the movement was not inspired, headed or even encouraged by the princes, and certainly not by Aleksandr:[80] the earliest source, the Lavrent'evskiy Chronicle, breathes no word of princely participation, and the author of Aleksandr's *Life*, eager to portray the future saint in as heroic and patriotic mould as possible, does not even mention the uprising, let alone Aleksandr's part in it.

Whatever the relationship between the various Mongol rulers may have been at the time – and it was clearly a period of stress and difficulty[81] – Berke, Ulaghchi's successor in the Golden Horde, could not permit the revolt to go unpunished. For his conflict with Hulagu, il-khan of Persia, and the war in Transcaucasia he needed troops, and he had relied on conscripts from Russia. Of all the Russian chronicles only the Sofiyskiy First talks of the immediate results of the uprising and the massacre of the Tatars in Suzdalia. 'Armies were sent to take the Christians [i.e. Russians] prisoner. And at that time there was distress caused by the pagans, and they persecuted the people and ordered them to go to war together with them.'[82]

Aleksandr had no choice but to go to the Golden Horde. In all probability he was summoned by Berke to explain away his failure to restrain the citizens of the towns in Suzdalia. His *Life* and the only chronicle to mention the reason for his visit say that he went to the Horde 'in order to beg the khan [to desist] from [causing] this misfortune', '*this* misfortune' referring to the immediately preceding phrase: 'they ordered [the people] to go to war together with them'.[83] How successful he was in either of his missions – saving the Russians from reprisals for the killing of the tax-collectors or talking the khan out of mass conscription for Suzdalia – we are not told. All we know is that Berke kept him in the Horde for the winter of 1262–63 and that he fell ill there. No mention is made of poison in any of the sources. He returned up the Volga. In Nizhniy Novgorod he stopped for a short while. Then, instead of returning to his capital Vladimir along the Oka and Klyaz'ma rivers, he journeyed further up the Volga to Andrey's town of Gorodets. There, having taken the extreme monastic tonsure, the *skhima*, he died on 14 November 1263.[84] The metropolitan and all the clergy met the funeral procession at Bogolyubovo, one-time residence of the grand princes, and brought the body of Aleksandr into nearby Vladimir, where on 23 November it was buried in the monastery of the Nativity of the Mother of God. The funeral oration of the metropolitan, quoted in the *Life*, was short and memorable: 'My children, know you that the sun of the land of Suzdal' has now set! For nevermore shall such a prince be found in the land of Suzdal'.'

*　　*　　*　　*

What conclusions can we draw from all we know about Aleksandr, his life and his reign? Was he the great hero, the great defender of the Russian frontiers against Western aggression? Did he save Russia from being overrun by the Teutonic Knights or the Swedish invaders? Was he the staunch protector of Orthodoxy against encroaching papacy? Did he, by means of his policy of appeasement, save the north of Russia from complete destruction at the hands of the Tatars? Were his acts of self-abasement, even humiliation, at the Golden Horde acts of pure altruism designed to save the fatherland and guarantee it a stable future? Of course we can never know the true answers to these questions. But what facts can be squeezed out of the thin and often deceptive sources, even from the silences of the *Life*, would lead us to think twice before answering any of these questions in the affirmative. For there was no concerted plan of Western aggression before or during Aleksandr's reign; there was no possible danger of a full-scale invasion, even though the papacy, the Germans, the Swedes, the Danes and the Lithuanians may have considered that northern Russia had been fatally weakened by the Tatar invasion, which in fact it had not been. All Aleksandr did was what numerous defenders of Novgorod and Pskov had done before him and what many were to do in the future – namely rush to the defence of a vast and vulnerable frontier against raiding parties. There is no evidence to show that the papacy had any serious designs on the

Orthodox Church or that Aleksandr did anything to defend the Russian Church's integrity. Indeed there was no question of his breaking with the Catholic West, even after 1242: he planned to marry his son Vasily to Christina, daughter of King Haakon of Norway, he drew up treaties with the Germans, he concluded one with Norway, he received embassies from the North and the West, he answered papal Bulls.[85] It is true, the Orthodox Church owed him a large debt, but not because its lands and possessions were secure and the clergy was immune from taxation and conscription. Religious toleration had been Mongol policy ever since the time of Chinghis Khan, and the khans of the Golden Horde, whether pagan or Moslem, always showed consideration and even generosity to the churches in the lands under their sway. Aleksandr had no need to intercede with Baty, Sartak or Berke for the Russian Church. But that a debt was owed him by the Church and that the Church felt this is evidenced by the metropolitan's devotion to him, by his local canonization in the monastery of the Nativity of the Virgin in Vladimir,[86] and by the fulsome praise contained in the *Life*.

Finally one may ask whether his policy of appeasement – for such it undoubtedly was – in any way ameliorated the position of the Russians vis-à-vis the Tatars. There were, it is true, no recorded punitive raids for a long time after Nevryuy's in 1252; Novgorod's disobedience and the uprising of 1262 went unpunished for the time being; interference in local Russian affairs was minimal; there is no evidence even of the stationing of Tatar officials or troops on Russian territory during Aleksandr's rule. But can this be ascribed to Aleksandr's policy? Was it not rather the result of Tatar preoccupation elsewhere – in Lithuania, South Russia and above all Iran?

One thing remains certain. As was said in the previous chapter, Aleksandr's intervention in 1252, his engineering of the crushing of his two brothers by the Tatars virtually spelled the end of effective Russian resistance to the Golden Horde for many years to come. What he did during his reign does nothing to alter this view of him.

Yet resistance there was. It did not die with the defeat of Andrey and Yaroslav. It was manifest in the hostility to Aleksandr in Novgorod and in the uprising of 1262. And Aleksandr did nothing to assist this spirit of resistance to the Golden Horde. It would indeed be generous to call his policy altruistic.

REFERENCES AND NOTES

1. For the granting of Suzdal' and Starodub to Svyatoslav and Ivan respectively, see *PSRL*, vol. 25, p. 130; vol. 2 (1843 edn), p. 338 (Gustinskiy Chronicle). Tatishchev, however, says that Ivan was given Starodub in 1212. *Istoriya*, vol. 4, p. 342.
2. According to *L* he was buried in Yaroslavl' in 1249 (*PSRL*, vol. 1, col. 472). *MAK*, which for its information 1239–1419 derives from a Suzdal'-Rostov source, calls him 'Vasily of Yaroslavl'' (ibid., col. 523). He died without male issue, and, although he may have had a brother, Konstantin (killed by the Tatars in 1255 or 1257: Baumgarten, *Généalogies*, vol. 2, p. 62), his widow Ksenia and daughter

Maria appear to have ruled Yaroslavl' in his place. In *c.* 1260 Fedor Rostislavich, brother of Gleb of Smolensk and ruler of Mozhaysk in the east of the principality of Smolensk, married Maria and became prince of Yaroslavl'. See *PSRL*, vol. 10, pp. 153–4.

3. *PSRL*, vol. 1, cols 472, 523.

4. Only Tatishchev (*Istoriya*, vol. 4, p. 359) gives his date of birth as 30 May 1220.

5. *PSRL*, vol. 1, col. 469 (also in *N4, S1, MAK*). The youngest son Vasily was born in 1241.

6. *Istoriya*, vol. 5, pp. 52, 56.

7. *PSRL*, vol. 1, col. 471; vol. 2, col. 795 (*s.a.* 1245); *NPL*, pp. 298–303.

8. *PSRL*, vol. 2, cols 805–8 (*s.a.* 1250).

9. *PSRL*, vol. 4, p. 228.

10. *PSRL*, vol. 1, col. 470.

11. For the attack on Kamenets, see *PSRL*, vol. 1, col. 469; vol. 2, col. 782 (*s.a.* 1238); vol. 30, p. 90 (*Vladimirskiy letopisets*, the only source to mention Mikhail's presence in the town: *a knyaz' Mikhail uteche*). For a slightly different interpretation, see Dimnik, 'Kamenec', pp. 26, 31–2.

12. *PSRL*, vol. 1, col. 469; vol. 25, p. 130.

13. *PSRL*, vol. 2, col. 806.

14. *PSRL*, vol. 1, col. 471; *The Mongol Mission*, pp. 58, 65.

15. *Pashuto, Ocherki*, pp. 268–9. As for Yaroslav's relations with Rome, Pashuto mentions Innocent IV's Bull to Aleksandr Nevskiy (1248) (*Historica Russiae Monumenta*, vol. 1, pp. 68–9).

16. Vernadsky, *The Mongols and Russia*, p. 148.

17. In 1238 it was agreed at the treaty of Stensby that the northern half of Estonia was to be under Danish control, while the south came under the Teutonic Order.

18. *NPL*, pp. 77, 289. See Pashuto, *Obrazovanie*, p. 376.

19. *NPL*, pp. 79, 304.

20. For details, see Pashuto, *Obrazovanie*, pp. 377 *et seq.*

21. *PIL*, p. 13; *P2L*, pp. 21, 81.

22. *NPL*, pp. 77 ('goroditsi'), 289 ('gorodets'').

23. *NPL*, pp. 79 (*s.a.* 1245), 304 (*s.a.* 1246).

24. *PSRL*, vol. 1, cols 471–2. Pashuto, not very convincingly, considers that the raids of 1245 and 1248 were one and the same and that the entry in *Ipat s.a.* 1252 to the effect that Mindovg 'sent his nephews Tovtivil and Edivid (Edividas) [of Zhemaytiya] . . . to Smolensk to wage war' refers to this campaign. *Obrazovanie*, pp. 377–8.

25. *P2L*, p. 14; Begunov, *Pamyatnik*, pp. 173, 192.

26. For an analysis of the *Life* of Aleksandr Nevskiy, see Fennell and Stokes, *Early Russian Literature*, pp. 107–21.

27. Shaskol'sky, *Bor'ba Rusi*, ch. VII. See also his 'Papskaya kuriya' and 'Novye materialy'.

28. Cf., however, Christiansen, *The Northern Crusades*, p. 128.

29. See *NPL*, p. 77. For the account in the *Life*, see *P2L*, pp. 11–13; Begunov, *Pamyatnik*, pp. 162–8, 188–91.

30. *NPL*, pp. 78, 294–5; *PSRL*, vol. 10, p. 123.

31. *NPL*, pp. 78, 295; *PSRL*, vol. 10, p. 125.

32. *NPL*, pp. 78–9, 295–6; *P1L*, p. 13 (date given 1 April); *P2L*, pp. 13–14, 82; *PSRL*, vol. 1, col. 470; vol. 5, pp. 226–9.

33. *PSRL*, vol. 1, col. 470.

34. *Ledovoe poboishche*, p. 227.
35. P. M. Tumler, *Der Deutsche Orden*, pp. 266–7. Note that according to the *S1* account (and Eisenstein's film *Aleksandr Nevskiy*) 'the Master' took part in the battle. *PSRL*, vol. 5, p. 227.
36. Note that the Order of Aleksandr Nevskiy ('For Toil and Fatherland') established by Catherine I in 1725 was resuscitated by Stalin on 29 July 1942 at the height of the great German offensive.
37. For a detailed investigation of the sources, see Fennell, 'Andrej Jaroslavič'.
38. *Pashuto, Ocherki*, p. 271.
39. *PSRL*, vol. 1, col. 473.
40. Aleksandr was in Vladimir at the time of the deaths of his cousins Vladimir Konstantinovich of Uglich (27 December 1249) and Vasily Vsevolodovich of Yaroslavl' (8 February 1250). *PSRL*, vol. 1, col. 472. For his arrival in Novgorod, see *NPL*, pp. 80, 304.
41. *PSRL*, vol. 2, col. 829, *s.a.* 1255.
42. Gumilev, *Poiski*, p. 381.
43. See Fennell, *The Emergence*, pp. 105 *et seq.*
44. Tatishchev, *Istoriya*, vol. 5, p. 40.
45. *PSRL*, vol. 1, col. 473.
46. Tatishchev says that he planned to go to Kiev from Novgorod but was dissuaded by the Novgorodians 'because of the Tatars'. *Istoriya*, vol. 5, p. 39.
47. The late Gustinskiy Chronicle calls Aleksandr at his death 'prince of Moscow [!] and Kiev' and Yaroslav Yaroslavich 'prince of Kiev'. *PSRL*, vol. 2 (1843 edn), pp. 342, 343, 344.
48. *L* merely says: 'Prince Boris went to the Tatars, and Prince Aleksandr sent gifts. And he returned to his patrimony with honour' (*PSRL*, vol. 1, col. 474). Tatishchev, however, states that Aleksandr 'sent his envoys [with Boris] to ask [forgiveness] for Andrey' and that Boris 'obtained forgiveness for Andrey'. *Istoriya*, vol. 5, p. 42.
49. Yur'ev Pol'skiy had been granted to Svyatoslav in 1213 (see above, p. 47). He was given Suzdal' in 1238 (see above, p. 98).
50. For Yaroslav's movements between 1252 and 1255, see *PSRL*, vol. 1, cols 473–4; *NPL*, pp. 80–1, 307.
51. Tatishchev, *Istoriya*, vol. 5, p. 42.
52. Ibid.
53. *PSRL*, vol. 1, col. 474; Tatishchev, *Istoriya*, vol. 5, p. 42.
54. Tatishchev calls him 'Grand Prince Andrey Yaroslavich of Suzdal'' (ibid.), while *T* talks of the death of 'Prince Andrey Yaroslavich of Suzdal'' in 1264 (*TL*, p. 328) (note that *L* breaks off in the middle of the entry for 1263).
55. *NPL*, p. 312 (Komissionnyy MS only).
56. *NPL*, pp. 81, 309 (1256).
57. *P2L*, p. 15; Begunov, *Pamyatnik*, pp. 178, 194.
58. It was in fact a joint bishopric with Southern Pereyaslavl'. Feognost, the successor of the first bishop Mitrofan was styled 'bishop of Russian Pereyaslavl' and Saray'. *TL*, p. 330 (*s.a.* 1269).
59. *P2L*, pp. 14–15; Begunov, *Pamyatnik*, pp. 175–6, 193. The mission of the two legates is presumably based on Pope Innocent IV's Bull to Aleksandr (1248). See note 15.
60. *PSRL*, vol. 1, cols 474–5.
61. *NPL*, pp. 83, 312. Pashuto, *Obrazovanie*, p. 382.

62. See *NPL*, pp. 84, 313. Pashuto, *Obrazovanie*, pp. 382–5.
63. *NPL*, pp. 80, 307.
64. *NPL*, pp. 83, 311–12.
65. Shaskol'sky, *Bor'ba*, ch. 8, section 2.
66. *NPL*, pp. 81, 308–309. The *'Svei, i Em', i Sum''* were accompanied by one Didman, who in the index of *NPL* is described as a 'vassal of Denmark'. Ibid., p. 576.
67. In 1253 Vasily was already 'leading' Novgorod troops against the Lithuanians at Toropets. *NPL*, pp. 80, 307.
68. *NPL*, pp. 80–1, 307–8.
69. For the events of 1257 in Novgorod, see *NPL*, pp. 82, 309. For the census in Suzdalia, Ryazan' and Murom, see *PSRL*, vol. 1, cols 474–5. On the Mongol census in Russia, see Allsen, 'Mongol Census Taking'.
70. *PSRL*, vol. 1, col. 475. The entry is duplicated (though without mention of Yaroslav) *s.a.* 1257 (ibid., col. 474). It is interesting to note that neither the *svod* of 1448 (i.e. N4 and SI) nor M mention this, Aleksandr's third trip to Saray.
71. The first entry for 6767 (1 March 1259–28 February 1260) concerns an eclipse of the moon which in fact took place on 1 December 1259. The subsequent entries cover the census. See Berezhkov, *Khronologiya*, p. 271.
72. *PSRL*, vol. 1, col. 475: the last entry under 6766, a year too early.
73. For a possible interpretation of the obscure *tuska*, see Vernadsky, *The Mongols and Russia*, pp. 220–1.
74. For the events of 1259–60 in Novgorod, see *NPL*, pp. 82–3, 310–11.
75. *PSRL*, vol. 1, col. 476.
76. S1 adds Pereyaslavl' (Zalesskiy) to the list (*PSRL*, vol. 5, p. 190): N4 has 'all the Russian towns' (ibid., vol. 4, p. 233).
77. The term given in L is *'tityam'* (or *'titam'* in T), which was incomprehensible to the compiler of the *svod* of 1448: S1 adds *poslom* (envoy); N4 has only the abbreviated version of *MAK*.
78. *PSRL*, vol. 10, p. 143.
79. *UL*, pp. 47–8.
80. See, however, Nasonov's view. *Mongoly i Rus'*, ch. 2, pp. 50 *et seq.*
81. See Vernadsky, *The Mongols and Russia*, pp. 71 *et seq.*; Nasonov, *Mongoly i Rus'*, ibid.; Spuler, *Die Goldene Horde*, pp. 39 *et seq.*
82. *PSRL*, vol. 5, p. 190. The second sentence is repeated in the *Life* of Aleksandr. See *P2L*, p. 15; Begunov, *Pamyatnik*, pp. 177, 193.
83. Ibid.
84. *TL*, p. 328; *NPL*, pp. 83, 312; *PSRL*, vol. 1, col. 524; vol. 5, p. 191; *P2L*, p. 15; Begunov, *Pamyatnik*, pp. 177–8, 193–4.
85. See Pashuto, *Ocherki*, p. 246.
86. Full canonization did not take place until 1547. See Klepinin, *Svyatoy . . . Aleksandr Nevskiy*, pp. 179 *et seq.*; Golubinsky, *Istoriya kanonizatsii*, pp. 65, 100.

CHAPTER SIX

Aleksandr Nevskiy's Successors

THE LAST OF THE YAROSLAVICHI 1263–1277

Aleksandr's legacy was a sorry one. At his death Novgorod had barely recovered from the census he had enforced on the city, and it was too early for the northern towns of Suzdalia to have forgotten the suffering and humiliation inflicted on them by the tax-collectors. Had he lived longer and had he had time to ensure that the patent for the grand-princely throne remained securely in the hands of his children and did not pass to his brothers, then at least he might have strengthened the authority of the ruler of Vladimir. But he died too young, at the age of 43 – was he poisoned like his father is alleged to have been and as his brother Yaroslav may have been? All three died 'travelling from the Tatars' and at the time of his death his eldest son Vasily, who had disgraced himself in the census affair of the winter of 1259–60 in Novgorod, seems to have been in some sort of political limbo from which he never emerged, while his second eldest, Dmitry, whom he groomed to take Vasily's place, cannot have been more than in his early teens, if that, when 'placed on the throne' of Novgorod in 1260 and put 'in command' of the Yur'ev expedition two years later[1] (see above, p. 114). The only hope for a powerful Suzdalia lay in the breaking of the system of lateral succession and the creation of a strong family nest in which power could be transmitted from father to eldest son; and this Aleksandr had been unable to achieve. Apart from leaving the country in disarray and doomed to weak rule as long as the present system survived, Aleksandr also left north Russia in a state of greater dependence on the Golden Horde than when he acceded to the throne in 1252.

At the death of Aleksandr northern Russia was ruled by a loose federation of princes. Konstantin Vsevolodovich's old principality, comprising Rostov, Yaroslavl', Beloozero and Uglich, was under the most homogeneous group, namely Konstantin's grandsons and Fedor Yaroslavich of Mozhaysk, who had taken over Yaroslavl' in about 1260 by marrying into the family (see above, Ch. 5, n. 2). The district of Pereyaslavl' Zalesskiy was the family possession of Aleksandr Nevskiy's children and the town itself was the headquarters of Dmitry Aleksandrovich, who at the time of his father's death was still prince of Novgorod as well. What, if anything, the other children of Aleksandr ruled cannot be said. Vasily remained in total obscurity – perhaps even in prison?

– until his death in 1271. As for Andrey, not more than eight years old at the time, and the two-year-old Daniil, the future ruler of Moscow, it seems hardly likely that their father had made any provisions for them before his death.[2] The second largest patrimony in Suzdalia proper, the east-Volga district of Suzdal', Gorodets and Nizhniy Novgorod, was by now the estate of Aleksandr's brother Andrey and the latter's son Yury. The westernmost principality, Tver', was ruled by Aleksandr's second eldest brother Yaroslav. The remaining minor districts of Starodub, Yur'ev Pol'skiy, Northern Galich and Kostroma were held by the families of Aleksandr's two uncles (Svyatoslav and Ivan Vsevolodovichi), his nephew (David Konstantinovich) and his younger brother Vasily respectively.

They were not exactly a cooperative family. Indeed they distinguished themselves by their lack of cohesiveness. As might be expected, as soon as Aleksandr died the succession to the grand-princely title became a matter of dispute between his eldest surviving brother, Andrey of Suzdal', and Yaroslav of Tver': neither, it seems, had been nominated by him as his successor. Both sent their envoys to the Horde with a request to Khan Berke to settle the question. Andrey as the instigator of resistance to the Tatars in 1252 was potentially the more dangerous of the two, and consequently Berke's choice fell on the younger Yaroslav, who was duly granted the patent. Throughout his brief reign, 1264–71,[3] he had difficulty in mustering his relatives and their armies in moments of need. Not once do we hear of any of the rulers of Rostov, Yaroslavl', Beloozero and Uglich rallying to his call to arms; indeed from the beginning of his reign to 1271 when he died there is practically no mention in the chronicles of their activities. In the great Suzdalian expedition which set out to capture the town of Rakovor in northern Estonia in early 1268 the only princes that Yaroslav and the Novgorodians could persuade to take part with their armies were Dmitry of Pereyaslavl', Yaroslav's two sons Svyatoslav and Mikhail of Tver', Yury of Suzdal' (his father Andrey had died in 1264), Konstantin Rostislavich (a minor prince of Smolensk) and Dovmont of Pskov (see below, p. 135). Vasily of Kostroma was conspicuous for his absence, and indeed two years later, in 1270, he was to emerge as the open opponent of his brother Yaroslav in the great 'upheaval' in Novgorod (see below, p. 129). The same lack of unity haunted Vasily during his reign (1272–77), especially in the bitter war over Novgorod in 1273 between Vasily and Yaroslav's son Svyatoslav on the one hand and Dmitry Aleksandrovich on the other (see below, pp. 138 et seq.).

The lack of cohesiveness could not be called unexpected in this strange twilight period of ineffectual leadership, one might say leaderlessness. Neither Yaroslav nor Vasily had strong or forceful enough characters to enable them to establish firm control over their nephews and cousins as well as over Novgorod and Pskov – and the same applies to the subsequent reigns of Aleksandr Nevskiy's two sons Dmitry and Andrey in the last two decades of the thirteenth century. Nor did any of them live long enough to achieve any aims of consolidating Suzdalia they may have had. But the looseness of control over the outlying districts of Vladimir must in the main be put down not so much to the feebleness of purpose of the grand princes, nor to the brevity of their reigns, not even to the aftermath of Aleksandr Nevskiy's disastrous policies, but rather to the fact that none of Aleksandr's successors in the thirteenth century had sufficiently strong bases from which to operate. First, they were not parochially-minded in any sense of the word. Yaroslav and Vasily did not, or could not, rule from Tver' and Kostroma, just as Dmitry and Andrey later were not to rule from Pereyaslavl' and Gorodets during their tenure of the grand-princely throne. This meant that they were unable to reside in for long, develop and expand their own provincial centres, to create major power bases which could eventually – like Moscow in the fourteenth century – share the grand-princely throne with Vladimir and which could be kept exclusively in their own families. Second, their principalities can only be described as economically and militarily backward by comparison with many of the other patrimonies in the 1260s and the 1270s.

The early history of the town and district of Tver' is obscure. Founded only in the late twelfth century, at the confluence of the Tvertsa river (the main river-route from Novgorod to the Volga) and the Volga itself, Tver' was originally the westernmost town of the district of Pereyaslavl'. All we hear of it in the first half of the thirteenth century is that in 1209 it was used as a base for a joint Suzdalian expedition against Mstislav Mstislavich in Novgorod (see above, p. 54). By 1215 it was part of the principality of Northern Pereyaslavl', probably having been left to Yaroslav by his father Vsevolod III in 1212.[4] The most likely date of Tver' as a separate principality is 1247, when Grand Prince Svyatoslav 'placed his nephews in towns'[5] according to Yaroslav Vsevolodovich's will: clearly Yaroslav Yaroslavich was given the large western slice of his father's patrimony of Pereyaslavl'. Of its dimensions at the time we know nothing, but as there is no information of any annexations made by its rulers during the whole of the history of Tver' as an independent principality, its boundaries were probably the same in the thirteenth century as they were in the fourteenth and fifteenth. It stretched on either side of the upper reaches of the Volga from Kashin in the east to Zubtsov in the west. In the south it included the entire Shosha river, a southern tributary of the Volga, and the Shosha's important tributary, the Lama, which flowed from the Novgorod outpost of Volok Lamskiy. In the east Tver' was linked with Northern Pereyaslavl' by the Western Nerl' river, which joins the Volga at Ksnyatin. We know of no important events which occurred in the principality during the reign of Yaroslav Yaroslavich or of his son Svyatoslav who died in the first half of the 1280s, except that a bishopric was founded there – some time before Yaroslav's death in 1271.[6]

Still less is know of Kostroma. Situated in the east of the district of Beloozero and Yaroslavl', to the south-west of Northern Galich and to the north of Suzdal', the remote land of Kostroma appears never to have been considered as the sole patrimony of any branch of the family. True, Vasily Yaroslavich was styled 'prince of Kostroma' and after his death it seems to have been held at one time by Andrey Aleksandrovich of Gorodets and at another by his nephew Ivan Dmitrievich, but it may well be that it was looked upon simply as an adjunct to the grand principality of Vladimir, just as Pereyaslavl' was to be at the end of the thirteenth century. In any case Vasily Yaroslavich never developed it as a military base. Too far removed from the Klyaz'ma and Oka basins and too long a journey from the borders of Novgorod, Kostroma remained a political backwater throughout the last decades of the thirteenth century.

Of course some sort of covenant between the grand prince of Vladimir and his relatives in Suzdalia must have existed, though none was ever recorded in the thirteenth century: some contract obliging the latter to provide military assistance to the former when required, in return for which the former would agree to protect the latter's interests – defence of frontiers against external aggression, for example, or protection against attack by neighbours. But apart from a system of mutual defence the relationship between the members of the princely family was a loose one. There was no question of the grand prince extending his authority in civil matters over the territories of his relatives; his power was limited to his own principality, to the town and district of Vladimir and, provided he was recognized as 'prince of Novgorod', to certain limited areas of control in Novgorod territory. He could not interfere in the internal affairs of lands belonging to his relatives. Furthermore, any agreements which may have existed between the princes in no way guaranteed obedience to the senior member of the family, who was, after all, nothing more than *primus inter pares*, the nominal head of a loose federation.

The ineffectualness of the leadership and authority of the two grand princes of Vladimir who succeeded Aleksandr Nevskiy is well illustrated by the part played by the Tatars of the Golden Horde in the 1260s and the 1270s. Even the description of Yaroslav's 'inauguration' as grand prince in Saray – given, it is true, only by Tatishchev, but none the less plausible for that – shows not only that the Horde was solely responsible for granting the patent, but also that the khan had by now devised some sort of ceremony for the installation of the grand prince:

When Yaroslav arrived at the Horde, the khan received him with honour, gave him his armour and ordered that he be instructed in the ceremony [of appointing him] to the grand principality. He ordered Vladimir of Ryazan' and Ivan of Starodub, who were in the Horde at the time, to lead his horse. And in August [1264] he let him go and sent him with his envoy (*posol*) Jani Beg and with the patent (*yarlyk*) for the grand principality.[7]

But far more important than the staging of this inauguration ceremony, if such it was, is the fact that the Tatars were now beginning to participate militarily in Russian affairs. In 1269 we have the first indication of a Tatar official taking part in what was otherwise a purely Russian foreign venture. The Novgorod First Chronicle describes how Yaroslav and the Novgorodians planned a massive campaign against Revel' (Tallinn) in Danish Estonia: Svyatoslav, Yaroslav's eldest son, was sent to the 'Lower Lands', i.e. Suzdalia, 'to collect regiments'.[8] 'Having collected all the princes and an army of innumerable size, he came to Novgorod. And with him was the great *baskak* of Vladimir, Amragan by name.' What exactly the function of the *baskaki* at this early stage was is not known: probably they were, as later, senior Tatar officials stationed in various centres of strategic importance with the function of maintaining order, quelling rebellions and overseeing the collection of taxes. For these purposes they presumably had under their command some Tatar troops or a mixed Russo-Tatar force. Evidently the 'great *baskak* of Vladimir' was the senior Tatar functionary in Suzdalia. He is the first *baskak* to be mentioned in the Russian sources, unless the 'Kutlu Beg' described as active in Yaroslavl' in 1262 was one (see above, p. 119). Presumably Amragan was present in Svyatoslav's army as the khan's watchdog, perhaps as the adviser of the commander-in-chief; his presence meant that this – and no doubt other foreign campaigns – were carried out with the approbation of the Tatars, and were in fact controlled by them.

More significant still, however, than the mere presence of a *baskak* in the Russian army in 1269 were the two occasions on which Russians actually called in Tatar troops to assist them in their political conflicts. In 1270, at the beginning of the great rebellion (*myatezh*) in Novgorod, Yaroslav, frustrated by the Novgorodians' obstinate refusal to retain him as their ruler, sent the *tysyatskiy* Ratibor Kluksovich to the Horde with a list of complaints against the Novgorodians and a request to send military aid. According to Ratibor's 'lying speech', as the biased chronicler called it, the Novgorodians were disobedient to the khan in that they refused to part with the tribute which Yaroslav and his agents were allegedly collecting. Ratibor managed to convince the khan of the misdeeds of the Novgorodians – and he could hardly have chosen a more compelling argument to persuade the authorities at Saray – and an army was sent to help Yaroslav. It was in fact deflected by the action of Vasily Yaroslavich, Yaroslav's brother, who went to the Horde accompanied by two Novgorod boyars. 'The men of Novgorod are right', he told the khan, 'and Yaroslav is to blame.' The khan believed him, and the army was ordered to return forthwith to Saray. In fact the Novgorod crisis was solved soon after by the intervention of the metropolitan and no Tatar troops were used to persuade the Novgorodians to yield to Yaroslav. Still, this was the fist time that a Russian prince is recorded as having sent to the Horde for military assistance.[9]

Three years later, in 1272 or 1273, we find two Russian princes, Vasily Yaroslavich, who had succeeded his brother Yaroslav as grand prince of Vladimir in 1272, and Yaroslav's son Svyatoslav of Tver', fighting against the then prince of Novgorod, Dmitry Aleksandrovich, with Tatar detachments on their side. It was a full-scale war on Dmitry and Novgorod. Again Amragan, 'the great *baskak* of Vladimir', was in evidence. 'Grand Prince Vasily Yaroslavich . . . with the great *baskak* of Vladimir Amragan and [his son-in-law] Prince Aydar and many of the khan's Tatars, waged war on the districts of Novgorod and returned with many prisoners to Vladimir.'[10] At the same time another Tatar force under Svyatoslav was also attacking the district of Novgorod: 'The grand [sic] prince of Tver' Svyatoslav Yaroslavich . . . marched with the khan's Tatars and waged war on Volok, Bezhichi and Vologda, the lands of Novgorod, and returned with many prisoners to Tver''.[11] In fact the pressure was such that Dmitry Aleksandrovich was obliged by the Novgorodians to yield the city to Vasily. 'The men of Novgorod were in confusion', so writes the sixteenth-century Nikon chronicler, 'and there was great fear and trembling, and they said: "We have trouble on all sides! Here is the grand prince of Vladimir, and here is the grand prince of Tver', and here is the khan's great *baskak* together with the Tatars, and all the Lower Land [i.e. Suzdalia] is against us." '[12] Well might they have felt anxiety: not only was the situation deeply confused, but also the summoning of Tatar military aid was all too reminiscent of the practice of prince fighting prince with the assistance of the Pechenegs, the Polovtsians and other steppe nomads during the previous three centuries, a practice which had contributed so significantly to the disastrous weakening of the Russian state.

* * * *

However well the instability of Aleksandr Nevskiy's two successors may be exemplified by the Tatar's growing participation in Russian affairs, it is still more vividly illustrated by the enormous difficulties both faced in the north-west – in Novgorod and, to a lesser degree, in Pskov. As always, strict control over Novgorod was essential for whoever ruled in Vladimir – essential for the economy of Suzdalia and essential for the defence of the north-west frontiers – and the events of the past fifty years or so had shown just how difficult it had often been for the grand prince to achieve and maintain this control. True, Yaroslav Vsevolodovich and his family had, from 1233 on, been recognized as the sole providers of princes for Novgorod: never any more was there question of other princely clans, even from amongst the other descendants of Vsevolod III, being summoned or accepted. And true, the grand prince always won the day by sheer military pressure. But again and again squabbles among the leading Novgorod families, or dissatisfaction with arbitrary rule, or disagreement over questions of local defence had led to internal opposition and had forced whoever was grand prince to quit.

If the first thirty years of the thirteenth century had witnessed few signs of a move towards Novgorodian independence, in the second thirty there was evidence of a new mood: of a determined effort to resist the more intolerable aspects of princely power. As has been shown in the previous chapter, Aleksandr Nevskiy, for all his authority and experience in Novgorod affairs, had great difficulty in maintaining firm control over the city; and it was only thanks to the support of the 'greater boyars' that he managed to solve the crisis of 1255 and only by sheer force of arms – and the threat of Tatar military reprisals – that he surmounted the subsequent crises of 1257 and 1259/60.

Yet for all the evident desire to curtail the prince's power and to resist his authority, it is still too early to talk of Novgorod as a 'republic'. Even though the contractual links between grand prince and city may have gone back at least to the time of Yaroslav Vsevolodovich's rule in Novgorod, if not earlier still, nevertheless the control of the prince over the military, legal, economic and administrative affairs of Novgorod was still such that, to use the expression of the great historian of Novgorod V. L. Yanin, one can only talk of a 'duality of power' (*dvoevlastie*), a sort of sharing of authority between city authorities (*posadnik, tysyatskiy*) archbishop and prince, for most of the thirteenth century.

However, in order to realize to what extent the grand prince's authority was gradually being whittled away in the second half of the thirteenth century, one has only to study the relations between Vladimir and Novgorod in the reigns of Yaroslav Yaroslavich and Vasily Yaroslavich.

The last three years of Aleksandr Nevskiy's reign as grand prince and nearly a whole year after his death were free from any sort of internal disturbance in Novgorod. There were no moves to unseat the prince. All we hear of, apart from the military operations of 1262, are severe frosts, church building, church repairs and a fairly destructive fire – routine events which the chronicler was wont to record in tranquil times or when nothing outside the city aroused his curiosity or interest. When Aleksandr had completed the census in early 1260, he felt strong enough to leave his youthful son Dmitry in the prince's residence as a sort of juvenile figurehead to keep the Novgorodians aware of his proximity in Pereyaslavl' or Vladimir, and although the Novgorod chronicle suggests that Dmitry was nominally in command of the large combined expeditionary force which captured Yur'ev in the autumn of 1262, the commander-in-chief was in fact Aleksandr's brother Yaroslav, and it was Aleksandr himself who signed the subsequent treaty with the Germans.[13]

It was not only the bitter memory of Aleksandr's no-nonsense treatment of the citizens in the second half of the 1250s that safeguarded internal peace in Novgorod from 1260 to 1264; it was also the fact that Mikhail Fedorovich, who had replaced the murdered Mikhalko Stepanovich as *posadnik* in 1257, was in control of the administration during the last three years of Aleksandr's life. As leader of the 'greater boyars', he facilitated Aleksandr's task in compelling the Novgorodians to submit to the census in 1260, and his son, it will be remembered, had, on Aleksandr's orders, protected the Tatars against guerrilla attacks by night (see above, p. 118). Small wonder, then, that from March 1260 to March 1261 'there was calm for a whole year',[14] to use the chronicler's set phrase for an eventless year, and that for the succeeding three years nothing disturbed the peace of the city. The opposition was lying low.

News of Aleksandr's unexpected death must have reached Novgorod by the end of November 1263. Yet no change took place for nearly a year: evidently Mikhail Fedorovich and his ruling party were waiting to see who would be granted the patent for the grand-principality, Andrey Yaroslavich, the eldest surviving brother of Aleksandr, or Yaroslav of Tver'. In the autumn of 1264 they knew. By then Andrey was already dead – no chronicle mentions the cause or circumstances of his death, just the year, 1264[15] – and Yaroslav had won the khan's approval. In September he arrived back from Saray and was solemnly enthroned in Vladimir by the khan's representative. The presence of the new grand prince's nephew Dmitry in Novgorod could now only embarrass the *posadnik* and his supporters. Yaroslav was known to the Novgorodians: ten years earlier he had been invited by Aleksandr's opponents, the 'lesser boyars', to rule in Novgorod (see above, p. 111), and now Mikhail Fedorovich had no desire to antagonize either his political opponents in the city or the new grand prince by harbouring the son of Aleksandr. A cooperative and well-disposed ruler in Vladimir was preferable to dissension among the boyars or a drawn-out struggle, civil war perhaps, over the question of who was to be prince in Novgorod. They sent Dmitry packing: 'drove him out' are the words used by the local chronicler; 'because he was too young' – the reason given. A delegation consisting of the *posadnik*'s son and the 'greater boyars' was sent to ask Yaroslav to be their prince. He agreed, and with alacrity, for on 27 January 1265 the Novgorodians sat him upon their throne.[16] Shortly afterwards he married the daughter of a local boyar.[17]

The early days of Yaroslav's rule in Novgorod were taken up with the drafting of a contractual agreement between prince and city. When exactly the transaction was completed and oaths were sworn on both sides is not known, but the text of the treaty – the first of its kind to have survived in manuscript[18] – would lead us to believe that the Novgorodians lost no time in obliging Yaroslav to accede to their terms. It was clearly not the first contract signed between prince and Novgorod; in the very first clause it stipulated that Yaroslav 'kiss the cross' on the same terms as his father had done before him, and indeed later treaties (1267, 1269) mention previous contracts with his 'father *and* grandfather'. The difficulty of course is to know what new restrictions on the prince were added in 1265 to the previous agreements. The treaty with Yaroslav, however, was clearly limitative in comparison with earlier transactions: it is hard to imagine an Aleksandr Nevskiy or a Yaroslav Vsevolodovich agreeing to all that Yaroslav Yaroslavich was compelled to agree to; indeed we know that Aleksandr treated Novgorod property in a somewhat off-hand manner, for Yaroslav had to 'yield those meadow-lands (*pozhne*) which [his] brother had confiscated from Novgorod'.

Apart from obliging the prince to abide by the terms of previous treaties, the Novgorodians insisted that there should be no princely interference in the affairs of the city and its dependent districts (*volosti*), all of which are meticulously listed. No part of Novgorod territory was to be appropriated by the prince, nor was any land to be distributed or property deeds drawn up without the agreement of the *posadnik*. The expulsion of Novgorodian citizens to Suzdalia was strictly forbidden, as was the control or ownership by the prince, his wife, his boyars and his servitors (*dvoryane*) of any territory recognized as forming part of Novgorodian *volosti*.

It was not all restrictive, however. The prince's property – unfortunately there is no mention of extent or location – was the prince's property and he could do with it what he liked. His servitors (*dvoryane*) were free to travel throughout Novgorod territory, perhaps to administer some form of justice (there is no talk of judicial limitations in the treaty) or to collect tax (*dar*), an unspecified amount of which was to be levied for the prince from all districts. Most important of all, the two frontier outposts of Volok Lamskiy and Torzhok, where Suzdalian troops earmarked for the defence of the western frontiers were stationed,[19] were to be administered jointly by representatives of Novgorod and by the grand prince's overseers (*tivuny*).

It was a tough treaty and there was little in it to encourage Yaroslav to remain for long in the city, married though he was to a local girl. Furthermore, there was soon to be a clash with the authorities. Two years earlier, as a result of the civil war in Lithuania which followed the murder of Grand Prince Min-dovg and his nephew Tovtivil of Polotsk,[20] the latter's son Konstantin had fled with his entourage to Novgorod. Konstantin had strong links with Novgorod. With his father and a Lithuanian detachment he had fought on the side of the joint Russian force in the successful campaign against Yur'ev in 1262 (see above, p. 114), and now, as adviser on Lithuanian affairs, he must have enjoyed a measure of support and authority amongst the boyars. So when some time in 1265 a group of three hundred pagan Lithuanian refugees, men, women and children, turned up in Pskov, the Novgorodians, acting no doubt on his advice, decided that the most convenient way of dealing with them was simply to put them all to death. Evidently they represented a faction opposed to the supporters of Mindovg and Tovtivil. But Yaroslav was determined to support them. Not only did his son Svyatoslav, whom he had appointed as governor of Pskov, arrange for and supervise their baptism, but somehow Yaroslav managed to prevent the authorities in Novgorod from taking action against them. He refused to have them handed over.[21]

What happened subsequently to Konstantin and his group in Novgorod and to the three hundred Lithuanians in Pskov is not known. But Yaroslav's brush with the Novgorodian authorities was probably enough to persuade him to quit the city and appoint Yury, the son of his old ally Andrey, as caretaker – prince in his place. There was, however, more trouble to come.

In 1266 yet another party of Lithuanians turned up in Pskov. This time they were led by the formidable figure of Dovmont (Daumantas), a princeling from the south-eastern corner of Lithuania (the district of Nal'sha (Nalšia)), but probably unrelated to Mindovg and his family. One of the instigators of the civil war in Lithuania – he had had a share in Mindovg's murder in 1263 – he had later fallen foul of Mindovg's son Voyshelk, who in 1264 emerged as the most powerful prince in Lithuania. Dovmont fled to Russia with the express intention of fighting Voyshelk and his vassals in Polotsk, which was now virtually a dependency of Lithuania. He settled in Pskov 'with his retinue (*druzhina*) and his household (*dom*)',[22] drove out Yaroslav's son Svyatoslav and, like the refugees of the year before, accepted Christianity.[23]

Before the year was out he was off on the first of his many campaigns fought with troops from Pskov. The objective was Polotsk, where one Erden', a minor Lithuanian prince and a creature of Voyshelk, was ruling. The tiny expeditionary force, a mere 270 Pskovites, captured Erden''s wife (who happened to be Dovmont's aunt) and her children, chased and soundly defeated Erden' and his army of 700, and returned victorious with the loss of only one soldier.[24] Not content with this he carried out a second expedition against the Lithuanians in the winter of 1266–7, but this time no details of the fighting are available.[25]

The reaction of the ruling boyar faction in Novgorod to Dovmont and his entourage was entirely favourable. The Lithuanians in Pskov clearly represented a group of an altogether different political persuasion to that of the three hundred refugees of the previous year. Konstantin, for the murder of whose great-uncle Mindovg Dovmont was partially responsible, had faded from the political scene: perhaps he had left Novgorod with Yaroslav? In any case the grand prince was determined to uproot the newcomer, who had not only demonstrated his military prowess in no uncertain way, but had also unceremoniously displaced Svyatoslav as prince of Pskov. For the second time in two years Yaroslav clashed with the Novgorodian authorities. In early 1267 he arrived in Novgorod with a Suzdalian army 'intending to march on Dovmont in Pskov'. This time it was the Novgorodians who prevented him from taking action. 'They forbade him', wrote the local chronicler, '. . . and the prince sent his troops back home.'[26]

If the Novgorodians' behaviour in the beginning of 1267 struck Yaroslav as provocative, then their action later in the year must have appeared as a positive gesture of dissent. Without consulting Yaroslav's representative Yury and in defiance of the grand prince's policy towards Dovmont, they mounted a military expedition together with the Pskovites. The immediate results are of little importance – in fact all we know is that it was directed 'against Lithuania' and that it was successful. What is important is that it was led not by Yury, but by a mere boyar, one Elevfery Sbyslavich, about whom Yaroslav was later to complain to the Novgorodians, and by Dovmont himself. It would be hard to imagine an action more calculated to rile the grand prince.[27]

It was probably at this time that the Novgorodians obliged Yaroslav to agree to a second contract with them. It was similar to that signed in 1265 and many of the clauses are the same. But this time there were more restrictions on the grand prince. Yaroslav was forbidden to tamper with any of the Novgorodian districts which Aleksandr Nevskiy or his son Dmitry had had at their disposal. He was to refrain from any violent behaviour such as had been perpetrated by Aleksandr. More specifically, he was not to interfere in the Novgorodian district of Bezhetskiy Verkh (Bezhichi), which bordered on Yaroslavl', Uglich and Tver'. Evidently Yaroslav had been attempting to infiltrate into this sensitive border area, for in the treaty it was laid down that he must own no lands in Bezhetskiy Verkh (Bezhichi), must not tamper with the legal privileges bestowed by his predecessors on Bezhetskiy Verkh and the district of Obonezh'e (between Lakes Ladoga and Onega) and must not abduct any of the citizens of the area.[28]

The events of the following two years did little to assuage Yaroslav's anger with Novgorod or the Novgorodians' mistrust of Yaroslav and his nephew Yury. They were years of intense military activity. Urged on though they were by Dovmont, the Novgorodians set their sights not so much on Lithuania as on Pskov's western neighbour Estonia, the southern half of which was effectively controlled by the Teutonic Knights, while the northern half, from Revel' (Tallinn) to Narva, had been in Danish hands since 1238. The prime objectives were the Baltic port of Revel' and the castle of Rakovor (Rakvere, Wesenburg), built by the Danes in 1252, half way between Revel' and Narva.[29]

The first campaign, which took place in 1267, was a total failure. The army lacked a leader, and nobody seemed to know just where they were heading for. The Novgorodians consulted with Yury, as well they might – he was after all the grand prince's deputy – but were unable to decide on their objective :

Lithuania, Polotsk or Danish-held Estonia? Eventually an army set off west-wards along the Shelon' river heading for Lithuania or Polotsk. But a disa-greement among the commanders arose. The army stopped, went back down the Shelon' and moved north-west. This time they crossed the Narova river and laid siege to the castle of Rakovor but were unable to take it. They returned to Novgorod thoroughly disillusioned with the grand prince's nephew.[30]

The conquest of Rakovor, and ultimately Revel', however, was still consid-ered a viable project, and at the end of 1267 the Novgorodians decided to mount a full-scale operation. This time they studiously avoided consultation with Yury and took advice from the *posadnik* Mikhail. So great was the army raised and so impressive the pieces of artillery refurbished in the archbishop's court that the Teutonic Knights even sent envoys begging the Novgorodians not to attack their lands (i.e. southern Estonia) and promising to remain neutral provided operations were confined to Revel' and Rakovor, a promise which they failed to keep. The operations (January–February 1268), which are described in great detail by an eye-witness in the Novgorod First Chronicle,[31] were conducted by Dmitry Aleksandrovich of Pereyaslavl', the first prince to be sent for. There were detachments from Tver', Smolensk and Pskov, as well as local Novgorod troops. Dovmont and Yury took part, as did the *posadnik* himself. But for all the preparation and for all the size of the army, little was achieved. Yury, not the chronicler's favourite prince by a long chalk, ran away on the battlefield; *Posadnik* Mikhail was killed; and the *tysyatskiy* was reported missing. Rakovor did not fall. Yaroslav, who permitted two of his sons to participate, can hardly have been pleased with the result.

Irritated by the restrictions of the treaty, annoyed by the treatment of his nephew Yury and worried by the fruitless fighting on the western frontiers and the resulting drain in manpower, Yaroslav appeared himself in Novgorod in June 1269 to voice his complaints. His anger is evident from the words put into his mouth by the chronicler: 'My men and my brothers and your men have been killed, and you have broken the peace with the Germans.' He laid the blame on three of the leading boyars, one of whom, Elevfery Sbyslavich, had usurped Yury's position and led the expedition against the Lithuanians in 1267 (see above, p. 134). He proposed confiscating their estates. How near to a complete breach both sides were is clear from the subsequent events. The Novgorodians under *Posadnik* Pavsha Onan'ich, who had replaced Mikhail, stood by the three boyars; Yaroslav threatened to break off all relations and to 'depart' (*iz goroda ekhati*); the Novgorodians attempted to avert what would have amounted to a declaration of war by arguing, somewhat unconvincingly, that they had 'not yet completed peace discussions with the Germans' – a ref-erence to negotiations with the Teutonic Knights following an unsuccessful German attack on Pskov in May 1269. Eventually Yaroslav lost patience and withdrew from the city. He was only persuaded to return and 'shed his anger' by a delegation consisting of the archbishop and several of the leading boyars. One of the conditions under which he agreed to come back was the eventual appointment of a close supporter of his, Ratibor Kluksovich, as *tysyatskiy* in place of Kondrat, who was still missing after the Rakovor campaign.[32]

The conflict between Novgorod and the grand prince was by no means over. For the rest of 1269 there was an uneasy peace. Tempers simmered on both sides. Another contract had to be drawn up. This time the tone of the representatives of Novgorod was slightly more conciliatory: Yaroslav was requested to 'lay aside his anger with the *posadnik* and all Novgorod', not to avenge himself either by judiciary measures or by any other means and not to bear a grudge against the archbishop. Two further clauses, however, still further restricted his rights: he was not to 'exercise judgment without the *posadnik*', a severe limitation on his previous juridical rights, nor were Novgorodians to be subject to Suzdalian law when outside their territory.[33]

In matters of foreign policy Yaroslav was unable to see eye to eye with the Novgorodians. After yet another major expedition against northern Estonia was begged off by the Danes, who agreed to yield the Narova river to Novgorod,[34] Yaroslav switched his attention to that bone of contention between Sweden and Novgorod, Karelia, the district north of the Neva and west of Lake Ladoga. This time the Novgorodians refused to cooperate, and Yaroslav was obliged to send home the large army he had gathered for the invasion of Estonia.

All was set for a major collision between the grand prince and Novgorod. The crisis came in 1270. Novgorod was split into two uneven parts, with the majority of the boyars opposed to Yaroslav. Events followed what was by now a traditional pattern. First, a *veche* was summoned, as a result of which one of Yaroslav's followers was murdered and others fled to the prince's residence at Gorodishche on the outskirts of the town. A list of complaints was drawn up at the *veche*: Yaroslav was abusing his hunting rights, illegally confiscating the property of others, expelling foreign merchants, committing unspecified 'violence' (*nasilie*). He was told to leave, and when he tried to reason with the *veche* and even agreed to amend his ways, he was threatened with force: 'All Novgorod will march against you and chase you out.' He had no alternative but to depart.

He was not, however, prepared to surrender Novgorod without a struggle, nor could Novgorod afford to remain for long without a prince. Both set about trying to rectify the situation. The Novgorodians appealed to Dmitry Aleksandrovich to be their prince, while Yaroslav sent Ratibor Kluksovich to Saray to ask for military assistance from the Tatars in order to stiffen the army that was being raised in Suzdalia. Neither was successful. Dmitry refused: he could hardly risk a war with his uncle; and Ratibor's mission to the khan was frustrated by Yaroslav's brother, Vasily of Kostroma, who for the first time appeared on the political scene to persuade the khan that the Novgorodians had right on their side and that Yaroslav was to blame for the crisis (see above, p. 129). Neither was prepared to give way. The Novgorodians erected fortifications around the city – a sure sign that they meant business – and took up a defensive position on the Shelon' river. Yaroslav moved to the town of Rusa on the river Polist' with his Suzdalian army, which included troops from Smolensk and Dmitry Aleksandrovich's patrimony of Pereyaslavl'. A final effort was made by Yaroslav to reach a compromise: he let the Novgorodians know that all the princes of Suzdalia were ranged on his side, but that he was still ready to meet their grievances. It was to no avail. The Novgorodians were adamant. 'Go, we do not want you', they repeated.

Had it come to a fight, Yaroslav and the forces of Suzdalia would have had little difficulty in overwhelming the Novgorodians who, apart from local troops and detachments from their northern provinces, could perhaps only count on the aid of Vasily of Kostroma, and his army was an unknown quantity. Yaroslav, as it turned out, had no need for arms. He had an even stronger weapon in the Church. While the two armies were facing each other waiting for hostilities to start, a message arrived in Novgorod from Metropolitan Kirill. It guaranteed the sincerity of Yaroslav's readiness to abjure 'all evil', it enjoined the Novgorodians to refrain from blood-letting, and, according to one version, it threatened the Novgorodians with the ultimate sanction should they not obey the metropolitan — excommunication.[35] It was not the first time a metropolitan had intervened in a political quarrel,[36] but it was the first and only recorded case in the thirteenth century of the head of the Church not only interceding on behalf of the grand prince but also achieving his aim by the threat of excommunication; and it was a pointer to the future support which the rulers of Moscow were to receive from the metropolitans of the fourteenth century.

The Church's intervention was successful. Yaroslav was reinstated on the throne of Novgorod in the presence of two envoys of the khan,[37] having submitted, it is true, to all the terms demanded of him by Novgorod. He agreed to abide by the conditions of the contract drawn up at the end of 1269 and to accept still further limitations on his authority: Novgorodian merchants were to be free to carry out their business 'in the land of Suzdal' without let or hindrance, according to the khan's charter' (presumably a concession extracted from Khan Mangu Temir by Vasily of Kostroma); there was to be no deportation of citizens from Novgorod to Suzdalia or from Suzdalia to Novgorod; and all hostages held by Yury, Yaroslav, Yaroslav's wife and Yaroslav's agents were to be released.[38]

In this the final struggle between Novgorod and Yaroslav the pattern of the future relationship between Novgorod and the grand prince was clearly emerging. True, Yaroslav seems to have won over to his side the powerful figure of Dmitry Aleksandrovich of Pereyaslavl' and true, he had the support of some of the princes of Suzdalia, or so he claimed. But Novgorod was manifestly strengthening its position and gaining more and more independence from the grand prince. The boyars were more cohesively opposed to their prince than in any earlier period of the history of Novgorod; there was no sign of support for the grand prince from the 'greater' or the 'lesser' boyars. Yaroslav's lieutenant-governor Yury was largely ignored, and his son Svyatoslav was ignominiously pushed out of Pskov. But worst of all, his authority was drastically eroded by the various treaties agreed to by both sides. If the first contract of 1265 was restrictive enough, the subsequent ones stripped him of even more of his privileges and power. By the time of his final assumption of control in 1270 he could do little without the consent of the *posadnik*, his juridical rights were curtailed and there were no new means whereby he could enrich himself at Novgorod's expense. He had become little more than a mercenary hired to defend the frontiers and unable to dictate how the real rulers of Novgorod should conduct their foreign policy.

The Novgorodians could hardly have welcomed Yaroslav's reinstatement. But they had no choice in the matter. The metropolitan's threat of excommunication was something they could not ignore. The presence of Mangu Temir's representatives was enough to ensure that Yaroslav was duly seated upon the throne. Not surprisingly, he left after the formalities were completed. This time he felt himself sufficiently secure to appoint in his place a mere boyar, one Andrey Vorotislavich, who had cooperated with him in the early stages of the *myatezh* of 1270. The unpopular Yury, presumably, had been sent back to his patrimony of Suzdal'. As for Pskov, Yaroslav sent one 'Prince Aygust' (Augustus?) to replace Dovmont.[39] Who Aygust was is not known – possibly a Lithuanian princeling opposed to Dovmont?[40] – but he only lasted a short time, as Dovmont was again in action in the spring of 1271, this time warding off a routine attack on Pskovite territory by the Teutonic Knights.[41]

Even though the question of Novgorod had been temporarily settled it was unlikely that there would be lasting peace in north-east Russia. Yaroslav and his brother Vasily were at loggerheads. Dmitry Aleksandrovich, despite his youth, was a figure to be reckoned with: his elder brother Vasily had ceased to play any role in the political life of Suzdalia since his expulsion from Novgorod in 1260, and when he died in early 1271 Dmitry automatically became the senior grandson of Yaroslav Vsevolodovich and next in the line for the grand-princely throne after the death of his uncles Yaroslav and Vasily. But it was not in the interest of the khan to allow the three leading princes to fight it out amongst themselves, and accordingly all three were summoned to the Horde in 1271. What happened there is not recorded: all we know is that in the winter of that year Yaroslav died while 'travelling from the Tatars' – the third time such a phrase had been used in connection with a grand prince's death in just over a quarter of a century – and that Vasily of Kostroma was installed upon the throne of Vladimir in 1271.[42]

Even if Mangu Temir sanctioned the accession of Vasily and gave him the patent, it was no guarantee that peace would ensue. The root of the trouble was, predictably, Novgorod. Although the Trinity Chronicle states, as it did six years previously with regard to Yaroslav, that Vasily 'became grand prince of Vladimir *and* Novgorod', his acceptance by Novgorod was anything but a foregone conclusion. Both he and Dmitry, 'intending to sit upon the throne', sent their representatives to Novgorod. After considering their applications the boyars sent not for the grand prince but for Dmitry, who 'accepted the throne' on 9 October 1272.[43] It was not just that Dmitry was popular and well-known to the Novgorodians, having 'ruled' there from 1259 to 1264 and having taken part in the Yur'ev and Rakovor campaigns in 1262 and 1268 respectively; there were other reasons as well. Tatishchev gives us a clue as to the cause of the Novgorodians' unwillingness to accept Vasily:

[Vasily] sent his lieutenants to Novgorod and ordered that the contracts of his brother Yaroslav be invalidated, saying 'wrongly did you extract these contracts from my

brother: from time immemorial such a thing has not happened . . .'. And the Novgorodians said 'it was you who devised this for us at that time [clearly a reference to
Vasily's intervention at the Horde in 1270]. If you do not wish to kiss the cross on
these conditions, then you are not the prince for us. We shall get a prince for
ourselves.'[44]

Although no other sources mention Vasily's demands, Tatishchev's version
was clearly not invented by him; and it has the ring of truth about it. Vasily's
unwillingness to rule in Novgorod on the same conditions as those imposed
upon his brother was without doubt the major reason for the boyars' choice of
Dmitry.

This time it was war. Vasily had no intention of letting Dmitry get away
with it. As soon as the news of Dmitry's enthronement reached him, he tried
military intimidation: he entered Torzhok, burned several buildings and placed
his representatives or lieutenant-governors (tiuny, namestniki) in the town. At
the same time he sent his voevoda, one Semen, to ravage the outlying districts
of Novgorod.[45] When neither of these actions had any noticeable effect, he
brought in Tatar troops. His nephew Svyatoslav of Tver' with an army of Tver-
ites and Tatars attacked the border districts of Volok Lamskiy, Bezhichi and
Vologda; while he himself, accompanied by the 'great baskak of Vladimir and
many of the khan's Tatars', invaded Novgorodian territory (see above,
p. 129). At the same time economic pressure was brought to bear on the Novgorodians: all their merchants who happened to be in Vladimir, Tver' and
Kostroma were arrested and their goods confiscated. As a result there was a
dramatic rise in the price of corn in Novgorod.[46]

The war and the food shortage were enough to move the Novgorodians.
There was nothing for it but for them to take counter-measures, and in the
winter of 1272–3 Dmitry and all the Novgorodian troops he could raise set
off eastwards towards Tver', the nearest Suzdalian district. Before risking a
clash with the combined Tatar-Suzdalian force, however, he sent three senior
boyars – one a future posadnik – to Vasily in Vladimir. The conditions they
laid before the grand prince amounted to four demands: return all captured
Novgorodian districts, stop trying to win the throne of Novgorod, free all the
merchants arrested and make peace. They were totally unacceptable. Vasily,
confident of his military superiority and aware of his inalienable right to the
throne of Novgorod as grand prince, dismissed the envoys and refused all offers
of peace. He had little more to do. When Dmitry and his army arrived in Torzhok en route for Tver', the entire town, already governed by Vasily's tiuny,
rose up in revolt against Dmitry and Novgorod. The citizens had had enough.
Menaced by the Suzdalians and the Tatars ('All the Lower Land is against us',
are the words put into their mouths by the Nikon chronicler), they settled for
Vasily. There was nothing Dmitry could do but relinquish Novgorod and retire
to Pereyaslavl', which he did in January 1273. He had been prince of Novgorod
for just three months.[47]

It was the end of the troubles in Novgorod, at least for the time being. A
certain amount of reorganization, of course, was inevitable. Pavsha Onan'ich,
posadnik since 1269, fled when Dmitry left, but later in the year made his peace

with Vasily and was reinstated; Ratibor Kluksovich, the *tysyatskiy* whose mission to the Horde in 1270 Vasily had so successfully foiled (see above, p. 136), was arrested; and those responsible for the *kramola* were summarily punished.[48] But apart from these measures nothing was done to settle any differences there may have been between Vasily and Novgorod. No fresh demands were made on Vasily, nor did Vasily attempt to alter the terms of his brother's contract, which presumably he accepted: at any rate no new treaties were drawn up. For the rest of Vasily's reign as grand prince nothing sufficiently ruffled the calm of the city to warrant mention by the chroniclers.

Vasily lived for another four years. During that period there were no more civil wars, no more signs of enmity between the rulers of north-east Russia. But the last four years of the reign were marked by a significant and wholly sinister increase of the dependence of the Russians on the Horde, or rather of the Tatars' growing control over Suzdalia. The number of Tatar troops now stationed in the country was considerable; this is evident from the ease with which both Vasily and his nephew Svyatoslav had been able to call upon Tatar reinforcements against Novgorod in 1272. But while these reinforcements had been under the control of Russian commanders and had acted solely in their interests, the Tatar detachments which took part in an unsuccessful joint Russo-Tatar attack on Lithuania in 1275 totally ignored their Russian commanders and acted on their own, causing considerable damage to the Russian lands they passed through both before and after the fighting in Lithuania:

In that year [1275] the Tatars and the Russians marched against Lithuania and having achieved nothing returned. But the Tatars did much wrong and much violence to the Christians [i.e. the Russian population] as they marched to Lithuania, and on their way back they did still more evil things . . . they plundered houses, took away horses, cattle and possessions, and whenever they met anyone they robbed him and sent him away naked . . .[49]

Of course parts of this passage may have been added to the original account at the beginning of the fifteenth century when the chronicle containing it (the Trinity Chronicle) was compiled, but the concluding sentence – 'This I have written so that people will remember and learn from it' – looks like the work of a contemporary, and it would seem that 1275 saw the first of a long series of destructive military actions carried out by the Tatars independently of the Russian princes.

Still more menacing were the signs of the Tatars' growing dissatisfaction with their Russian subjects. In 1275 Vasily was summoned to the Horde. He took with him the Tatar tribute. According to Tatishchev, the only source to give what looks like reliable information on the affair, the khan objected to the paucity of the tribute collected.[50] Vasily countered by saying that the number of taxpayers was according to the previous census. The result was that the khan ordered a second census of all the Russian land with the exception of the clergy. This time no chronicle records any reaction of any Russian district. Opposition to the census officials was a thing of the past. Indeed, only a handful of chronicles mention the census at all.[51] Resistance was dead.

Vasily returned from the Horde in 1276. In January 1277 he was dead. He was buried in his town of Kostroma, thirty-five years old and heirless. In the events of his and his brother's reigns Aleksandr's legacy became manifest. Neither Yaroslav nor Vasily had been able to take any positive steps to strengthen the authority of the grand prince or in any way to secure the future for an independent north-east Russian state. There was little effective unity among the descendants of Vsevolod III. The Novgorodians were gradually establishing the independence of their local forces from the grand prince in an attempt to make the appointment of the prince-mercenary less of a defence necessity; they were trying to settle the inter-boyar conflicts which had previously damaged opposition to the prince; they were restricting the prince's activities by written agreements; and they were evolving a system which was to lead eventually to the establishement of a 'Council of Lords' (*Sovet gospod*) consisting of representatives of the five city districts (*kontsy*) and to the annual appointment of *posadniki* (see below, p. 157). All this greatly diminished the risk of in-fighting between various groups supporting this or that candidate for the throne, markedly decreased the arbitrary powers of whoever ruled Novgorod and paved the way towards what might be called oligarchic republicanism.

Nothing was done by Yaroslav or Vasily to spread their influence to the south or west of Suzdalia. True, Novgorod's western frontiers, and all of Suzdalia's, remained undented, and true, the attacks of the Teutonic Knights on Pskovite territory slackened noticeably during this period. But all the time the nascent state of Lithuania was gaining strength, penetrating, both peacefully and militarily, into the north-western districts of the old Kievan empire and establishing control over the ethnically Russian territories of Polotsk, Black Rus' (the lands watered by the upper Neman river), northern Volynia (the lands of Berest'e and Dorogochinin) and the western half of what had once been the principality of Turov and Pinsk.[32] Taking advantage of the impotence of the rulers of Suzdalia, Mindovg's successors were quietly laying the foundations of the huge Lithuanian state which was later to embrace most of White Russia and the Ukraine. Had support and encouragement been given to Dovmont in pursuit of his Lithuanian ventures, then perhaps the boundaries of eastern Europe in the fourteenth and fifteenth centuries might have been very different. But, as has been shown, Yaroslav actively discouraged him and was only prepared to support his military activities in northern Estonia – and these turned out to be fruitless in the end.

The most lasting results of Aleksandr Nevskiy's policies, however, are to be seen in the growing enthralment of Suzdalia by the Tatars. There was no longer any question of resistance to Tatar domination. Instead, the Russians were beginning to look to the Horde for military aid in their own internal squabbles, and the Tatars were beginning to show an increasing interest in Russian affairs and to realize that the wealth of the Russian land was there to be ravished. The last quarter of the thirteenth century was to witness a series of particularly ruinous Tatar interventions, raids and invasions.

CIVIL WAR AND TATAR DOMINATION 1277–1304

During the last twenty-seven years before the beginning of the great struggle between the rival principalities of Moscow and Tver' for supremacy in north-east Russia, the downward political trend noted in the previous section continued undiminished. Most of the negative features of the rule of Aleksandr Nevskiy's two successors were emphasized in this grim age of civil war and growing Tatar domination. Neither of the two grand princes who followed Vasily Yaroslavich on the throne of Vladimir had the strength, the single-mindedness, the ability or just the luck to unite the princes of Suzdalia or to challenge the nascent authority of the families of their brother Daniil of Moscow or their cousin Mikhail Yaroslavich of Tver'. Nor did they have the good fortune to form dynasties. Indeed, by 1304 their families had fizzled out: the male heirs of both Dmitry and Andrey were dead.[53]

There was as little unity as before among the various princes of Suzdalia. Towards the end of the period, it is true, there were signs of powerful alliances being tentatively formed amongst the principalities, but in the main these turned out to be only temporary and were invariably directed not against external enemies but against political opponents within Suzdalia.

By far the most sinister symptom of the disintegration of the grand prince's power was the ever-increasing subservience to the Tatar khan. The invasions, the raids, the occupations, the repeated summoning of princes to the Horde, and above all the eagerness of the Russian rulers to call in Tatar armies merely to help them achieve their own political ends – all this illustrates the impotence and the bondage of north-east Russia at the end of the thirteenth century.[54]

When Vasily Yaroslavich died childless in 1277, the genealogical pendulum swung back to the family of his eldest brother, and he was succeeded by his nephew, the eldest surviving son of Aleksandr Nevskiy, Dmitry of Pereyaslavl'. The descendants of the senior branch of the Vsevolodovichi, the grandchildren and great-grandchildren of Konstantin of Rostov, were, as has been pointed out above (p. 110), debarred from succession and were never considered as candidates for the grand-princely throne, nor did they ever lay claim to it. As for the princes of the tiny and relatively insignificant districts of Yur'ev Pol'skiy and Starodub, the descendants of Svyatoslav and Ivan Vsevolodovichi respectively, they too seem to have been out of the running for the succession.[55]

With the death of Vasily Yaroslavich little changed in the distribution of the Russian lands among the princely families. The northern principalities of Rostov, Yaroslavl', Beloozero and Uglich were still independent of the grand prince of Vladimir and were held as before by the descendants of Konstantin Vsevolodovich. On acceding to the throne of Vladimir, Dmitry Aleksandrovich retained his hold on what was by now considered to be his patrimony, Northern Pereyaslavl'. His next eldest brother, Andrey, had to make do with the distant district of Gorodets on the Volga, which had been carved out of the former holding of the prince of Suzdal' and now formed an awkward wedge between Suzdal' and its eastern dependency of Nizhniy Novgorod, the patrimony of the sons of Andrey Yaroslavich, Yury and Mikhail.[56] Moscow, Tver' and Northern Galich (to which, incongruously, had been added the district of Dmitrov, west of Pereyaslavl') remained in the hands of their former owners, Dmitry's younger brother Daniil, the sons of Yaroslav Yaroslavich and the insignificant David Konstantinovich respectively. As for Kostroma, it is hard to say what happened to it when Vasily died in 1277. At one time we find Andrey Aleksandrovich's *voevoda* Semen Tonilovich hiding, and being murdered, there (1283); ten years later Dmitry's son Ivan 'sat upon the throne of Kostroma', and in 1303 Andrey's son Boris died there. Evidently it formed part of the grand-princely territory and was at the disposal of the grand prince. For most of the period Novgorod was held by whoever was grand prince or by his appointee, while Pskov was still ruled by the longeval and tough Lithuanian Dovmont, who died only in 1299.

Very little is known of the lands south of the Oka. Smolensk continued to be ruled by members of the clan of the Rostislavichi, and indeed Fedor Rostislavich of Mozhaysk, who had become prince of Yaroslavl' in 1260 by marrying into the family of the Konstantinovichi (see above, Ch. 5, note 2), followed his two elder brothers, Gleb (died 1277) and Mikhaylo (died 1279), on the throne of Smolensk (1280) and remained ruler of both principalities until 1297 when his nephew Aleksandr Glebovich ousted him in Smolensk. Ryazan' and Murom to the south-east of Vladimir seem to have carried on under their own princely families and led an existence quite independent of Vladimir. As for the heartlands of the old Kievan empire – Kiev, Chernigov and Southern Pereyaslavl' – we have practically no information on their history in the last quarter of the thirteenth century. There were survivors of princely families, especially of the Chernigov clan, but it seems likely that most of the south was under strict Tatar control and that considerable fragmentation of territory was the general rule.

South-west Russia, during the last quarter of the thirteenth century, ceased to be of any interest whatsoever to the chroniclers of the north; at any rate no mention of the old principalities of Volynia and Galicia is made by them. Only the Ipat'evskiy Chronicle continues its confused and haphazard narrative about the descendants of Daniil and Vasil'ko Romanovichi. The northerners' lack of interest in the district south-west of them is not really surprising. Suzdalia was far removed from the frontiers of Volynia and Galicia, separated from them by the lands of Smolensk and the old principality of Turov and Pinsk; there were no longer any marriages to link the dynasty of the Vsevolodovichi with that of the Romanovichi; and politically Volynia and Galicia were absorbed by their relations with their neighbours: in the north the Lithuanians: in the west the Poles and the Hungarians: and in the south the Tatars.

Ever since Khan Berke's general, Burunday, had overrun Volynia and Galicia in 1260, the two principalities had been virtual vassals of the Horde. There was no further resistance to the Tatars. Yet for the time being the princes were still able to lead an existence reasonably independent of the khan and his local agents, even though they were obliged to obtain his patents for their throne.[57] At Daniil's death in 1264 south-west Russia was divided between his sons,

Shvarn and Lev, and his brother Vasil'ko, who retained Vladimir, the capital of Volynia. For a time even, Shvarn, who held eastern Galicia and much of the west bank of the upper Bug river, managed to rule Black Rus' (the area of the upper Neman river) as well: he acquired the territory from his brother-in-law Voyshelk of Lithuania, but it reverted to Lithuania on Shvarn's death (1267). Of the other Romanovichi, Lev Danilovich emerged as the most powerful, ruling, as he did, most of Galicia and the lands on the west bank of the Bug. His relations with Lithuania were on the whole peaceful – Grand Prince Troyden (Traidenis), it is true, seized Dorogochinin on the Bug, only to lose it to Lev, who retrieved it with Tatar help in 1279 – but this was because for much of the period Lithuania was fully occupied with the Teutonic Order. In fact, during the last three decades of the thirteenth century, Lithuania acquired no more land at the expense of Volynia and Galicia. As for the Tatars, their hold over the south-west increased considerably at the time of their devastating raids of 1286 and 1287. These drastically undermined the authority of the princes and paved the way for the ultimate surrender of their lands to their northern and western neighbours. But it was not until the mid-fourteenth century that the Tatars' control over south-west Russia faded and Galicia and parts of western Volynia fell into Polish hands, while the great Ol'gerd of Lithuania annexed the remainder of Volynia together with its capital Vladimir.[58]

*   *   *   *

In order to understand the reasons for the political decline of north-east Russia in the last quarter of the thirteenth century, the growing subservience of the princes to the Tatars and the debilitating civil wars which preceded the emergence of Mikhail of Tver' as grand prince in 1304, we must look briefly to the political situation in the Pontic steppes during this period. The story of the successors of Khan Berke, who died in 1267, is a complex and intriguing one. A straightforward narrative of events would lead one to believe that this, as an age of internecine war amongst the Juchids, was one of decline. Yet for all their internal disorders the khans managed to maintain an ever stricter control over their Russian subjects and to increase their authority in Hungary and spread it to the Balkans. However much the power of the Kipchak Horde may have splintered in the 1280s and the 1290s, the Russians were totally unable to exploit what might have appeared to them as a slackening of the authority of their masters in the south.

During the khanate of Baty's grandson, Mangu Temir, who ruled in Saray from Berke's death in 1267 to 1280, the star of yet another Juchid prince was in the ascendant. This was Nogay, a great-grandson of Juchi, but of a cadet branch. His horde stemmed from the area of the river Yaik, which flows into the Caspian Sea east of the Volga, yet his main sphere of activity was west of the Golden Horde – on the northern banks of the Black Sea and in the Balkans. Gradually he built up his great empire, which stretched westwards from the Dnepr and embraced Bulgarians, Wallachians on the lower Danube, Moldavians, and, later on, Serbs. He ranged across the northern shores of the Black Sea. His armies fought in Transcaucasia, Transylvania, Serbia, Bessarabia and

Asia Minor. At times he had close diplomatic links with Egypt and Constantinople. Two princesses of his family were married to László IV of Hungary, while he himself was married to an illegitimate daughter of Emperor Michael VIII Palaeologus.[59] Is it surprising that this immensely energetic conqueror, this Chinghis Khan of the Pontic steppes, became the rival of his cousins in Saray, the officially elected khans of Kipchak?

The great dichotomy began in 1280 when Tuda Mangu succeeded his brother Mangu Temir as khan of the Golden Horde and Nogay established himself as virtual co-ruler. Gradually Tuda Mangu lost ground, delegating much of his authority to his nephew Tula Bugha (Telebuga in the Russian sources), who himself became khan in 1287 after Tuda Mangu's abdication. Relations between Tula Bugha and Nogay soon soured. Tula Bugha's two campaigns against the il-khans of Persia (1288, 1290), the aim of which was the capture of Azerbaijan, both ended in failure and led to yet another split: this time Tula Bugha's enemies at Saray favoured a rival in Mangu Temir's son Toktu, who, when threatened with arrest by Tula Bugha, sought asylum with Nogay. Together, Nogay and Toktu had Tula Bugha murdered (1291) and Toktu was proclaimed khan. Toktu, however, was made of sterner stuff than his cousin or his uncle. Determined to be sole ruler amongst the Tatars of the Pontic steppes, he built up his army, reasserted his authority in Russia, and, in 1293 or 1294, led his armies against Nogay. He was, however, beaten and it was not until 1299 that he marched again against Nogay. This time Nogay was killed and his army defeated. It was the end of the period of dual rule. Toktu established himself as sole khan in the Golden Horde. His rival's horde disintegrated. His reign (until 1312) and that of his nephew Uzbeg (1312–41) marked 'the apogee of Mongol rule in Russia'.[60]

* * * *

The extraordinary and bitter civil strife which raged in Russia in the 1280s, the 1290s and the first few years of the fourteenth century seems at first sight to have been based merely on the rivalry and enmity of different princes and different groups of princes. It looks as though it was a vast family squabble to acquire power and land, with no thought whatsoever for the common weal. But much of the bitterness of the strife arose from Tatar policy, and the course of events in Russia was clearly influenced by the fluctuations of power in the Kipchak steppes.

The civil war did not start immediately after Vasily's death. For nearly five years there was no fighting amongst the princes; indeed no chronicles mention any immediate rivalry for the throne between the eldest sons of Aleksandr Nevskiy, Dmitry and Andrey. Both were old enough to rule: Dmitry was at least 27 and Andrey probably 22.[61] It seems likely that Dmitry took the law into his own hands and, as senior claimant, simply pronounced himself grand prince. At any rate he did not go to the Horde for the patent, nor is there any evidence to show that the khan's envoys 'placed him upon the throne', as was normally the practice. The majority of the remaining princes were summoned to Saray in 1277, not, it seems, to be confirmed as rulers of their patrimonies,[62] but to be obliged to take part in a Caucasian campaign under Mangu Temir's command.[63] As Andrey was one of them, it explains why Dmitry was not challenged for the first two or three years of his reign. It was as well for him that he was not, for most of the time he was busily engaged in Novgorod (see below, p. 156). By 1281 Dmitry had settled affairs in the west to his liking and was back in Suzdalia. It was then that the storm broke.

In 1281 Andrey Aleksandrovich set off to the Horde. The aim of his journey may have been to pay his respects to the new khan Tuda Mangu, but it was also to request the patent for the grand principality. Tuda Mangu's reaction was favourable. He sent Andrey back to Russia with a Tatar army. Andrey was joined by a number of princes – the Trinity Chronicle mentions Fedor Rostislavich of Yaroslavl', Mikhail Ivanovich of Starodub and Konstantin Borisovich of Rostov – and the combined force set about ravaging the country in no uncertain manner. Murom, Pereyaslavl', Vladimir, Yur'ev and Suzdal' were the first areas to suffer. The army then moved north to the Rostov district and west as far as Tver' and Torzhok and proceeded to lay them waste. The author of the largest account of what he calls 'Andrey's first campaign' (Trinity Chronicle), strongly biased against Andrey, pulls out all the stops and stresses the horror, misery and slaughter with a run of well-worn clichés: men, women and children killed or led off into captivity; nuns and priests' wives raped; towns, villages, monasteries, churches sacked; ikons, books, jewels, chalices looted, 'and there was great fear and trembling among the Christians'.[64] Even though little credence can be given to these descriptions of universal disaster, which are so commonly paralleled in the pages of the early chronicles, nevertheless their degree of intensity is equal to, if not greater than, that of the accounts of Baty's invasion in 1237–40. 'Andrey's first campaign' was clearly one of the major Tatar inroads of the thirteenth century.

There was little Dmitry could do. Somehow he managed to escape from Pereyaslavl'. Realizing that Novgorod was unlikely to offer him asylum, he fled to the fortress he had built in the previous year in Kopor'e, north-west of Novgorod. Even here he was unsafe. The Novgorodians made it clear that he would receive no help from them. Instead they allowed him to flee the country. On 1 January 1282 he went 'across the sea', evidently to Sweden, just like his uncle Andrey had done thirty years earlier. Not even his son-in-law, the great Dovmont of Pskov, could save him, although he succeeded in transferring many of his possessions from Kopor'e to Ladoga, which he had seized on the day Dmitry had fled.[65] In February 1282 the Novgorodians showed still more clearly where their sympathies lay. They levelled Dmitry's fortress to the ground, chased out those of his followers who were still there and sent to Vladimir for the new grand prince. Andrey lost no time; he sent his Tatar army back to the Horde, came straight to Novgorod and was solemnly installed on the throne.[66] His position, however, was anything but secure.

The Tatar expedition of 1281 could hardly have endeared Andrey to the population of Suzdalia, and, as was to be expected, Dmitry soon returned, doubtless with Swedish reinforcements,[67] to his former capital of Pereyaslavl', which he proceeded to rebuild and refortify. Refugees flowed in, much to the alarm of Andrey, who quit Novgorod and made his way back to Vladimir, because, as the chronicle puts it, 'he was afraid of his brother Dmitry, who at that time was in Pereyaslavl''.[68] There was nothing he could do, given the meagre local resources, to stand up to the threat of Dmitry, whose first aim was to regain control of Torzhok and then to win back Novgorod. Semen Mikhaylovich, the *posadnik* of Novgorod, who had accompanied Andrey to Vladimir, was sent to Torzhok with instructions not to admit Dmitry's men or his governors. Andrey himself went to his patrimonial town of Gorodets on the Volga and from there proceeded once again to Saray.

Andrey's second visit to Tuda Mangu was just as successful as his first. In order to press his claim he complained about his elder brother's attitude to the khan: Dmitry had no intention not only of obeying the khan, but also – the most effective crime Andrey could think up   of paying tribute.[69] His arguments were immediately effective. Tuda Mangu provided him with a second army, and with it Andrey proceeded to ravage the same districts in Russia as before. Once again the pendulum swung back in favour of Andrey. Dmitry, for all the strength of his position in Pereyaslavl', realized that he could not stand up to his brother, the second Tatar army, the Novgorodians and most of the Russian princes. Indeed, earlier in 1282, a combined army from Novgorod, Tver' and Moscow had marched against him and had only been dissuaded from attacking Pereyaslavl' after five days of negotiations while the two armies faced each other near Dmitrov.[70] His answer was to exploit the dichotomy amongst the Tatars and to seek support from Nogay.

So Dmitry went to Nogay and returned to Russia with yet another Tatar expeditionary force. Brother faced brother, each supported by rival Tatar detachments. The chaos which ensued only too clearly illustrates the weakness and instability of the two brothers and their inability to do anything more than call in outsiders, Swedes and Tatars, to help solve the incessant struggle for power. So chaotic was the situation that the contemporary Suzdalian chronicle, which supported Dmitry, and the Novgorod chronicle, which at the time, remembering Novgorod's previous conflicts with Dmitry, favoured Andrey, give different and conflicting accounts of what actually happened. Their attitude eloquently expresses the feeling of unrest and confusion which gripped the whole of the north of Russia at the time.

Andrey's first reaction to Dmitry's arrival from Nogay's horde was to secure the friendship of Novgorod. He met with Semen Mikhaylovich, the *posadnik*, in Torzhok and signed a treaty according to which Andrey was not to yield Novgorod, nor was Novgorod to seek any other prince than Andrey.[71] But, as was so often the case in the thirteenth century, Novgorodian military support was hardly enough to tip the scales in Andrey's favour. Dmitry's Tatar army and whatever support he may have received from Sweden or from other principalities in Suzdalia was sufficient to oblige Andrey to yield not only Novgorod but also the grand-princely throne of Vladimir. Yet Novgorod refused to accept Dmitry; it was to pay dearly for its stubbornness. In the winter of 1283–84 'all the princes' led by Dmitry and Andrey together with a Tatar army invaded Novgorod territory. It was one of those rare occasions in the second half of the thirteenth century on which 'the whole Suzdalian land' cooperated against Novgorod and the only one on which they did it with Tatar backing. Of course it was successful. After 'much evil' and the ritual burning of towns and villages peace was concluded. Dmitry was once again not only grand prince but also ruler of Novgorod.[72]

Clearly it was only under extreme pressure that Andrey yielded to Dmitry, and if Dmitry hoped that his troubles were over now that he had regained the throne he was sorely mistaken. Andrey had no intention whatsoever of giving up his quest for power, still less so when he learned of the fate of his senior boyar Semen Tonilevich. Semen, according at least to the anti-Andrey Trinity Chronicle, was Andrey's evil genius, his 'aid and accomplice', 'the false instigator of sedition'; it was he who was partially responsible for raising Andrey's first Tatar expeditionary force in 1281 and was one of the generals, if not the commander-in-chief, of the second Tatar army which invaded Russia in 1282. Dmitry himself was only too aware of Semen's role and after his installation as grand prince sent two of his boyars to Kostroma, where Semen had taken refuge after his master's capitulation. The Nikon Chronicle gives a vivid account of their interrogation of Semen, perhaps invented, but none the less plausible for all that. They accused him of 'raising the khan of the Horde' and of 'leading Tatars against our master, Grand Prince Dmitry Aleksandrovich'. Semen denied responsibility and advised his torturers to ask *his* master, Andrey: 'He will answer you about all this'.[73] The boyars' predictable reaction was to put him to death in spite of his protestations of innocence.

The murder of Semen Tonilevich sparked off another phase of inter-princely hostility and warfare. Again Andrey went to the Golden Horde, and again he returned to Russia (1285) with yet a third Tatar army. The programme was much as before. Andrey and his Tatars set about laying waste the countryside. This time, however, he was up against more formidable opposition. Dmitry had managed to rally his cousins behind him: they drove the Tatar army out of the country and arrested a number of Andrey's boyars.[74]

The collapse of Andrey's third Tatar invasion was followed by some eight years of relative calm. For the time being no fighting between the two brothers is recorded in any of the sources. Dmitry was intent on consolidating his position. In 1286 he allied himself with one of the princes of Rostov, Dmitry Borisovich, whose daughter was married to his son Ivan.[75] The only sign of opposition came from Tver'; but in 1287 Dmitry, together with Andrey, Daniil of Moscow, Dmitry Borisovich and the Novgorodians, marched on Tver'. The town of Kashin in the eastern part of the principality was besieged for nine days and neighbouring Ksnyatin was burned. Dmitry Aleksandrovich, it seemed, was now in control of all north-east Russia.[76]

It looked as though his problems were solved, even more so when his patron Nogay joined forces with Mangu Temir's son Toktu and had the official khan of Saray, Tula Bugha, removed in 1291. But, as has been mentioned above, Toktu showed no inclination to occupy a position secondary to Nogay and soon established himself as supreme ruler of the eastern Kipchak steppes. At the same time Andrey was busy forging a new anti-Dmitry alliance in Russia.

Toktu's growing power in Saray and Andrey's success in attaching to his side a number of princes anxious to see Dmitry removed from both his thrones led eventually to the most serious outburst of civil war since Andrey's first campaign of 1281. Again it was a question not of Russian armies pitted against each other, but of a major Tatar invasion summoned by one side to help force the issue.

'Dyuden''s campaign', as the great invasion of 1293 is called in the chronicles, was oppressive and onerous. As with the events of 1281, the Trinity Chronicle uses all available disaster clichés to describe the destruction wrought. Even the chronicler of Novgorod, who was by no means ill-disposed towards the instigator of the invasion, Andrey, felt called upon to exclaim when listing the 'innocent towns' sacked by the Tatars: 'Oh, much was the evil done to the Christians!' Once again it all started with a visit paid by Andrey to the khan. It was the fourth time he had been to the Horde on such a mission. On this occasion he was accompanied by all the princes from the Rostov area,[77] as well as by the bishop of Rostov himself. Evidently Dmitry Aleksandrovich's alliance of 1286 with Dmitry Borisovich of Rostov was now a dead letter. Andrey recited what by now must have been a familiar list of complaints against his brother. The khan's first plan was to send for Dmitry,[78] but he was persuaded instead to take instant action. The army this time was headed by one 'Dyuden'' (Tudan?[79]), described by the Novgorod chronicler as Khan Toktu's brother.

The invasion followed a familiar pattern. A number of towns were attacked, besieged or destroyed by the combined Tatar Russian army: Suzdal', Vladimir, Murom, Yur'ev, Pereyaslavl', Moscow, Kolomna, Mozhaysk, Dmitrov, Uglich, Volok Lamskiy are all mentioned as having suffered. Needless to say Andrey's town of Gorodets was left intact, as were the northern cities belonging to the princes of Rostov. At the beginning of the invasion Pereyaslavl' clearly expected the worst. There was general panic. Many of the townsfolk fled and and neighbouring towns and villages were vacated. Together with his army Dmitry left Pereyaslavl' and fled as far west as he could, to Pskov. 'All Suzdalia was in confusion (*zametesya*)', wrote the compiler of the Trinity Chronicle account.

The last town in Suzdalia which Andrey and his Tatars planned to take was Tver'. It was crowded with refugees from districts already overrun and its inhabitants were in a state of deep anxiety, as their prince and commander-in-chief, Mikhail Yaroslavich, was absent in the Horde – no doubt on a mission to seek aid from Nogay. He came back, however, just in time to save the town and district, for Andrey and Dyuden' decided not to attack when they heard of his presence there. Instead they marched on the border town of Volok Lamskiy as a prelude to invading Novgorod territory. Volok was seized and all the inhabitants who had fled to the surrounding forests were rounded up. Sensing that an attack was imminent, the Novgorodians took the only step they could to save themselves. They bribed the Tatars to quit Volok, just as they had bribed the census officials to quit Novgorod 36 years earlier (see above, p. 117). At the same time they requested Andrey to become their prince once more. It was enough for him. He sent the Tatar army back to the steppes and went himself to Novgorod where he ascended the throne for the second time.[80]

Dyuden''s campaign was over, but the inter-princely squabbles dragged on and on. Firstly, there was the question of the fugitive grand prince. What was he to do? He saw no future in remaining in Pskov. His one hope was to join his newly-found ally Mikhail Yaroslavich in Tver' and then to return to Pereyaslavl'. He reached Tver' by the skin of his teeth. On the way he was nearly captured by Andrey and a party of Novgorodians who had gone to Torzhok to intercept him. All he lost was his baggage train. The war might well have flared up again, but, as was so often the case in the last quarter of the thirteenth century when Russians faced Russians without Tatar backing, a compromise was reached and some sort of peace was patched up between the two brothers.[81] Dmitry once more yielded the grand principality to his brother and in return was given back his old patrimony of Pereyaslavl', which Fedor Rostislavich, the joint ruler of Yaroslavl' and Smolensk, had occupied in February 1294.[82] He never regained his capital. On the way he died near Volok Lamskiy. No chronicle, not even the Suzdalian chronicle, which had shown a glimmering of sympathy for him in his struggle with Andrey, contained even a sentence of praise, or a hint of an obituary. His son Ivan, whom he had earlier placed in Kostroma,[83] took over Pereyaslavl', which Fedor Rostislavich burned to the ground in a fit of pique as he left it at the grand prince's behest.[84] Andrey had only one more task left to round off his highly successful venture: Tver' had to be punished and temporarily quelled. It was done by yet another Tatar khan or prince (*tsar'* and *tsarevich* are the terms used to designate him) – 'Toktomer' (Tok-Temir?)[85] – who marched on the town, 'causing great grief, killing some and leading others off to captivity'.[86] With the suppression of Tver', temporary though it turned out to be, Andrey Aleksandrovich had at last reached the height of his power. There was no one left physically capable of offering him any resistance, or so it seemed at the time.

Andrey managed to survive as grand prince for another ten years. But his days as supreme ruler were numbered. His strength, such as it was, resided in the fact that Nogay was unwilling or unable to support his enemies. His weakness was twofold: his only allies, apart from the Golden Horde, were the Rostov group of princes, the Konstantinovichi, none of whom had either sufficient political muscle or any claim to supremacy over the other princes of Suzdalia; second, his kowtowing to the khans of Saray and the ruinous Tatar invasions which resulted from his reliance on their military aid caused unprecedented suffering and bitter resentment amongst the population of northern Russia and made his political opponents even more determined to stick together and to resist him. Furthermore, as has been mentioned above, Andrey had no power base from which to operate. Gorodets, his patrimony, was too remote and probably still underpopulated.[87] Besides, Andrey rarely had the time to 'care for his patrimony', as the pharase ran, let alone to reside in it and build up its resources and its army. More time was spent by him in the capital and in Novgorod than in the eastern fringes of Suzdalia. The bases of the oppositional princes on the other hand were being carefully nurtured by their owners, who, having no business to tie them to Novgorod or Vladimir, were able to concentrate on their local resources. Tver' and Moscow were emerging in the last decade of the thirteenth century as the true centres of power in north-east Russia, and their rulers, Mikhail Yaroslavich and Daniil Aleksandrovich, together with the old grand prince's son Ivan Dmitrievich, were to prove too strong a combination for Andrey.

It might of course be asked what Andrey could possibly have been hoping to achieve, apart from control over Vladimir and Novgorod and the nominal title of grand prince. The answer surely is that he realized the need for a strong patrimony close to the centre of power in Suzdalia. Gorodets was too out of the way. So too was Kostroma (presumably at the disposition of the grand prince since Vasily Yaroslavich's death), where eventually Andrey placed his son Boris. The only patrimony to which he clearly considered that he had a right and which it would have been in his interest to build up as a family possession was Dmitry's old stronghold, the extremely fertile and strategically important district of Pereyaslavl'.[88] Much of the internal conflict that flared up from time to time and bedevilled princely relations for the last ten years of Andrey's reign was connected with Pereyaslavl', occupied since Dmitry's death by his son Ivan.

It was with the question of Pereyaslavl' uppermost in his mind that Andrey went to Toktu in 1295. This time he did not succeed in persuading the khan to provide him with an army to batter his opponents with. Instead he came back in the following year with a plenipotentiary agent (*posol*) of the khan. A congress was immediately summoned in Vladimir at which 'all the princes' were present. The chronicles describe it as though it were a battle: 'they stood opposite each other: on one side Grand Prince Andrey, Fedor Rostislavich of Yaroslavl' and Konstantin of Rostov; on the other Daniil of Moscow, his cousin Mikhail of Tver' and all the men of Pereyaslavl''. Indeed it nearly came to bloodshed; only the intervention of the bishops of Vladimir and Saray prevented them from fighting it out.

The decision reached at the Congress of Vladimir – that Pereyaslavl' was the patrimony of Ivan Dmitrievich – was totally unacceptable to Andrey. He attempted to bluster. He planned to attack first Pereyaslavl' – Ivan Dmitrievich had already set off to Saray to obtain his patent – and then Moscow and Tver'. But Daniil and Mikhail blocked his way at Yur'ev Pol'skiy, and both sides, showing traditional unwillingness to fight without Tatar backing, made peace and confirmed the findings of the Vladimir congress.[89] At the same time Andrey's position in Novgorod was considerably weakened by a treaty drawn up between Tver' and Novgorod, according to the terms of which Novgorod agreed to assist Tver' in case of 'adversity (*tyagota*) on the part of Andrey or the Tatars or anyone else' – in other words, should Andrey or the Tatars attack Tver' – while Mikhail obliged himself to assist, 'should there be any offense against Novgorod'. Significantly enough, Mikhail named as his allies ('I am at one with . . .') his 'senior cousin' Daniil of Moscow and 'Ivan [? of Pereyaslavl']'.[90]

Despite his failure in 1296 to deprive Ivan of his 'patrimony' either by negotiation or by force, Andrey persevered for the rest of his life in his effort to secure a foothold in Pereyaslavl'. He tried again, in 1298, to capture it, and again was thwarted by the joint efforts of Daniil and Mikhail.[91] In 1300 he summoned a second congress, this time in the small town of Dmitrov, to the west of Vladimir and equidistant from Moscow and Tver'. All that was discussed was the distribution of principalities, in other words who was to hold Pereyaslavl'. There was 'great confusion', and although Ivan and Mikhail failed to agree over some unspecified point,[92] Daniil of Moscow's support for Ivan was enough to guarantee him future control over Pereyaslavl' in the face of opposition from Andrey, and perhaps from Mikhail as well. It was a pointer to the great increase of authority of the prince of Moscow. It was not of course that Daniil had any desire to strengthen his nephew's hold on Pereyaslavl'; rather it was a shrewd political gambit on his part, for it ingratiated him with the inhabitants of the district and endeared him to Ivan.

Andrey had still not given up hope of acquiring Pereyaslavl'. As soon as Ivan Dmitrievich died childless in May 1302, he was quick to post his lieutenants in the town and hurry off to the Horde to press his claim for the vacant principality. He was too late. The pro-Moscow compiler of the Trinity Chronicle version of Ivan's death, no doubt with an eye to justifying Moscow's subsequent seizure of the district, says that Ivan 'gave his blessing to Prince Daniil of Moscow to rule in his place in Pereyaslavl', for he loved him more than all others'. Whether this was true or not, Daniil moved in as soon as Andrey had left for Saray and quickly replaced the grand prince's lieutenants with his own.[93] It was the end of Andrey's aspirations. He could no longer hope to win Pereyaslavl'. Even when Daniil died in 1303 the situation became no rosier for him. According once more to the Trinity Chronicle, the people of Pereyaslavl' immediately opted for Daniil's eldest son Yury; so anxious indeed were they that he should protect them against a possible attack by Andrey that they refused to let him go to his father's funeral in Moscow.[94] Nor was Andrey any more successful at the Horde. When he returned at the end of 1303 together with the khan's agents (*posly*), he called yet another congress of princes, this time in Pereyaslavl' itself. But again he got no joy from his relatives. For all the khan's patents (*yarlyki*) which were read out, Yury remained firmly in control of Pereyaslavl', which from now on was never to leave Muscovite hands.[95]

On 27 July 1304 Andrey died and a new era of interprincely rivalry began. This time the participants – the princes of Tver' and Moscow – were of a very different calibre from Aleksandr Nevskiy's brothers and sons. The struggle was no longer between seemingly rootless princes with no patrimonies behind them strong enough to enable them to build up a lasting *family* claim to the supreme throne. The struggle was now between dynasties capable of conducting their business from powerful hereditary bases without having to rely solely on the glamour of Vladimir and the economic advantages of Novgorod.

The civil war which raged off and on from 1281 to 1304 and which tore Suzdalia apart was centred largely around the restless figure of Andrey Aleksandrovich. The north-western districts of Rostov, Uglich, Yaroslavl' and

Beloozero, however, suffered relatively little from the violent Tatar depredations to which again and again the central Suzdalian areas were subjected as a result of Andrey's inability to rule without Tatar support. Although we find the prince-rulers of these lands involved from time to time in the inter-princely conflicts of Suzdalia proper, the actual management of their *otchiny* had little to do with the quest for the throne of Vladimir or the struggle for Pereyaslavl'. Yet their conflicts and their principalities were in many ways microcosms of those of the sons of Aleksandr Nevskiy.

Rostov, the old capital of Konstantin Vsevolodovich, was the largest of the towns and the most important political centre. Since Konstantin's death it had remained in the hands of the senior branch of the family: Konstantin's eldest son Vasil'ko had held it and his son Boris had held it after him. When Boris died in 1277, his brother Gleb, to whom the remote *otchina* of Beloozero in the north had been allocated, took over Rostov. But when he died a year later, Boris's sons, Dmitry and Konstantin, became joint rulers. It was the beginning of a long and painful family squabble, which lasted off and on for fourteen years and which contributed to the subjugation of the area to Tatar control. As in the quarrel which had embroiled Aleksandr Nevskiy's two eldest sons, so here one brother, Konstantin, showed himself not averse to seeking Tatar aid to help him achieve his political ends, while the other, Dmitry, took a resolutely anti-Tatar stance. An initial clash in 1281 between the two, which nearly ended in armed hostilities, was settled amicably by Bishop Ignaty of Rostov,[96] but later in the same year we find Konstantin taking part in Andrey's first Tatar expedition, which ravaged, amongst others, the town of Rostov — clear evidence that Dmitry Borisovich was there in sole control of the principality. Konstantin's links with the Tatars stood him in good stead. When his cousin from the cadet branch of the family, Roman Vladimirovich of Uglich, died heirless in 1285, leaving no one to follow him on the throne, Uglich reverted to the two senior members. This time Konstantin, no doubt with the blessing of Khan Tuda Mangu, took over Rostov, while Dmitry was obliged to satisfy himself with the lesser principality of Uglich. But Dmitry was far from out of the race for power. He allied himself to the grand prince Dmitry Aleksandrovich by marrying his daughter to the latter's son in 1286 and by joining his expedition against Tver' in the following year (see above, p. 148). Two years later he ousted his brother, who in his turn was relegated to Uglich. Dmitry's return to Rostov coincided with — or sparked off — what can only have been an upsurge of anti-Tatar feeling amongst the populace: a *veche* was held and as a result the numerous Tatars in the city, whose presence there can only be explained by Konstantin having invited them in the first place, were driven out. Modelling himself, as it were, on the behaviour of Andrey Aleksandrovich, Konstantin predictably hurried to Saray to lodge complaints against his brother. He was not so successful as Andrey — and not surprisingly in view of the confusion at the Horde — and no Tatar army followed him back to Uglich.[97]

In spite of a whole decade of feuding, the two brothers somehow or other managed to coexist for another four years. Evidently some sort of *modus vivendi* was worked out, for in 1293 all the princes from the old Rostov area, even Dmitry Borisovich, followed Andrey Aleksandrovich to the Horde and took part in Dyuden''s ruinous campaign. In spite of his support for Andrey, Konstantin was unable to prevent the Tatars from including Uglich in their itinerary. However, he did not have long to wait for his ultimate triumph: in 1294, the same year that Dmitry Aleksandrovich died and Andrey became grand prince again, Dmitry Borisovich died heirless and Konstantin once more became prince of Rostov, having settled his son in Uglich. He remained in Rostov until his death in 1307, still *persona grata* at the Golden Horde, indeed so much so that in 1302 he married a Tatar princess. His support for Andrey – he sided with him at the Congress of Vladimir in 1296 – and his readiness to avail himself of Tatar aid were as damaging to Rostov as were Andrey's futile policies to Suzdalia.

During the squabbles for control over Rostov, Beloozero remained aloof from its neighbours. Dmitry Borisovich, it is true, tried to discredit his uncle Gleb Vasil'kovich of Beloozero when the latter died in 1278: nine weeks after his death, Bishop Ignaty had his corpse exhumed from the cathedral in Rostov[98] in an attempt to demonstrate that he and his descendants had from then on no claims to Rostov and to dissociate Dmitry from Gleb's servile attitude to the Tatars – Gleb is described in his otherwise laudatory obituary as 'serving them'[99]; and in the following year Dmitry confiscated parts of the district of Beloozero, which now belonged to Gleb's son Mikhail.[100] But apart from these two incidents nothing is known of the relations between Beloozero and Rostov. Either the chronicles lost interest in the principality after the good Gleb's death, or else no clashes took place. At any rate by the end of the thirteenth century Beloozero had virtually disjoined itself from the other principalities which had originally formed Konstantin Vsevolodovich's inheritance.

The same applies to Yaroslavl'. Fedor Rostislavich, who ruled the principality he had obtained by marriage for nearly forty years (1260–99), seems to have had no close links with Rostov, Uglich or Beloozero.[101] Much of his long reign was spent elsewhere, either in the Golden Horde or fighting on the side of the Tatars in Russia and abroad, or managing the principality of Smolensk, which he acquired in 1279 when his brother Mikhaylo died and which he nominally 'held' until 1297 when his nephew Aleksandr Glebovich took it from him 'by cunning'.[102] Like Beloozero, Yaroslavl' had broken free from Konstantin Vsevolodovich's inheritance and was to remain independent until finally absorbed by Moscow in the fifteenth century.

For all their independence from each other, the rulers of Rostov-Uglich, Beloozero and Yaroslavl' were linked by an identical relationship with the Golden Horde. All the princes, with the one exception of Dmitry Borisovich, were remarkable for their unwillingness, or inability, to show the slightest resistance to Tatar pressure and for their readiness to accept whoever was khan as their natural overlord. This is not of course to say that the population of the towns in any way shared the opinions of their princes: the popular upheaval in Rostov in 1289, for instance, which resulted in the expulsion of the Tatars from the city, although it may have been connived at by Dmitry, looks like a repetition of the mass uprisings which swept Suzdalia in 1262 and which did not enjoy the backing of any princes (see above, pp. 118–19).

Perhaps the princes had little choice? Perhaps their behaviour was governed by contracts with the khans which have not come down to us? Whatever the reason, they behaved as though they had even less freedom of action than their cousins in the rest of Suzdalia. The khan was their master. They fought abroad in Tatar wars: four of them took part in the Caucasian campaign of 1277 (see notes 62, 63); two, Fedor of Yaroslavl' and Mikhail of Beloozero, helped crush an anti-Tatar uprising among the Danubian Bulgars in 1278[103]; they marched with Andrey's first Tatar expedition of 1281; they followed Andrey to the Horde in 1293; and they assisted Dyuden' in the resulting invasion of Suzdalia. Perhaps even they took part in the three recorded Tatar invasions of Lithuania (1279, 1282 and 1289).[104] Twice their bishop went to the Horde 'on behalf of the clergy'.[105] Three of them married Tatar princesses[106] – not yet the frequent practice it was to become in the fourteenth century. And one of them, Fedor Rostislavich of Yaroslavl' and Smolensk, spend many years at the court of the khan, married his daughter, became his cupbearer and favourite, was looked upon by him as his 'vassal and servitor' (*ulusnik i sluzhebnik*) and, if we can believe the words of his hagiographer – Fedor was later canonized – was given thirty-six towns and sent back to Yaroslavl' with a Tatar army.[107]

As for the other districts of northern Russia, almost nothing is known of their history in the last quarter of the thirteenth century. Suzdal', Northern Galich, Dmitrov, Yur'ev Pol'skiy, Starodub and Murom might not have existed for all the notice the chroniclers give them. The silence of the sources is not, however, all that surprising. Apart from Novgorod, the only districts to maintain their own chronicles were Vladimir and Rostov. There *were* embryonic annals kept in Moscow and Tver' and these were reflected in the Vladimir-Rostov compilation which was later incorporated in the Lavrent'evskiy and Trinity Chronicles, as were the fragmentary ecclesiastical jottings that have survived – transactions and itineraries of the senior clergy. Only one area outside the purview of the grand prince of Vladimir managed to keep up a semblance of record-keeping, and that was Ryazan'; but only the barest details – two Tatar invasions (1278, 1288)[108] and an attack by Daniil of Moscow (1300)[109] – have survived.

*   *   *   *

Under the last two Yaroslavichi the bonds that tied Novgorod to the grand prince had gradually been working loose. Novgorod had imperceptibly been worming its way towards the distant goal of independence. But military support was still essential, if not to protect the western frontiers, then at least to help resist Tatar occupation and devastation. The threat had always been there, ever since Aleksandr Nevskiy's enforcement of the census in the 1250s: Yaroslav Yaroslavich had been within a whisker of raising a Tatar army to quell Novgorod in 1270, and in 1272 Vasily had brought in Tatars to tear the land apart and drive out his nephew. A prince, or his deputy, had to be there – and with an army.

During Dmitry Aleksandrovich's first period of rule as grand prince his relationship with Novgorod was trouble free. He still enjoyed the enviable position of a prince who had twice been invited to rule by the Novgorodians and who had never led a Tatar army across their frontiers. There were no clashes with the authorities, only cooperation. In early 1278 he led a highly successful joint Novgorodian-Suzdalian expedition to Karelia – the vast and vaguely defined area between Lake Ladoga and Swedish Finland and stretching further to the north – which succeeded in 'punishing the Karelians and taking their land by the sword', and in the same year he obtained permission to build a fortress in the town of Kopor'e near the Gulf of Finland, a possible refuge and a stepping-stone to Sweden in case of personal danger and civil war.[110]

The turning-point in his relations with the city came in 1280 when a quarrel flared up. No reasons are given, just the results. An attempt by the archbishop to pacify him failed, and in the winter of 1280–81 Dmitry for the first time invaded Novgorod territory with a Suzdalian army. As was so often the case when Russians faced Russians, nothing came of the invasion. Somehow or other peace was patched up. Bur the damage had been done. The Novgorodians were never again to welcome Dmitry as their prince. They refused him refuge during Andrey's first Tatar campaign, they flattened his fortress of Kopor'e, they called in his brother in 1282 and they only received him back when force of circumstances and extreme military pressure were brought to bear (1283–84) (see above, pp. 147–8). His second period of rule (1284–94) was passed over largely in silence by the circumspect Novgorod chronicler, who gives little indication of his activity – it is hard even to tell whether he was in Novgorod for most of the time or whether a deputy was there in his place. It is true, he did manage to force the Novgorodians to join his army and march against Tver' in 1287 (see above, p. 148), but there were also three violent upheavals in the city (1287, 1290, 1291) indicative of a fierce struggle between boyar groupings supporting and opposing Dmitry.[111]

By contrast, Andrey's last spell as prince of Novgorod (1294–1304) was almost as tranquil and uneventful as his first (1281–84). There was, it is true, the treaty between Novgorod and Tver' (between 1295 and 1298) in which 'Andrey or the Tatars' were specified as possible enemies of Tver' (see above, p. 151), and there was also one occasion when, during Andrey's absence, the Novgorodians expelled his 'governors' (*namestniki*) and called in Daniil of Moscow for a short spell,[112] but it never came to the crunch and Novgorod was never obliged to 'protect' Tver' against Andrey. There were none of the violent upheavals which had marked Dmitry's last term of office, there were no treaties further to limit the prince's power. Nor were there any threats of violence from the grand prince. Instead, Andrey performed his military duties on the frontiers, assisting the Novgorodians in their periodic clashes with the Swedes and the Danes.[113] Perhaps it was the memory of Andrey's formidable skill in raising Tatar armies to fight his wars that caused the Novgorodians to use restraint in their dealings with him. At any rate they suffered their last prince of the thirteenth century quietly, and perhaps even with a modicum of deference. At least the local chronicler did not show the antagonism towards him that he had shown towards his brother.

Novgorod's seemingly amicable relations with Andrey were not a retrograde step in the slow but steady move towards independence. Far from it. From 1294 onwards a new system in the election of *posadniki* was instituted. Hitherto there had been no limit to the *posadnik's* period of office: he could hold the job for life, or until he was physically removed, or, as was often the case, until such time as the prince demanded his dismissal. Now, *posadniki* were elected annually from a special 'Council of Lords' (*Sovet gospod*) consisting of life members of each of the city's five administrative districts (*kontsy*). The very fact that such a council was established and that no one boyar held the post as long as he was capable of holding it or willing to hold it meant that the boyar fraternity within the city became more united and more controllable and that an organ now existed capable of more cohesive action than before against any obstreperous prince. Yet complete boyar solidarity was still a thing of the future in so far as there was as yet no system of *regular* succession to the office of *posadnik*. It did not pass annually from *konets* to *konets* but remained with only those contestants who were powerful, cunning or rich enough to sway whoever did the electing, and indeed for most of the period between 1294 and 1304 it appears to have alternated between the two brothers Semen and Andrey Klimovichi.[114] Novgorod was not yet a republic, but it was on the way to becoming one.

REFERENCES AND NOTES

1. There is no record of the date of his birth. According to the eighteenth-century Russian genealogist Mal'gin, he was born in 1250 (*Zertsalo*, p. 292), but he was probably older than 10 when left as prince of Novgorod in 1260.

2. The sixteenth-century *Stepennaya kniga* says that Daniil was given Moscow by Aleksandr (*PSRL*, vol. 21, p. 296); according to the west-Russian Suprasl'skiy Chronicle, in 1303 Daniil had ruled in Moscow for only eleven years (*PSRL*, vol. 17, p. 27); *N1*, however, mentions Daniil as an independent prince of Moscow in 1283 (*Danilo . . . s moskvitsi. NPL*, p. 325). According to *Tv.sb.*, *s.a.* 1408, Yaroslav Yaroslavich's *tiuny* governed Moscow for seven years and Daniil was 'brought up' by Yaroslav (*PSRL*, vol. 15, col. 474); in other words, Moscow was part of the grand principality of Vladimir from 1264 to 1271. See Kuchkin, 'Rol' Moskvy'.

3. Tatishchev says that he left the Horde in August 1264 and was enthroned in Vladimir in September. *Istoriya*, vol. 5, p. 44. Andrey died some time in 1264. *TL*, p. 328.

4. In 1212 Yaroslav imprisoned two Novgorodians in Tver' (*NPL*, pp. 53, 252). According to the second redaction of Tatishchev's History, Yaroslav was left 'Pereyaslavl', Tver' and Volok' (*Istoriya*, vol. 3, p. 186). Only Pereyaslavl' is mentioned in the first redaction, however (ibid., vol. 4, p. 342).

5. *PSRL*, vol. 1, col. 471. Yaroslav Yaroslavich and Tver' are not mentioned here, but *s.a.* 1254, when Yaroslav fled to Ladoga 'leaving his patrimony', he is called 'Yaroslav, prince of Tver''. Ibid., cols. 473–4.

6. The first bishop was Simeon. He buried Yaroslav in Tver'. *TL*, p. 331.

7. Tatishchev, *Istoriya*, vol. 5, p. 44. Who Vladimir of Ryazan' was is not known.

Ivan of Starodub was presumably Yaroslav's only surviving uncle.

8. The word *polk* is used by the chroniclers usually to denote a body of soldiers, more rarely a campaign. It could be translated as force, detachment, regiment, corps, army. Mostly I have used 'regiment' with no consideration of the size of the body.

9. *NPL*, pp. 88–9. Two Tatar 'envoys' (*posly*) performed the ceremony of 'placing' (*sazhat*) Yaroslav once more on the throne of Novgorod in 1270. See *GVNiP*, p. 11.

10. Only in *Nik* (*PSRL*, vol. 10, p. 151). The entry, *s.a.* 1273, is detailed, bears little trace of padding or invention and probably reflects a non-extant Novgorod or Tver' source. Aydar is also mentioned, *s.a.* 1269 (ibid., p. 147), as the son-in-law or brother-in-law (*zyat'*) of Amragan.

11. Again, the only mention of Tatar participation is in *Nik*. Ibid. Cf. *NPL*, p. 322.

12. *PSRL*, vol. 10, p. 151. Cf. *NPL*, p. 322.

13. *NPL*, p. 312; *GVNiP*, No. 29, pp. 56–7.

14. *NPL*, pp. 83, 311.

15. *TL*, p. 328 (note that *L* has no entries from 1263 to 1284).

16. *NPL*, pp. 84, 313.

17. *TL*, p. 328.

18. Printed in *GVNiP*, No. 1, pp. 9–10.

19. See Zimin, 'Novgorod i Volokolamsk', pp. 104–5.

20. See Pashuto, *Obrazovanie*, pp. 383 *et seq.*

21. *NPL*, pp. 85, 314.

22. *P2L*, p. 16.

23. Pashuto thinks that in fact he came with the 300 Lithuanian refugees in 1265. *Obrazovanie*, p. 384.

24. *P2L*, pp. 16–17; *NPL*, pp. 85, 314–15.

25. *NPL*, pp. 85, 315.

26. *NPL*, pp. 85, 315. According to *Nik*, Yaroslav left his nephew Dmitry Aleksandrovich in Novgorod (*PSRL*, vol. 10, p. 145). This seems unlikely as Yury was prince in Novgorod in 1267 and the Novgorodian sources make no mention of it. *Nik* also adds that there was an uprising (*myatezh usobnoy*) in 1267, again not mentioned in *N1*.

27. *NPL*, pp. 85, 315. The later chronicles (*N4* and *Nik*) add that Erden' was killed (*PSRL*, vol. 4, p. 236; vol. 10, p. 145).

28. *GVNiP*, No. 2, pp. 10–11. The treaty mentions *Posadnik* Mikhail and *Tysyatskiy* Kondrat, both victims of the second Rakovor campaign (1286). It must therefore have been concluded between 1265 and 23 January 1268 (the date Mikhail and Kondrat left Novgorod with the army). For a discussion of the early treaties with Yaroslav, see Cherepnin, *RFA*, vol. 1, pp. 251–66.

29. See Christiansen, *The Northern Crusades*, p. 108.

30. *NPL*, pp. 85, 315.

31. Ibid., pp. 85–7, 315–18.

32. Ibid., pp. 87–8, 318–19.

33. *GVNiP*, No. 3, pp. 11–13. Cherepnin (*RFA*, vol. 1, pp. 263–6) considers that the last three clauses of the treaty printed in *GVNiP* were added in 1270 after the second major confrontation with Yaroslav.

34. *NPL*, pp. 88, 319.

35. See the versions stemming from the '*svod* of 1472–9' (*M*, *E*, *L'v* and *Nik*) (*PSRL*, vol. 25, p. 149; vol. 23, p. 88; vol. 20, p. 167; vol. 10, p. 149). The original story of the *myatezh* (without the threat of excommunication) is in *NPL*,

pp. 88–9, 319–21.

36. For example see above, p. 71.

37. On the back of the treaty of 1269–70 are the words '*Posly* from Khan Mangu Temir arrived to enthrone Yaroslav with a document (*gramotoyu*: presumably a *yarlyk*). *GVNiP*, p. 11.

38. These were the last three clauses of the treaty (*GVNiP*, No. 3), which, in Cherepnin's opinion, were added in 1270. See above, n. 33.

39. *NPL*, pp. 89, 321.

40. See Pashuto, *Obrazovanie*, pp. 54, 387.

41. *PSRL*, vol. 4, p. 241; vol. 5, p. 197; *P2L*, pp. 17, 85.

42. *TL*, p. 331.

43. *NPL*, pp. 89–90, 321–2.

44. *Istoriya*, vol. 5, p. 50.

45. *NPL*, p. 322; *PSRL*, vol. 10, p. 151.

46. *PSRL*, vol. 10, p. 151.

47. *NPL*, pp. 322, 471 ('having sat for three months he left the town'); *PSRL*, vol. 10, pp. 151–2.

48. For Pavsha's flight, replacement (by Mikhail Mishinich) and reinstatement, see *NPL*, p. 322. For Ratibor and the *kramol'niki*, see Tatishchev, *Istoriya*, vol. 5, p. 51.

49. *TL*, pp. 332–3.

50. 'Half a *grivna* for each *sokha* (lit. 'plough', taxation unit), and each *sokha* two working men.' *Istoriya*, vol. 5, p. 51. See Kochin, *Sel'skoe khozyaystvo*, pp. 92–3.

51. *Nik*, *N4* and the early *Letopisets Nikifora vskore* (the latter two *s.a.* 1273, clearly the wrong date). *PSRL*, vol. 10, p. 152; vol. 4, p. 219; Tikhomirov, 'Zabytye . . . proizvedeniya'.

52. See Pashuto, *Obrazovanie*, pp. 387 *et seq.*; Alekseev, *Polotskaya zemlya*, pp. 285 *et seq.*

53. But see Kuchkin, 'Nizhniy Novgorod', p. 239.

54. Kargalov, *VFR*, pp. 167–8.

55. Svyatoslav's son Dmitry predeceased his cousin Vasily of Kostroma; his descendants, therefore, lost the right of succession. Ivan's son Mikhail, however, was still alive in 1281 (*TL*, p. 339), but neither he nor his descendants ever laid claim to the throne.

56. Cf., however, Kuchkin's view that Nizhniy Novgorod was part of the district of Gorodets at the end of the thirteenth century. 'Nizhniy Novgorod', p. 239.

57. See Vernadsky, *The Mongols and Russia*, pp. 158–9.

58. For a detailed survey of the history of Volynia and Galicia from the death of Daniil to the end of the thirteenth century, see Pashuto, *Ocherki*, pp. 289–302.

59. Vernadsky, *The Mongols and Russia*, pp. 164 *et seq.*; Meyendorff, *Byzantium*, p. 36.

60. Meyendorff, *Byzantium*, p. 68. For the events of 1280–1300, see Vernadsky, *The Mongols and Russia*, pp. 174–89; Spuler, *Die Goldene Horde*, pp. 64–77; Fedorov-Davydov, *Obshchestvennyy stroy*, pp. 68–74.

61. Mal'gin, *Zertsalo*, p. 296 – the only 'evidence' for the date of his birth.

62. *Nik* says that they went 'each concerning their principalities' (*PSRL*, vol. 10, p. 154), but this is probably a later addition to the original account of *T*.

63. They took 'the glorious Ossetian town of Dedyakov' (Vladikavkaz? – see Vernadsky, *The Mongols and Russia*, p. 173) in February 1278. *TL*, p. 334.

64. *TL*, pp. 338–9. The author of the *N1* account clearly favoured Andrey and merely says that 'Andrey . . . raised a Tatar army and took Pereyaslavl' by

storm'. (*NPL*, p. 324). The account found in *N4* and *S1* gives the names of the two Tatar generals 'Kovadyy' and 'Alcheday' (*PSRL*, vol. 4, p. 244; vol. 5, p. 199).

65. For a confused account of Dovmont's activities, see *N1*, *N4* and *S1* (*NPL*, p. 324; *PSRL*, vol. 4, p. 244; vol. 5, p. 200). *Nik* makes a little more sense of the whole episode (*PSRL*, vol. 10, pp. 159–60).

66. *TL*, pp. 338–9; *NPL*, p. 324; *PSRL*, vol. 10, pp. 159–60.

67. See Tatishchev, *Istoriya*, vol. 5, p. 57.

68. *PSRL*, vol. 25, p. 154.

69. *PSRL*, vol. 10, p. 160.

70. *NPL*, p. 325 (*s.a.* 1283); *PSRL*, vol. 25, p. 154; vol. 10, p. 160 (both *s.a.* 1282).

71. *NPL*, p. 325 (*s.a.* 1284).

72. Ibid., pp. 325–6 (*s.a.* 1284).

73. *PSRL*, vol. 10, p. 161.

74. Only reported in *N4* and *S1* (and derivative chronicles), but not in *T* or *N1*. *PSRL*, vol. 4, p. 246; vol. 5, p. 201.

75. *TL*, p. 344.

76. Ibid., p. 344 (*s.a.* 1287); p. 326 (*s.a.* 1289). The most detailed account is found in *Nik s.a.* 1288 (*PSRL*, vol. 10, p. 167).

77. Dmitry and Konstantin Borisovichi (*N4* only), Mikhail Glebovich of Beloozero and Fedor Rostislavich of Yaroslavl' (and Smolensk). The sources which cover the campaign most fully are *T*, *L*, *N1*, *N4*, *S1*, *MAK* and *Nik*. See *TL*, pp. 345–6; *PSRL*, vol. 1, cols 483, 527; vol. 4, p. 248; vol. 5, pp. 201–2; vol. 10, pp. 168–9; *NPL*, p. 327. Note that *Nik*, clearly in error, adds 'Ivan Dmitrievich' (Dmitry Aleksandrovich's son) to the list of princes accompanying Andrey.

78. *Nik* only. *PSRL*, vol. 10, p. 169.

79. Spuler, *Die Goldene Horde*, pp. 73–4.

80. *PSRL*, vol. 1, cols 483, 527; *TL*, pp. 346–7. See Berezhkov, *Khronologiya*, pp. 120–1.

81. *PSRL*, vol. 1, col. 483; *NPL*, p. 328. According to *N1*, Dmitry sent Bishop Andrey of Tver' and 'Svyatoslav' to negotiate terms. However, Mikhail's eldest step-brother, Svyatoslav Yaroslavich, was probably dead by 1294, as Mikhail was clearly the senior prince in Tver'.

82. For Fedor Rostislavich's occupation of Pereyaslavl', see *TL*, p. 346; *PSRL*, vol. 1, col. 483 (where Yaroslavl' is given in error for Pereyaslavl').

83. Mentioned only in *N4*, *MAK* and *Nik* (*PSRL*, vol. 4, p. 248; vol. 1, col. 527; vol. 10, p. 170).

84. *PSRL*, vol. 1, col. 484; *TL*, p. 347.

85. See Spuler, *die Goldene Horde*, p. 74, n. 51.

86. *PSRL*, vol. 1, col. 483; *TL*, p. 347.

87. On Gorodets, see Kuchkin, 'Nizhniy Novgorod', pp. 234–5.

88. On Pereyaslavl''s importance, see Sakharov, *Goroda*, pp. 34 *et seq.*, and Tikhomirov, *Drevnerusskie goroda*, pp. 413–15.

89. For Andrey's visit to the Horde in 1295, the Congress of Vladimir and the abortive attack on Pereyaslavl', see *PSRL*, vol. 1, col. 494; vol. 4, p. 249; vol. 5, p. 202; vol. 10, p. 171; *TL*, pp. 347–8. Note that *Sim* begins its account for 1296 with the words: 'There was a Tatar *invasion*: Oleksa Nevryui came . . .' (*PSRL*, vol. 18, p. 83). *N4* and *S1*, however, make it clear that Nevryuy was the name of Tokhta's *posol*.

90. The Tver' version of the treaty is printed in *GVNiP*, No. 4, pp. 13–14. No date is given, but the treaty was probably concluded at a time when Andrey was not in Novgorod, i.e. between 1295 and 1298. Cf., however, Cherepnin's views (*RFA*, vol. 1, pp. 266–70). Kuchkin considers that the 'Ivan' mentioned in the Tver' copy of the treaty (*GVNiP*, No. 4) was Daniil of Moscow's son, who at the end of 1297 was sent to Novgorod by his father after the Novgorodians had temporarily removed Andrey's *namestniki* and that the treaty was concluded between 1 September 1296 and 28 February 1297 (Kuchkin, 'Rol' Moskvy').

91. Only mentioned in *N4* and *S1*. *PSRL*, vol. 4, p. 250; vol. 5, p. 202.

92. The Rostov Chronicle (*MAK*) vaguely mentions a military conflict between Ivan and Konstantin of Rostov in 1301, probably over frontiers. It was settled by Bishop Simeon. *PSRL*, vol. 1, col. 528.

93. *PSRL*, vol. 1, col. 486; vol. 4, p. 252; vol. 5, pp. 203–4; *TL*, p. 350.

94. *TL*, p. 351.

95. Ibid.

96. Ibid., p. 338.

97. The events of 1289 in Rostov (Dmitry's return, the expulsion of the Tatars and Konstantin's visit to the Horde) are only reported in *MAK* (*PSRL*, vol. 1, col. 526). In *Nik* Konstantin is called prince of Uglich in 1289 (*PSRL*, vol. 10, p. 168).

98. *TL*, p. 337. Ignaty was excommunicated for his action by Metropolitan Kirill in 1280, but was pardoned after Dmitry Borisovich interceded for him.

99. *TL*, p. 335.

100. Ibid., p. 336.

101. Except for the fact that a daughter of his married Mikhail of Beloozero in 1278. *TL*, p. 335.

102. For his accession to Smolensk, see *TL*, p. 337; for Aleksandr's takeover, see *PSRL*, vol. 4, p. 250; vol. 5, p. 202. For much of Fedor's absentee 'rule' in Smolensk it appears that he appointed prince-governors from the Smolensk dynasty to control the principality. See Baumgarten, *Généalogies*, pp. 97–8.

103. *TL*, p. 335; Kargalov (*VFR*, ch. 3) supplies the object of the campaign, which is not mentioned in the Russian sources.

104. *PSRL*, vol. 10, pp. 157, 161, 168.

105. *PSRL*, vol. 15, col. 405; vol. 1, col. 525 (= *MAK*).

106. Fedor Rostislavich (*PSRL*, vol. 21, p. 309); Konstantin Borisovich (1302) and Fedor Mikhaylovich of Beloozero (1302) (*PSRL*, vol. 1, col. 528 (=*MAK*).

107. See *PSRL*, vol. 21, pp. 307–11. On his *vitae*, see Serebryansky, *Drevnerusskie . . . zhitiya*, pp. 222–34. It would seem as though Fedor spent at least six years at the Horde – three years before his marriage, and three after (two sons were born to him). He was probably there some time between 1281 (Andrey's first Tatar expedition) and 1293 when he returned with Andrey Aleksandrovich to the Horde.

108. *PSRL*, vol. 10, pp. 156, 167. In 1288 Murom and the land of the Mordvinians were also attacked.

109. *PSRL*, vol. 10, p. 173; vol. 1, col. 486.

110. *NPL*, p. 323.

111. Ibid., pp. 326, 327.

112. See Kuchkin, 'Rol' Moskvy', pp. 60–2.

113. *NPL*, pp. 91, 328, 330, 331.

114. See Yanin, *Novgorodskie posadniki*, pp. 165 *et seq.*

CHAPTER SEVEN

Conclusion

When Andrey Aleksandrovich died, an epoch died with him. It was the end of an age of leaden hopelessness and seemingly utter purposelessness in strife-torn Russia. The rulers appear to have lost all sense of direction. It was the end of an age of chaotic disunity, fragmentation and disintegration, of feeble-ness of endeavour, of military unpreparedness and inefficiency. The sickness of thirteenth-century Russia was caused not so much by any external factor or by the so-called 'yoke' imposed by the Tatars, as by the innate and devastating conservatism of the ruling clans, by their unwillingness and inability to change an outmoded and creaking system and by the sheer impotence of most of the rulers. By 1304 the grand prince enjoyed less authority and less real power in terms of national solidarity than at any time previously. The old Kievan empire lay in ruins; it was a thing of the past, only much later to be lamented and remembered with regret and a certain nostalgia. South-west Russia looked to Eastern Europe and, by the end of the century, had few ties with Suzdalia. Nowhere was there a glimmer of a thriving economy, except in Novgorod. The only known links with the outside world, apart from mercantile contacts with the East, were conducted either with the West by the traders of Novgorod and to a lesser extent of Smolensk, or with a tattered and tottering Byzantium by the Church, and that only rarely and spasmodically. It might have appeared to anyone possessed at the time of a knowledge of the overall situation that there were only two possible futures for Russia, or rather for Suzdalia-Nov-gorod: either to be physically neutralized by the Kipchak Horde, put in a state of political limbo (rather as Kiev and Chernigov had been after 1240) and eventually to be occupied by a virile and aggressive Lithuania; or to be resus-citated by a tough single-minded ruler or clan of rulers who knew how to exploit Tatar policy and not simply to rely on the khans as their military allies, much as their ancestors had relied on the Polovtsians.

What passed away at the end of the century? Most important by far was the by now hopelessly outmoded system of rule by seniority, which for two and a half centuries had gnawed away at Russian unity. The principle of lateral succession – brother succeeding brother to the senior throne either of the coun-try or of the clan, then the sons of the eldest brother followed by the sons of the second eldest brother, and so on – was a sure guarantee of ineffectual government and political disunity. Yet most of the descendants of Yaroslav Vladimirovich (so-called 'the Wise') seem at any rate to have recognized and accepted the principle, and many of them even attempted to adhere to it, sometimes with mistrust and often with modifications.[1] In the second half of the eleventh century, when the surviving members of the house of Ryurik in the Kievan confederation had been virtually reduced to the three eldest living sons of Yaroslav, it may have seemed to some people an ideal form of management: Kiev, the supreme principality, to be held as it were by a triumvirate, the heirs of the 'wise' ruler, the upholders of family loyalty; the country to be ruled not by an *individual* but by a whole *clan*. But however viable a system it may have appeared to Yaroslav, if indeed it was he who instituted it, or to his sons, it was doomed to failure. After twenty years the triumvirate was disrupted by internal feuding, and although the rota system was looked upon as the basic principle of succession and although for much of the time it was actually observed for accession both to the throne of Kiev and to individual patrimonies – and even to cadet branches of individual principalities – nevertheless it could not but collapse from time to time. The bigger the family grew, the more impossible it became to follow any such complex rules. Yet in the two and a half centuries of its existence how many of the princes, from Izyaslav to Andrey, attempted to alter or abrogate it? Neither Vladimir Monomakh, nor Vsevolod III, nor Yaroslav Vsevolodovich, to mention but three of the most realistic and practical of the rulers, appear to have taken any steps other than confine the succession to their own children and grandchildren, thus drastically limiting the number of claimants. But the same system was still observed in *their* families. It seems as though they could not rid themselves of it.

If the original aim of the system was to ensure that all transfers of authority should take place peacefully and that the family *as a whole* should rule the state, it was soon to prove disastrously unrealizable. It was too much to expect that a sense of family loyalty would hold together the ever-swelling numbers of the descendants of Yaroslav 'the Wise', that cousins and nephews would automatically recognize the authority of the 'head' of the family, who might be far separated from them genealogically. The system inevitably bred greed and envy. It led to round after round of civil war. Prince fought against prince either for the throne of Kiev or Vladimir or for a place close to the senior holding of the patrimony concerned. And as the inevitable weeding-out process took place and as branches of the family were automatically excluded from the struggle for supremacy either by some decision of the senior prince or because the head of the branch in question predeceased his ruling brother or uncle, so fragmentation of the country increased. By the end of the thirteenth century the disintegration of Suzdalia was well under way with more than a dozen principalities virtually separated from Vladimir, their rulers out of the running for the grand-princely throne. There was no effective central authority and no comprehensive military command, just as there had not been on the eve of the Mongol invasion or at any other time in the thirteenth century. Resistance to a determined external enemy was unthinkable, and it was Suzdalia's good fortune that potential enemies were otherwise engaged – Lithuania, for example, with the consolidation of its territorial gains in what had been the western sector of the old Kievan state , the Teutonic Knights with the subjugation of the Baltic tribes. All Suzdalia could hope for was that either the Church might provide some sort of unifying process by means of its supra-parochial metropolitan – and there are precious few signs of *that* happening in the thirteenth century – or that the system might die a natural death.

The latter happened. As has been frequently pointed out above, no grand prince of Vladimir in the thirteenth century was able sufficiently to develop his own patrimony so that eventually it might emerge as the uncontested supreme principality of Suzdalia. Either the *otchina* was too insignificant – Yur'ev Pol'skiy, for example, or even Suzdal' – or premature death and perhaps sheer bad luck prevented the grand princes from developing what might have turned out to be a strong centre, such as Pereyaslavl', the patrimony of Yaroslav Vsevolodovich, Aleksandr Nevskiy and Dmitry Aleksandrovich. Already in the last years of the thirteenth century Moscow and Tver', both splendidly situated from a strategic, economic and geographical point of view, were building up their resources. Both had intelligent, single-minded and tough princes. Both were as yet unaffected by fragmentation. And Moscow, by 1304, had already increased its territory almost threefold by annexing the districts of Pereyaslavl', Kolomna and Mozhaysk. All that was necessary for a strong centralized state to emerge was for one of the two to absorb the majority of the remaining principalities of Suzdalia and eventually to take over the territory of Vladimir, the grand principality itself, and with it the title of grand prince. It was Moscow that eventually achieved this supremacy. By 1371 Dmitry Donskoy had already obliged the Tatars and his Suzdalian cousins to recognize him as 'grand prince of Moscow *and* Vladimir'.[2] In other words, the 'grand principality' had become his *otchina*, the inalienable possession of the descendants of Daniil of Moscow. In his will of 1389 he was able to bequeath his 'patrimony, the grand principality' to his eldest son.[3]

The system had been broken. It is true, in the early years of the fourteenth century the title of grand prince of Vladimir did pass twice to the house of Tver' (1304–18, 1322–27) and once to a grandson of Andrey of Suzdal' (1327–31), and later yet another descendant of Andrey of Suzdal' (Dmitry Konstantinovich) did manage to hold it for a short time (1360–62). But for three quarters of the fourteenth century the title and all that went with it were firmly in the hands of the Danilovichi and it only passed from brother to brother when there was no male heir. From Ivan II (1353–59) to the extinction of the line at the end of the sixteenth century, fathers were succeeded by eldest sons, except during the brief period of civil war in the mid-fifteenth century. The principle of primogeniture had ousted the archaic system of lateral succession.

* * * *

The enfeeblement of the grand princes in the thirteenth century, from the powerful Vsevolod III to the impotent Andrey Aleksandrovich, and the steady diminution of centralized authority are amply reflected in and illustrated by the gradual strengthening of the position of Novgorod vis-à-vis its rulers. It might appear that in the first thirty years of the century Novgorod enjoyed a degree of independence and even strength in that its choice of prince-mercenary was much as it had been in the twelfth century, that is to say not confined to any one family branch. Between 1200 and 1230 representatives of Vsevolod III's family, of the Rostislavichi of Smolensk and of the Ol'govichi of Chernigov all ruled in Novgorod at one time or another. True, a weak prince could be, and often was, unceremoniously bundled out by the Novgorodians, and that too might be construed as a sign of strength. But in the pre-1230 period princes were imposed on Novgorod by strong outsiders, or imposed themselves, and in any case the supplying of princes by rival clans led continuously to debilitating clashes between their supporters in Novgorod, between rival groups of boyars. Furthermore, it is obvious that a strong prince on the throne was able to lay down his own terms, and in general the authority of the princes was not noticeably slackened in the first three decades of the thirteenth century, while the boyars, chronically split for much of the time, were unable to evolve any sort of effective or lasting restraining influence on the prince. During the last alternation of Vsevolodovichi and Ol'govichi between 1224 and 1230 one can discern slightly more cohesiveness amongst the boyars, slightly more inclination to limit the prince's power and an attempt to demand that he attend more assiduously to his military obligations, but it was not until much later in the century that boyar solidarity really manifested itself or that active measures could be taken to curtail the prince's power.

In the two and a half decades following the Tatar invasion of 1237–38 Novgorod was unable to strengthen its position or to make any significant advance towards independence. There is little evidence as yet of a greater boyar cohesiveness. During the immediate post-invasion period, when the western and north-western frontiers came under slightly more pressure than before from the Teutonic Knights, the Lithuanians and the Swedes, there are signs that a 'pro-German' (that is to say pro-foreign) party existed within the city. Furthermore, the repeated disagreements between Aleksandr Nevskiy and Novgorod are clear pointers to inter-boyar rivalry at the time. The split between rival groups becomes still more evident during Aleksandr Nevskiy's rule as grand prince: it will be remembered how the 'lesser' boyars supported his brother Yaroslav in 1255 and together with the bulk of the population opposed the two attempts at census-taking at the end of the 1250s, and how the 'greater' boyars stood firmly behind Aleksandr in all his ventures. Any endeavour on the part of the Novgorodians to assert their independence was met with resoluteness by Aleksandr. The uprising of 1255 was put down with firmness and threats; resistance to the census was crushed with ferocity. Aleksandr was not the man to brook any hint of opposition in unruly Novgorod. Yet it was only with difficulty that he surmounted the crises that he faced, and in Novgorod there were clear signs of a desire and an ability to stand up to the more intolerable demands of the prince. The mood was changing.

It was only when a succession of weaker and less determined rulers followed Aleksandr that resistance to unpopular rule increased to such an extent as to oblige the prince to reconsider his attitude towards the city. Novgorod now began to show positive signs of strengthening its position vis-à-vis the prince. Stringent limitations were placed on the prince's rights; contracts were drawn up increasing the power of the *posadnik* and circumscribing that of the prince; and the boyars at last achieved some sort of agreement amongst themselves, if not cohesiveness, by the establishment of an oligarchic 'Council of Lords' from which *posadniki* were annually appointed.

Although the rulers of the fourteenth century were incomparably stronger than their predecessors and although the power of whoever was grand prince was more firmly based than that of any of Aleksandr Nevskiy's brothers or sons, nevertheless the authority of Novgorod continued to grow while that of the prince or his deputy shrank. Altogether, Novgorod's history in the fourteenth century is marked by a new feeling of confidence, at times even of a certain insouciance towards the grand prince. There were still extreme measures that the rulers of Moscow or Tver' could take and did take to cow Novgorod, such as the cutting off of grain supplies by blocking the Tvertsa river or the holding of hostages. But Novgorod remained undaunted. The time of annexation was a long way off.

Yet for all Novgorod's growing confidence, there was still a considerable amount of shilly-shallying amongst the boyars during the first half of the fourteenth century. From 1304 to 1331, when the grand princely throne was hotly disputed and the outcome of the struggle between Moscow and Tver' was still in the balance, the boyars were split into pro-Moscow and pro-Tver' groups. During the rule of Ivan I (1331–40), who was notoriously irresolute when it came to dealing with Novgorod, the main parties were those who supported Moscow and those who threw in their lot with Lithuania. Under Semen the Proud (1340–53), who kept a firmer grip on the city than his father had done – albeit a weakened Lithuanian faction still existed – the boyars were now divided by parochial interests in their quest for land and power. All this affected the authority of the *posadnik* and weakened the *boyarstvo* as a governmental element: the Council of Lords could hardly prove an effective counterpart to the prince while its members squabbled for power. Eventually in the 1350s a new system of collective *posadnichestvo* was instituted, whereby six *posadniki* were elected for life , one senior *posadnik* being chosen annually. There was still an element of competition among the aspirants for power, but the main grounds for party strife were now virtually removed. This 'complete renovation of the ruling élite of Novgorod', as a Soviet historian has called it,[4] marked the beginning of 'boyar' or 'oligarchic' republicanism in Novgorod; the greatest step ever taken towards the independence of the city and its colonies from the rule of Suzdalian princes. If only the new republic had been able to maintain an army strong enough to cope with its enemies in the west, Novgorodian independence would have been complete.

*   *   *   *

The end of the thirteenth century saw not only the demise of the lateral system of succession in Russia and the gradual diminution of Novgorod's dependence on its prince, but also the passing of what appears to have been an abject and aimless subordination to the Tatar Horde. If the squabbles among the princes and the futility of the succession system facilitated the Tatars' task in over-running northern and southern Russia, then Aleksandr Nevskiy's policy of appeasement conditioned future relations between Suzdalia and Saray. The second half of the thirteenth century was, as has been amply illustrated above, an age of gradually increasing Tatar pressure — invasions, raids, occupations, humiliations. This regime of Tatar toughness, which grew in intensity in the last thirty years of the thirteenth century, was part of the legacy of Aleksandr Nevskiy. But his successors were also to blame, for it was they who had no hesitation in following his example and calling in Tatar troops to help them achieve their political ends. They paid for it, of course, by having to fight in the Tatars' own wars , by having to watch the armies they asked for ravage their lands and by having to put up with the burdensome presence of Tatar officials and Tatar troops in their towns and villages. Resistance there was — witness the popular uprisings of 1262 and 1289 — but, as has been pointed out earlier, resistance was never planned or coordinated by the rulers themselves; they were unable, or too scared, to do anything to lessen the suffering and the indignity. Perhaps by the end they had simply grown used to it?

A new attitude to the Tatars soon became noticeable in the fourteenth century. True, concessions were still made to the Tatars; princes still pleaded their causes and remorselessly blackened their rivals at the Horde, still wheedled armies out of the khans to settle local scores. But now the rulers of Suzdalia were acting with more purpose and circumspection. The aim of their dealings with the Tatars was not just to ingratiate themselves or to secure the removal of rivals; but to dig themselves in and so to strengthen their position as to guarantee immunity from Tatar inroads and a cessation of inter-princely feud-ing. It was done with skill and tact. And it was successful. By the end of the 1320s Moscow had won the struggle for supremacy; from 1331 onwards no more princely rivalries were encouraged by the Tatars and Moscow was allowed to flourish and to provide a barrier to Lithuanian expansion. Eventually, at the end of the 1370s, this defensive and somewhat negative attitude towards the Tatars changed to one of offensive aggression. Moscow had become a power capable of dealing with the Horde on equal — or nearly equal — terms.

* * * *

At the beginning of the thirteenth century it might have appeared to an observer in Suzdalia that the whole of what had once been the Kievan state could somehow or other be held together; it might have been believed that the grand prince of Vladimir was the one person capable of stopping the disinte-gration which had been threatening for much of the twelfth century. It is true that during the early years of the thirteenth century Smolensk, Chernigov and Volynia-Galicia were embroiled in a seemingly endless struggle for control over Kiev and the south of Russia; but the ever-watchful Vsevolod III in Suzdalian Vladimir exerted a strong influence over the south. Often the operative figure in the solution of the squabbles of the south-Russian princes, he was recognized, respected and even feared by them. Yet he was not able to do more than step in from time to time to redress the damaged balance of power. When he died in 1212 the authority the grand prince of Vladimir had over the south seemed to evaporate. His sons Konstantin and Yury, absorbed by their own power struggle in the north, were unable to bring any noticeable influence to bear on what went on in Kiev, Chernigov and Smolensk, and for over twenty years the southern principalities were virtually unaffected by the policies of the grand prince of Vladimir: stability had been achieved thanks to the skill and cohesiveness of the Rostislavichi and the eclipse of the Ol'govichi. As for Volynia and Galicia, in spite of temporary annexations by both Ol'govichi and Rostislavichi and in spite of Daniil Romanovich's ambitious plans to unite Kiev and Galicia, south-west Russia in the post-1212 period gradually broke away both from Kiev and from Suzdalia.

The final breach between north and south occurred at the time of the Tatar invasion. After 1240, except for the metropolitan's sporadic peregrinations between his see in Kiev and Vladimir-on-the-Klyaz'ma, Suzdalia had virtually no more connections with Kiev and Chernigov; and after the foundering of the short-lived alliance between Daniil Romanovich and Andrey Yaroslavich in the beginning of the 1250s Volynia and Galicia broke off all relations with the north: their future lay with the countries of Eastern Europe.

Only one south-Russian district managed, after the Tatar invasion, to maintain a precarious life of its own, and that was the principality of Ryazan'. It was, miraculously, neither sucked into the Lithuanian empire along with Kiev and with its elder-sister state Chernigov, nor was it fully annexed by Moscow – indeed, it retained its independence until the sixteenth century – but somehow it survived throughout the fourteenth century, battered though it was by Tatar armies passing through it en route to the north.

The breach between north and south was not healed in the fourteenth century. The whole of the south and the south-west of Russia were outside the sphere of influence of Moscow and Tver'. Bit by bit Southern Russia, from Volynia and Galicia in the west to Kiev, Chernigov and Southern Pereyaslavl' in the east fell into the ever-receptive hands of Lithuania and Poland, and were only slowly, painfully and partially retrieved by Muscovy in the course of the three succeeding centuries.

REFERENCES AND NOTES

1. For a somewhat different view, see Stokes, 'The System of Succession'.
2. Fennell, *The Emergence of Moscow*, p. 306. *DDG*, p. 22.
3. *DDG*, p. 34.
4. Yanin, *Novgorodskie posadniki*, p. 200

Appendix A: Chronicles

The following brief notes are intended merely as a guide to the origins and history of those chronicles which I have used in this book as my main sources.

[1] THE LAVRENT'EVSKIY CHRONICLE (abbr. *L*)

This is the chief source for the history of Suzdalia, particularly in the thirteenth century. It was copied by a monk, one Lavrenty, in 1377 from an ancient and defective MS which takes events as far as 1305. It was therefore copied from a *svod* or compilation of 1305 probably completed at the court of Grand Prince Mikhail. Many of the earlier redactions were carried out in Vladimir and in Rostov; thus, for the thirteenth century, *L* is based in the main on the official grand-princely annals of Vladimir as well as local Rostov records.

L also contains evidence of south-Russian sources (for the period up to 1240) similar to those used by *Ipat* (see below, [2]).

There are lacunae in the thirteenth century *s.a* 1263–84 and 1286–94: these can be filled from the reconstructed Trinity Chronicle (*T*), which goes as far as 1409 and which itself derives from the *svod* of 1305.

[2] THE IPAT'EVSKIY CHRONICLE (*Ipat*)

Ipat consists of three parts: the so-called 'Primary Chronicle' (up to 1117); 1118–99: a south-Russian *svod*, the final redaction of which was carried out in 1200 in the Vydubetskiy Monastery near Kiev and which represents the family chronicle of Ryurik Rostislavich; 1200–92: the chronicle of Galicia and Volynia, including one or two items of Suzdalian interest.

The second part clearly derives from a south-Russian source which was also used by *L*; at the same time it appears that *Ipat* had access to a source of *L*.

169

[3] THE CHRONICLE OF PEREYASLAVL'-SUZDAL'SKIY (*LPS*)

LPS covers events from 1138 to 1214 and is very close to *L*, from a source of which it largely derives. It also contains information not found in *L* or elsewhere.

[4] MOSCOW ACADEMY MS OF THE SUZDAL' CHRONICLE (*MAK*)

MAK derives from *LPS* (see above, [3]) up to 1206; from 1207 to 1238 *MAK* derives from *S1* (see below, [6]); from 1239 to 1419 *MAK* represents the text of an abbreviated Rostov chronicle which also influenced the *svod* of 1448 (see below, [6]) and which derived from *T*.

The following stemma illustrates the relationship of the above sources (note that unshaded circles represent hypothetical redactions and sources):

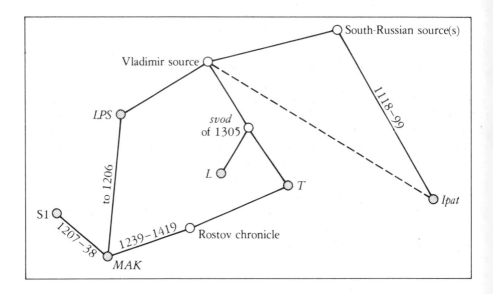

[5] NOVGOROD FIRST CHRONICLE (*N1*)

N1 is an abbreviated version of non-extant Novgorod archiepiscopal chronicle-writing. It has survived in two redactions: the 'older redaction' (*starshiy izvod*) which takes events up to 1330, and the 'younger redaction' (*mladshiy izvod*) – up to 1446/7. Both *izvody* are much the same for events of the thirteenth century, but occasionally the 'younger redaction' can be used to fill in gaps occurring in the 'older redaction'.

[6] THE SVOD OF 1448

This hypothetical compilation derives both from *T* (and *L*) and from *N1*, as well as from various other sources (Suzdal'-Rostov, south-Russian, Tver' and Pskov) and is reflected in the Novgorod Fourth and Sofiyskiy First Chronicles (*N4* and *S1*).

[7] THE MOSCOW SVOD OF 1479 (*M*)

This major grand-princely compilation represents a collation of most of the previous available chronicles. Its main sources are: (a) the *svod* of 1448 ([6]) or perhaps *S1* direct; (b) an independent hypothetical *svod* (*svod* of 1472–79) which itself derives from the *svod* of 1448 and from *T* and which is the indirect source of the later Ermolinskiy (*E*), L'vov (*L'v*) and Nikon (*Nik*) Chronicles.

The following stemma illustrates the relationship between [5], [6] and [7]:

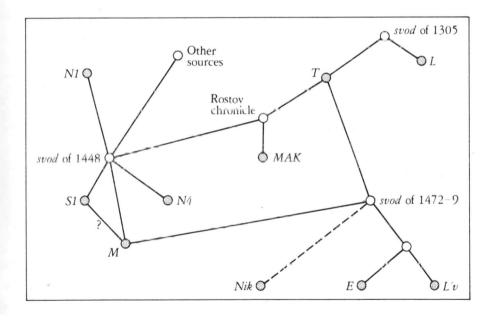

Appendix B: Genealogical tables

Note: Only those princes and khans mentioned in the text are given in these Tables.

Capitals denote those who occupied the thrones of Kiev or Vladimir-on-the-Klyaz'ma.

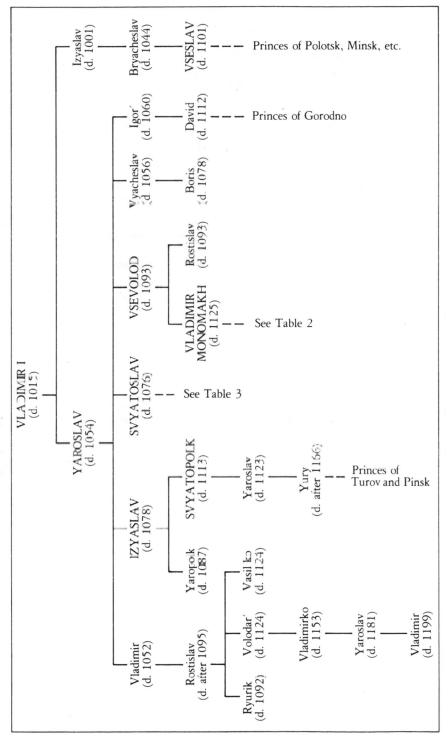

Table 1. The descendants of Vladimir 1

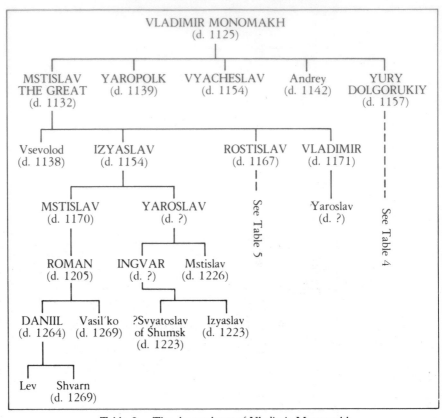

Table 2.   The descendants of Vladimir Monomakh

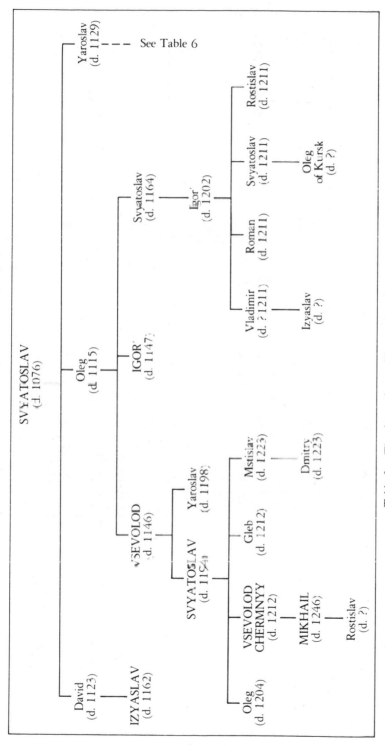

Table 3.   The descendants of Svyatoslav of Chernigov

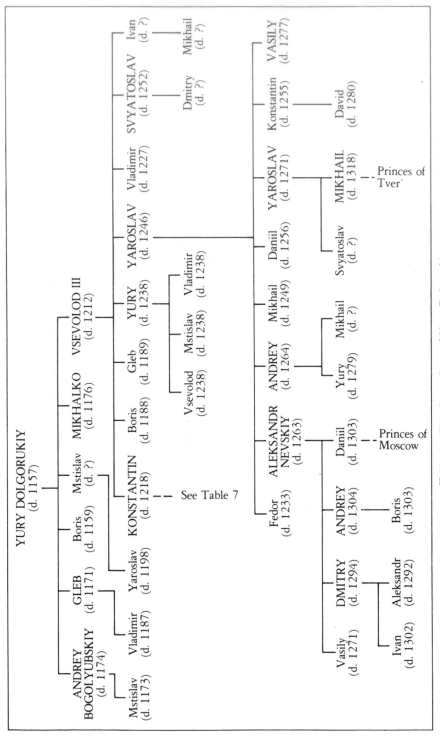

Table 4.   The descendants of Yury Dolgorukiy

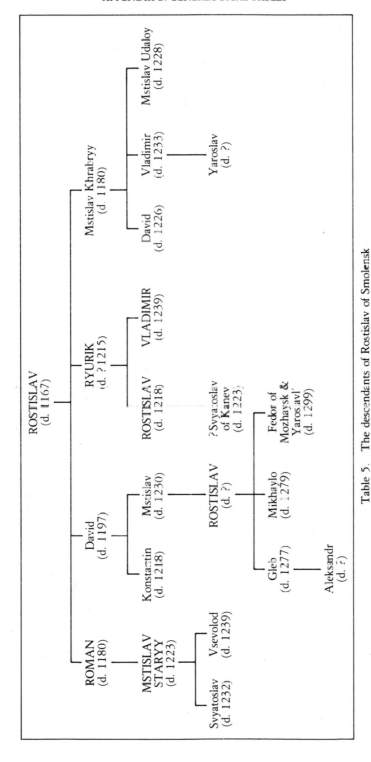

Table 5. The descendants of Rostislav of Smolensk

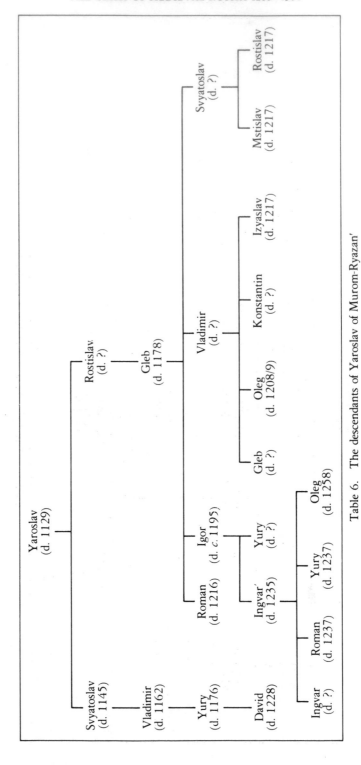

Table 6. The descendants of Yaroslav of Murom-Ryazan'

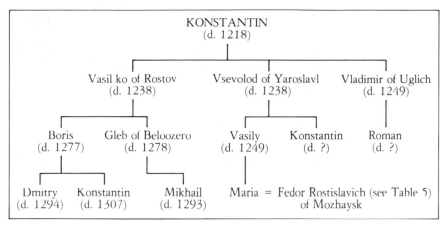

Table 7.   The descendants of Konstantin of Rostov

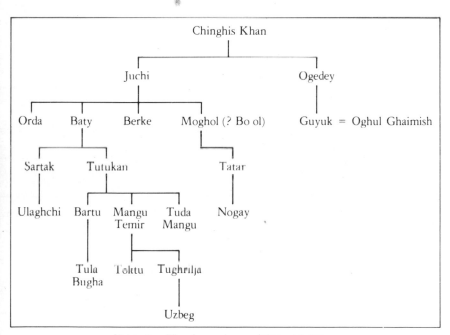

Table 8.   The descendants of Chinghis Khan

Maps

Map 1. Russia in the thirteenth century

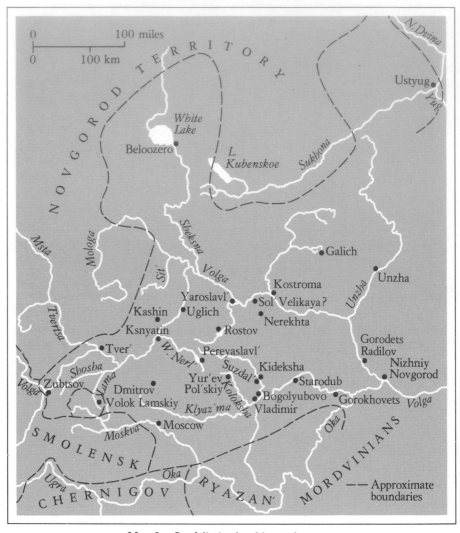

Map 2.   Suzdalia in the thirteenth century

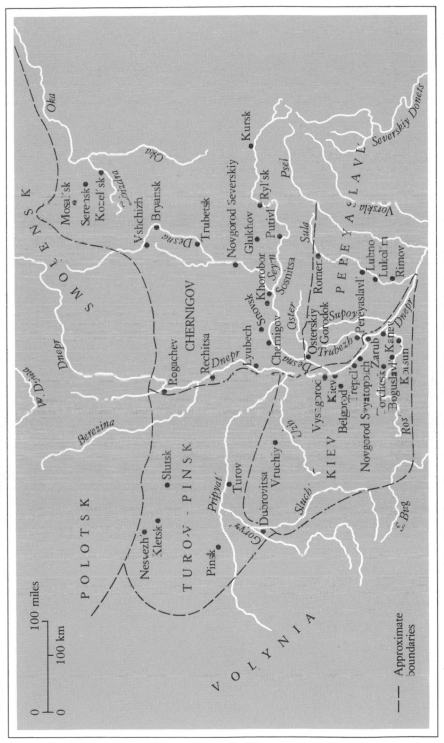

Map 3. Kiev, Cherrigov, Pereyaslavl', Turov-Pinsk in the thirteenth century

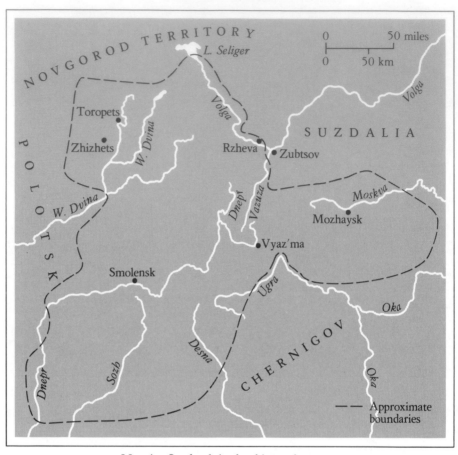

Map 4.   Smolensk in the thirteenth century

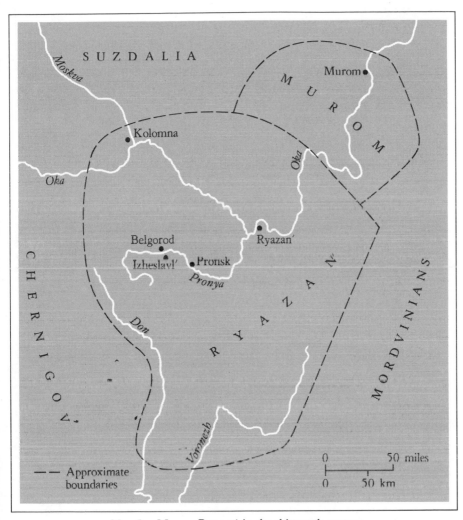

Map 5. Murom-Ryazan' in the thirteenth century

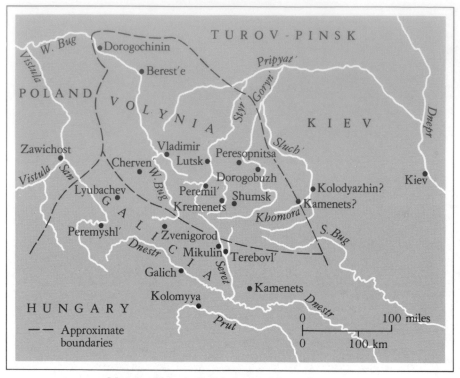

Map 6.   Volynia-Galicia in the thirteenth century

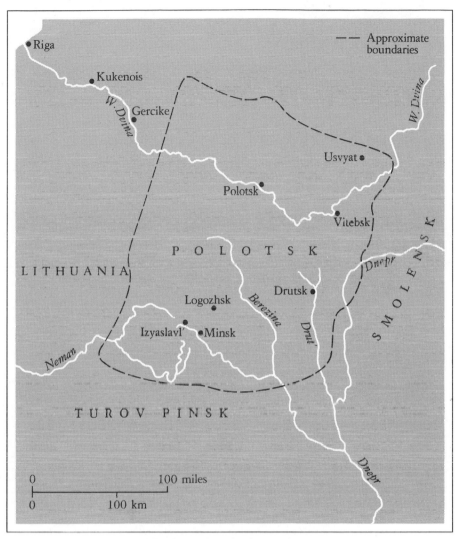

Map 7.   Polotsk in the thirteenth century

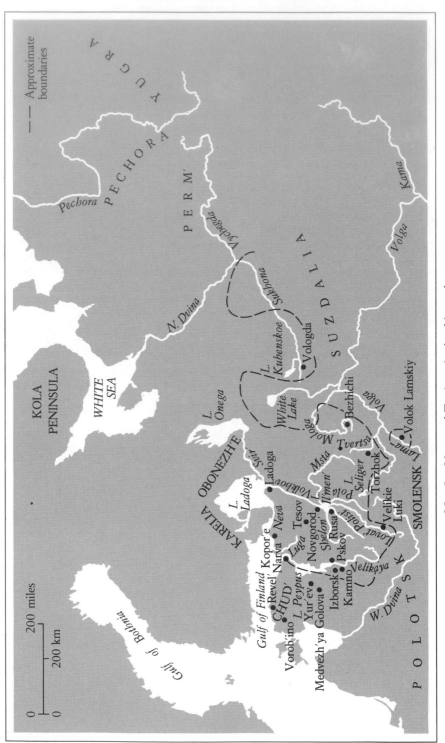

Map 8. Novgorod Territory in the thirteenth century

Bibliography

Albrici monachi Triumfontium Chronicon, in: *MGH*. Scriptorum tomus XXIII (Hanover, 1874).

Alekseev, L. V., 'Nekotorye voprosy zaselennosti i razvitie zapadnorusskikh zemel' v IX–XIII vv', in: *Drevnyaya Rus' i slavyane*, pp. 23–30.

Alekseev, L. V., *Polotskaya zemlya* (Moscow, 1966).

Alekseev, L. V., 'Polotskaya zemlya', in: *Drevnerusskie knyazhestva*, pp. 202–39.

Alekseev, L. V., *Smolenskaya zemlya v IX–XIII vv. Ocherki istorii Smolenshchiny i Vostochnoy Belorussii* (Moscow, 1980).

Allsen, T. T., 'Mongol Census Taking in Rus', 1245 1275', *Harvard Ukrainian Studies*, vol. v, no. 1, March 1981, pp. 32–53.

Allsen, T. T., 'Prelude to the Western Campaigns: Mongol Military Operations in the Volga-Ural Region, 1217–1237'. Forthcoming.

Anninsky, S. A., 'Izvestiya vengerskikh missionerov XIII veka o tatarakh v Vostochnoy Evrope', *Istoricheskiy arkhiv*, vol. 3 (Moscow-Leningrad, 1940), pp. 71–112.

Baumgarten, N. de, *Généalogies et mariages occidentaux des Rurikides russes du Xe au XIIIe siècle (Généalogies*, vol. i) (*Orientalia Christiana*, vol. ix, No. 35, 1927).

Baumgarten, N. de, *Généalogies des branches régnantes des Rurikides (Généalogies*, vol. ii) (*Orientalia Christiana*, vol. XXXV, No. 94, 1934).

Begunov, Yu. K., *Pamyatnik russkoy literatury XIII veka 'Slovo o pogibeli Russkoy zemli'* (Moscow-Leningrad, 1965).

Berezhkov, N. G., *Khronologiya russkogo letopisaniya* (A. N. SSSR, 1963).

Brundage, J. A., *The Chronicle of Henry of Livonia* (Madison, Wis. 1961)

Cherepnin, L. V., 'Mongolo-Tatary na Rusi (XIII v.)', in: *Tataro-Mongoly v Azii i Evrope*, pp. 186–209.

Cherepnin, L. V., *Russkie feodal'nye arkhivy XIV–XV vekhov (RFA)*, 2 vols (A. N. SSSR, 1948, 1951).

Christiansen, E., *The Northern Crusades. The Baltic and the Catholic Frontier 1100–1525* (London, 1980).

Dimnik, M., 'Kamenec', *RM*, vol. 4, 1979, pp. 25–34.

Dimnik, M., *Mikhail, Prince of Chernigov and Grand Prince of Kiev 1224–1246* (Toronto, 1981).

Dimnik, M., 'Russian Princes and their Identities in the First Half of the Thirteenth Century', *Mediaeval Studies*, vol. xl (Toronto, 1978), pp. 157–85.

Dimnik, M., 'The Siege of Chernigov in 1235', *Mediaeval Studies*, vol. xli (Toronto, 1979), pp. 387–403.

Dimnik, M., 'The Struggle for Control over Kiev in 1235 and 1236', *Canadian Slavonic Papers*, vol. xxi, 1979, pp. 28–44.

Drevnerusskie knyazhestva X–XIII vv., ed. L. G. Beskrovnyy (Moscow, 1975).

Drevnyaya Rus' i slavyane (Moscow, 1978).

Dukhovnye i dogovornye gramoty velikikh i udel'nykh knyazey XIV–XV vekov (DDG), ed. S. V. Bakhrushin and L. V. Cherepnin (A. N. SSSR, 1950).

Ermolinskaya letopis' (E), in: *PSRL*, vol. 23 (St Petersburg, 1910).

Fedorov-Davydov, G. A., *Kochevniki Vostochnoy Evropy pod vlast'yu Zolotoy Ordy* (Moscow, 1973).

Fedorov-Davydov, G. A., *Obshchestvennyy stroy Zolotoy Ordy* (Moscow, 1973).

Fennell, J. L. I., 'Andrej Jaroslavič and the Struggle for Power in 1252: an Investigation of the Sources', *RM*, vol. 1, 1973, pp. 49–63.

Fennell, J. L. I., 'Russia on the Eve of the Tatar Invasion', *Oxford Slavonic Papers* (New Series), vol. xiv, 1981, pp. 1–13.

Fennell, J. L. I., *The Emergence of Moscow 1304–1359* (London, 1968).

Fennell, J. L. I., 'The Last Years of Rjurik Rostislavich'. Forthcoming.

Fennell, J. L. I., 'The Tale of Baty's Invasion', *RM*, vol. 3, 1977, pp. 41–78.

Fennell, J. L. I., 'The Tale of the Death of Vasil'ko Konstantinovič: a Study of the Sources', in: *Osteuropa in Geschichte und Gegenwart*, pp. 34–46.

Fennell, J. L. I., 'The Tatar Invasion of 1223', *Forschungen zur osteuropäischen Geschichte*, vol. 27 (Berlin, 1980), pp. 18–31.

Fennell, J., and Stokes, A., *Early Russian Literature* (London, 1974).

Golubinsky, E., *Istoriya kanonizatsii svyatykh v russkoy tserkvi* (Moscow, 1903).

Gorski vijenats. A Garland of Essays offered to Professor Elizabeth Mary Hill, ed. R. Auty, L. R. Lewitter, A. P. Vlasto (Cambridge, 1970).

Gorsky, A. D., 'K voprosu ob oborone Moskvy v 1238', in: *Vostochnaya Evropa v drevnosti i srednevekov'e*, pp. 176–84.

Gramoty Velikogo Novgoroda i Pskova (GVNiP), ed. S. N. Valk (Moscow-Leningrad, 1948).

Grousset, R., *L'Empire des Steppes* (Paris, 1939).

Grushevsky, M., *Ocherk istorii Kievskoy zemli ot smerti Yaroslava do XIV stoletiya* (Kiev, 1890).

Gumilev, L. N., *Poiski vymyshlennogo tsarstva* (Moscow, 1970).

Gustinskaya letopis', in: *PSRL*, vol. 2 (St Petersburg, 1843).

Historica Russiae Monumenta, ed. A. T. Turgenev, vol. 1 (St Petersburg, 1841).

Ilovaysky, D., *Istoriya Ryazanskogo knyazhestva* (Moscow, 1858).
Ipat'evskaya letopis' (*Ipat*), in: *PSRL*, vol. 2 (St Petersburg, 1908; photoreproduction Moscow, 1962).
Istoricheskaya geografiya Rossii XII–nachalo XX v. Sbornik statey k 70-letiyu professora Lyubomira Grigor'evicha Beskrovnogo, ed. A. L. Narochnitsky (Moscow, 1975).
Istoriya russkoy literatury X–XVII vekov, ed. D. S. Likhachev (Moscow, 1980).

Juvaini, *The History of the World-Conqueror by 'Ala-al-Din 'Ara-Malik*, 2 vols Transl. from the text of Mirza Muhammad Qazvini by John Andrew Boyle (Manchester, 1958).

Kargalov, V. V., *Vneshnepoliticheskie faktory razvitiya feodal'noy Rusi. Feodal'naya Rus' i kochevniki* (*VFR*) (Moscow, 1967).
Khoroshev, A. S., *'Tserkov' v sotsial'no-politicheskoy sisteme Novgorodskoy feodal'noy respubliki* (Moscow, 1980).
Klepinin, N. A., *Svyatoy i blagovernyy knyaz' Aleksandr Nevskiy* (Paris, no date).
Kloss, B. M., *Nikonovskiy svod i russkie letopisi XVI–XVII vekov* (Moscow, 1980).
Kochin, G. E., *Sel'skoe khozyaystvo na Rusi kontsa XIII–nachala XVI v.* (Moscow-Leningrad, 1965).
Kuchera, M. P., 'Pereyaslavskoe knyazhestvo', in: *Drevnerusskie knyazhestva*, pp. 118–43.
Kuchkin, V. A., 'Nizhniy Novgorod i Nizhegorodskoe knyazhestvo v XIII–XIV vv.', in: *Pol'sha i Rus'*, pp. 234–60.
Kuchkin, V. A., 'O marshrutakh pokhodov drevnerusskikh knyazey na gosudarstvo volzhskikh bulgar v XII–pervoy treti XIII v.', in: *Istoricheskaya geografiya Rossii*, pp. 31–45.
Kuchkin, V. A., 'Rol' Moskvy v politicheskom razvitii Severo-Vostochnoy Rusi kontsa XIII v.', in: *Novoe o proshlom nashey strany. Pamyati M. N. Tikhomirova*, pp. 54–64.
Kuchkin, V. A., 'Rostovo-Suzdal'skaya zemlya v X – pervoy treti XIII v. (tsentry i granitsy)', *Istoriya SSSR*, 1969, No. 2, pp. 62–94.
Kuz'min, A. G., *Ryazanskoe letopisanie. Svedeniya letopisey o Ryazani i Murome do serediny XVI v.* (Moscow, 1965).

Lavrent'evskaya letopis' (*L*), in: *PSRL*, vol. 1 (Leningrad, 1926; photoreproduction, Moscow, 1962).
Lederer, F., 'Vengersko-russkie otnosheniya i tataro-mongol'skoe nashestvie', in: *Mezhdunarodnye svyazi Rossii*, pp. 181–202.
Ledovoe poboishche. Trudy kompleksnoy ekspeditsii po utochneniyu mesta Ledovogo poboishcha, ed. G. N. Karaev (A.N. SSSR, 1966).
Letopisets Nikifora vskore, in: Tikhomirov, 'Zabytye ... proizvedeniya',

pp. 234–43.

Letopisets Pereyaslavlya-Suzdal'skogo, sostavlennyy v nachale XIII v. (mezhdu 1214 i 1219 gg.) (LPS), ed. M. A. Obolensky (Moscow 1851).

Limonov, Yu. A., 'Iz istorii vostochnoy torgovli Vladimirovo-Suzdal'skogo knyazhestva', in: *Mezhdunarodnye svyazi Rossii*, pp. 55–63.

Lur'e, Ya. S., 'Lavrent'evskaya letopis' – svod nachala XIV v.', *TODRL*, vol. xxix (Leningrad, 1974), pp. 50–67.

Lur'e, Ya. S., *Obshcherusskie letopisi XIV–XV vv.* (Leningrad, 1976).

Lur'e, Ya. S., 'Povest' o bitve na Lipitse 1216 g. v letopisanii XIV–XVI vv.', *TODRL*, vol. xxiv (Leningrad, 1979), pp. 96–115.

L'vovskaya letopis' (L'v), in: *PSRL*, vol. 20 (St Petersburg, 1910).

Lyaskoronsky, V. G., *Istoriya Pereyaslavskoy zemli* (Kiev, 1897).

Lysenko, P. F., *Goroda Turovskoy zemli* (Minsk, 1974).

Mal'gin, T. S., *Zertsalo rossiyskikh gosudarey* (St Petersburg, 1794).

Matuzova, V. I., *Angliyskie srednevekovye istochniki IX–XIII vv.* (Moscow, 1979).

Meyendorff, J., *Byzantium and the Rise of Russia* (Cambridge, 1981).

Mezhduknyazheskie svyazi Rossii do XVIIv. Sbornik statey, ed. A. A. Zimin, V. T. Pashuto (Moscow, 1961).

Mongayt, A. L., *Ryazanskaya zemlya (Istochniki istorii ryazanskoy zemli i istoriografiya)* (A. N. SSSR, 1961).

Mongayt, A. L., *Staraya Ryazan' (Materialy i issledovaniya po arkheologii SSSR, 49)* (Moscow, 1955).

Monumenta Germaniae Historica (MGH) (Hanover).

Moskovskiy letopisnyy svod kontsa XV veka (M), in: *PSRL*, vol. 25 (Moscow-Leningrad, 1949).

Nasonov, A. N., *Istoriya russkogo letopisaniya XI–nachalo XVIII veka* (Moscow, 1969).

Nasonov, A. N., *Mongoly i Rus'* (A. N. SSSR, 1940).

Nasonov, A. N., *'Russkaya zemlya' i obrazovanie territorii drevnerusskogo gosudarstva* (A. N. SSSR, 1951).

Nazarov, V. D., '"Dvor" i "dvoryane" po dannym novgorodskogo i severo-vostochnogo letopisaniya (XII–XIII vv.), in: *Vostochnaya Evropa v drevnosti i srednevekov'e*, pp. 104–23.

Nikonovskaya letopis', see *Patriarshaya ili Nikonovskaya letopis'*.

Noonan, T. S., 'Suzdalia's Eastern Trade in the Century before the Mongol Conquest', *Cahiers du Monde russe et soviétique*, xix (4), (Oct.–déc., 1978), pp. 371–84.

Novgorodskaya chetvertaya letopis' (N4), in: *PSRL*, vol. 4, Part 1 (Petrograd, 1915).

Novgorodskaya pervaya letopis' starshego i mladshego izvodov (NPL) (A. N. SSSR, 1950).

Novoe o proshlom nashey strany. Pamyati M. N. Tikhomirova (Moscow, 1967).

Ocherki istorii SSSR perioda feodalizma IX–XV vv. Part 1 (Moscow, 1953).
Osteuropa in Geschichte und Gegenwart. Festschrift für Günther Stökl zum 60. Geburtstag (Vienna, 1977).

Pashuto, V. T., 'Mongol'skiy pokhod v glub' Evropy', in: *Tataro-Mongoly v Azii i Evrope,* pp. 210–27.
Pashuto, V. T., *Obrazovanie Litovskogo gosudarstva* (A. N. SSSR, 1959).
Pashuto, V. T., *Ocherki po istorii Galitsko-Volynskoy Rusi* (A. N. SSSR, 1950).
Pashuto, V. T., *Vneshnyaya politika Drevney Rusi* (Moscow, 1968).
Patriarshaya ili Nikonovskaya letopis' (Nik), in: *PSRL,* vol. 10 (St Petersburg, 1862; photoreproduction, Moscow, 1965).
Pletneva, S. A., 'Polovetskaya zemlya', in: *Drevnerusskie knyazhestva,* pp. 260–300.
Polnoe sobranie russkikh letopisey (PSRL).
Pol'sha i Rus', ed. B. A. Rybakov (Moscow, 1974).
Poppe, A., 'On the Title of Grand Prince in the *Tale of Ihor's Campaign',* *Harvard Ukrainian Studies,* vol. iii/iv, 1979–1980, pp. 684–9.
Presnyakov, A. E., *Obrazovanie Velikorusskogo gosudarstva* (Petrograd, 1918).
Pskovskie letopisi (P1L, P2L), ed. A. N. Nasonov, 2 vols (Moscow-Leningrad, 1941; Moscow, 1955).

Rapov, O. M., *Knyazheskie vladeniya na Rusi v X–pervoy polovine XIII v.* (Moscow, 1977).
Rashid ad-Din, *Sbornik letopisey,* vol. 1. Transl. from Persian by O. I. Smirnov (Moscow-Leningrad, 1952).
Rashid ad-Din, *The Successors of Genghis Khan.* Transl. by J. A. Boyle (New York and London, 1971).
Rhode, G., *Die Ostgrenze Polens,* vol. 1 (Köln-Graz, 1955).
Russia Mediaevalis (RM), ed. J. L. I. Fennell, L. Müller, A. Poppe (Munich, 1973–).
Russkie povesti XV–XVI vekov, ed. B. A. Larin (Moscow-Leningrad, 1958).
Rybakov, B. A., *Remeslo drevney Rusi* (A. N. SSSR, 1948).

Sakharov, A. M., *Goroda severo-vostochnoy Rusi* (Moscow, 1959).
Serebryansky, N., *Drevne-russkie knyazheskie zhitiya* (Moscow, 1915).
Shaskol'sky, I. P., *Bor'ba Rusi protiv kretonosnoy agressii na beregakh Baltiki v XII–XIII vv.* (Leningrad, 1978).
Shaskol'sky, I. P., 'Novye materialy o shvedskom pokhode 1240 na Rus'', *Izvestiya Akademii nauk SSSP, Seriya ist. i fil.,* vol. 8, no. 3, 1951, pp. 267–76.
Shaskol'sky, I. P., 'Papskaya kuriya – glavnyy organizator krestonosnoy agressii 1240–1242 gg. protiv Rusi', *Istoricheskie zapiski,* 37, 1951, pp. 169–88.
Simeonovskaya letopis', (Sim), in: *PSRL,* vol. 18 (St Petersburg, 1913).
Smirnov, A. P., *Volzhskie bolgary* (Moscow, 1951).
Sofiyskaya pervaya letopis' (S1), in: *PSRL,* vol. 5 (Leningrad, 1925).
Soiov'ev, S. M., *Istoriya Rossii s drevneshikh vremen,* 15 vols (Moscow, 1959–66).

Spuler, B., *Die Goldene Horde. Die Mongolen in Russland 1223–1502* (Wiesbaden, 1965).

Stokes, A. D., 'The System of Succession to the Thrones of Russia 1054–1113', in: *Gorski vijenats*, pp. 268–75.

Suzdal'skaya letopis' po Akademicheskomu spisku (MAK), in: *PSRL*, vol. 1 (Leningrad, 1926; photoreproduction, Moscow, 1962).

Tataro-Mongoly v Azii i Evrope, ed. S. L. Tikhvinsky, 2nd edn (Moscow, 1977).

Tatishchev, V. N., *Istoriya Rossiyskaya*, 7 vols (Moscow-Leningrad, 1962–8).

The Hypatian Codex. Part Two: The Galician-Volynian Chronicle, transl. and ed. G. A. Perfecky (Munich, 1973).

The Mongol Mission, ed. C. H. Dawson (New York, 1955).

Tikhomirov, M. N., *Drevnerusskie goroda* (Moscow, 1956).

Tikhomirov, M. N., 'Zabytye i neizvestnye proizvedeniya russkoy pis'mennosti', in: *Arkheograficheskiy ezhegodnik za 1960 g.* (Moscow, 1962).

Tizengauzen, V. G., *Sbornik materialov, otnosyashchikhsya k istorii Zolotoy Ordy* (St Petersburg, 1884).

Tolochko, P. P., *'Kiev i Kievskaya zemlya v epokhu feodal' noy razdroblennosti XII–XIII vekov* (Kiev, 1980).

Tolochko, P. P., 'Kievskaya zemlya', in: *Drevnerusskie knyazhestva*, pp. 5–56.

Troitskaya letopis' (TL). Rekonstruktsiya teksta, ed. M. D. Priselkov (A. N. SSSR, 1950).

Trudy Otdela drevnerusskoy literatury Instituta russkoy literatury (Pushkinskiy Dom) Akademii nauk SSSR (TODRL).

Tumler, P. M., *Der Deutsche Orden* (Vienna, 1955).

Tverskaya letopis' (Tverskoy sbornik, Tv.sb.), in: *PSRL*, vol. 15 (St Petersburg, 1863, photoreproduction, Moscow, 1965).

Ustyuzhskiy letopisnyy svod, ed. K. N. Serbina (Moscow-Leningrad, 1950).

Vernadsky, G. , *The Mongols and Russia* (Newhaven, Conn., 1953).

Voinskie povesti Drevney Rusi, ed. V. P. Adrianova-Peretts (Moscow-Leningrad, 1949).

Voronin, N. N., *Zodchestvo severo-vostochnoy Rusi*, 2 vols. (Moscow, 1961–2).

Vostochnaya Evropa v drevnosti i srednevekov'e, ed. L. V. Cherepnin (Moscow, 1978).

Yanin, V. L., 'Mezhdunarodnye otnosheniya v epokhu Monomakha i "Khozhdenie Daniil"', in: *TODRL*, vol. xvi (Leningrad, 1960), pp. 112–31.

Yanin, V. L., *Novgorodskie posadniki* (Moscow, 1962).

Zaytsev, A. K., 'Chernigovskoe knyazhestvo', in: *Drevnerusskie knyazhestva*, pp. 57–117.

Zimin, A. A., 'Novgorod i Volokolamsk v XI–XV vekakh', *Novgorodskiy istoricheskiy sbornik*, vol. 10 (Novgorod, 1961), pp. 97–116.

Index

195